Creature Features

ALSO BY WILLIAM SCHOELL

*The Horror Comics: Fiends, Freaks
and Fantastic Creatures, 1940s–1980s*
(McFarland, 2014)

*The Opera of the Twentieth Century:
A Passionate Art in Transition*
(McFarland, 2006)

Creature Features

Nature Turned Nasty in the Movies

WILLIAM SCHOELL

McFarland & Company, Inc., Publishers

Jefferson, North Carolina

The present work is a reprint of the illustrated casebound edition of Creature Features: Nature Turned Nasty in the Movies, *first published in 2008 by McFarland.*

LIBRARY OF CONGRESS CATALOGUING-IN-PUBLICATION DATA

Schoell, William.
Creature features : nature turned nasty
in the movies / William Schoell.
p.   cm.
Includes bibliographical references and index.

ISBN 978-0-7864-9562-7 (softcover : acid free paper) ∞
ISBN 978-1-4766-1072-6 (ebook)

1. Monsters in motion pictures.   2. Animals
in motion pictures.   I. Title.
PN1995.9.M6S36 2014   791.43'67—dc22   2008029408

BRITISH LIBRARY CATALOGUING DATA ARE AVAILABLE

On the cover: Poster art for the 1977 film *Empire of the Ants* (American International Pictures/Photofest).

Printed in the United States of America

McFarland & Company, Inc., Publishers
Box 611, Jefferson, North Carolina 28640
www.mcfarlandpub.com

When I was a boy, my father, William T. Schoell, took me to a twin-bill of *Ghidrah the Three-Headed Monster* and Elvis Presley's *Double Trouble*. I couldn't have cared less about the Presley pic but we had to sit through it to get to the monster movie. It is hard to remember which of the two movies was more awful. I think Dad took me to the double-feature because he felt guilty that he would usually only drop me off at the movie theater and pick me up two or three hours later, so I either saw *King Kong vs. Godzilla* with friends or by myself. Dad wouldn't even sit through *The Birds*, which is too bad. We did see *Jason and the Argonauts* together and I think Dad enjoyed that wonderful picture as much as I did — how could he help it? After a double helping of *Ghidrah* and Elvis, however, Pop was back to dropping me off and picking me up later, and I couldn't blame him. For sitting through that atrocious double-bill with me, my late father deserves the dedication of this book.

Acknowledgments

Thanks to 20th Century–Fox, Allied Artists, Warner Brothers, Republic Pictures, Universal, Taft, Sunn Classic, Stan Winston Studios, American International, Toho, Embassy, MGM, Eugene Lourie, Ray Harryhausen, United Artists, RKO, Dino De Laurentiis Productions, Hal Roach Productions, Hammer Films, 7 Arts, Bing Crosby Productions, and Orion. All of the photographs in this book are from private collections.

Table of Contents

Preface

While it may not be true that everyone loves a good monster movie — or creature feature — these films are among the most popular ever made. Some monster movies, such as *Jaws* and *Alien* (*Jaws* is definitely a monster movie), even attract people who normally wouldn't go to a monster movie. In general, critics have never been too fond of monster movies, unless they are parodies or have a strong sense of humor or have something else to offer besides a bad-tempered creature. Science fiction fans usually excoriate monster movies, because they don't understand that movies about resuscitated dinosaurs and gigantic, impossible insects are not science fiction, but *horror* (or dark fantasy if you want to get technical). Most monster movie fans couldn't care less if the science doesn't add up, although even we have to pause and scratch our heads from time to time at the sheer illogic of a certain movie.

This book concentrates on *creatures*, but in general you won't find the likes of *Creature from the Black Lagoon* or *Frankenstein* or other monstrosities in its pages. The monsters in this book are either behemoths (discovered in time-lost worlds or ancient societies and somehow unleashed upon modern civilization) or normal-sized animals such as birds and bears that behave in strange ways. The chapter on dragons also covers other mythological creatures, as well as dinosaurs. The chapter on big bugs is self-explanatory. The chapter on "humongous" creatures looks at ordinary animals that grow to giant-size, while the three chapters on nature turned nasty movies look at creatures that crawl or fly (birds, bugs, and bats); creatures at home in the water (fish, alligators); and all other animals (wolves, dogs and so on). The final chapter examines movies about creatures that aren't as easy to classify: blobs and demons and other weird things that go *thump* in the night. In general, I discuss the films in each chapter in chronological order, although I sometimes lump related films or sequels together with the original film.

I have generally eliminated discussion of films that were made for TV or for cable or as direct-to-video releases, not only because there's no room for them but because most are pretty bad. The Sci Fi Channel shows dozens and dozens of original and direct-to-video monster movies, but while the creature feature may be *alive* on Sci Fi it's rarely *well*; occasionally a decent or even better-than-decent creature movie may be shown on the cable network but most of its offerings are dismal. The low budgets only allow very crude FX work and the movies are padded with boring subplots that often have little to do with the monster in question.

There have been a lot of changes to the creature feature over the years. Although many other methods were employed, stop-motion was the FX technique of choice in bringing dinosaurs and other monsters to life until the advent of computer technology, which relies on the work of stop-motion artists to make the computer-generated beasties look and move with that certain "veracity." But not all computer imagery is created equal, and cheap movies often offer monsters that are far below the level of *Jurassic Park* (whose effects seems less impressive today than when it was first released). In most Sci Fi Channel movies the monsters seem not so much to move in a realistic way but to *stretch* unnaturally, their size changing from shot to shot, looking in some ways more like cartoon figures (or video game animation) than stop-motion or anything approximating reality. Whatever you call it, the monsters just don't look *good*. Indeed the great stop-motion FX in older movies can still hold their own with the effects that many monster movies offer today.

Another change has to do with the amount of ugliness on screen. In the fifties nobody had to see chewed-up bodies or body parts left behind by big bugs, hydras and the like because everyone could more or less imagine what happens when man meets monster and the man loses. Who wanted or needed to see severed limbs strewn about (which was senseless in the first place since a large predator would either carry off the body or devour everything, including the bones). Modern monster movies often cater to a disaffected gorehound sensibility; as long as the limbs keep flying, who cares if the monster resembles Silly Putty? There was a time when special effects technicians couldn't outdo the audience's imagination, but those days seem to be long gone, with sometimes clever, sometimes idiotic grossouts occurring on a regular basis. This has led to some happily ingenious moments of gruesomeness — the chest-bursting scene in *Alien*, for instance — but also to scenes that leave you wondering if somebody oughta check with his or her psychiatrist. Sometimes the grisly slaughter and upchuck sequences work against what should be the sheer *fun* of the creature feature. And if a monster movie isn't fun, what's the point of it?

In a 2007 Sci Fi Channel offering entitled *Megasnake*, there is a scene in which the giant snake enters an amusement park and rises up over a roller coaster full mostly of happy younger teenagers. *Splat*— the snake lunges out and the coaster attendant is spattered with blood. He looks up in horror to see that most of the young people on the roller coaster are now *missing their heads*; the few shocked, screaming survivors are covered in gore. It's one thing to see a loathsome villain torn up by a monster; another to see innocent kids out for a happy afternoon get beheaded. The filmmakers, and geeks of all ages, probably thought the scene was macabre, "cool," delightfully gruesome (and it certainly has an fiendishly grotesque quality to it), but *Megasnake* is proof positive that today's monster movies are increasingly geared toward a slasher or "splatter movie" sensibility that has little to do with — and cares little about— the ghoulish but rarely sadistic delights of creature features. True, there have always been "shock" scenes in movies, and the deaths of innocents (which were frequently mined for pathos) that offended the sensitive — Suzanne Pleshette's gouged-out eyes in *The Birds* was disturbing to many in 1963 on both of those levels and *The Flesh Eaters* certainly scored on the gross-out meter in 1964 and still does today. But contemporary filmmakers almost seem too intent on outdoing one another in nastiness while at the same time making films that are generally devoid of the artistry, class and humanity of the best of Hitchcock. Hitchcock could be very tasteless and gruesome when he wanted to be (and indeed *Psycho* helped open the floodgates) but he was on a much higher level than the typical monster movie maker of the 21st century.

The point of monster movies is that they help us forget our real problems for an hour or two by showing us fictional characters who have utterly impossible (or, at the very least, highly improbable) and horrific challenges to deal with that we ourselves are unlikely to ever have to face. Monster movies reassure us, that no matter how bad things may get in our own lives, there are *worse* things out there in the dark.

Much worse.

ONE

Here There Be Dragons

One theory goes that it was ancient man's discovery of dinosaur bones that led to the myths about dragons. Whatever the reality, dinosaurs are our real dragons, capturing our imagination every bit as much as the supernatural, fire-breathing menaces who devoured virgins and set fire to whole villages. And mythology is full of fearsome, terrible creatures — gorgons, harpies, hydras — that haunt mankind's nightmares. There have been so many films that have exploited our interest in these real and mythical creatures that sometimes the line between fact and fantasy has been blurred...

Speaking of dragons ... Fritz Lang's *Siegfried* is the first half of his epic *Die Nibelungen* (1924), based on German mythology. It features one of the first and most impressive dragons in the movies. Siegfried (Paul Richter) sets off for Burgundy where he hopes to win the hand of King Gunther's (Theodor Loos) fair sister Krienhild (Margarete Schon). Encountering the dragon Fafnir, Siegfried slays the beast and bathes in its blood, gaining invulnerability except for one spot that has been covered by a falling leaf. From Alberich, the King of the Dwarves, Siegfried gains a cap of invisibility. Siegfried importunes Gunther for the hand of his sister, but Krienhild cannot marry until her brother wins the heart of Brunhilde (Hanna Ralph), the queen of Iceland. Using his cap and natural prowess, Siegfried makes it look as if Gunther has defeated Brunhilde, and later disguises himself as the king when he goes to Brunhilde's bedchamber, again hoping to impress the queen. In this he succeeds. When Brunhilde learns of the deception, she demands that her new husband, Gunther, have Siegfried killed, and reminds him that when he disguised himself as the king (a plan of which Gunther actually approved) he "took what was rightly yours." After Siegfried has been killed by a spear thrown at his vulnerable spot by Gunther's uncle, Brunhilde laughingly tells Gunther that Siegfried never had his way with her. Part two of *Die Nibelungen* is the story of *Krienhild's Revenge*.

Siegfried starts out as a fairly silly adventure story, but as it proceeds gains in interest and intensity until it becomes a powerful and fascinating study of betrayal and revenge. Adding to the interest are the elaborate scenic designs of woodlands, castles, mountains and bridges, as well as atmospheric settings such as the literally fiery rocks that surround Brunhilde when she first appears. Most of the special effects, such as when Alberich and his dwarves turn into stone, are achieved with simple dissolves and superimpositions, but Fafnir the dragon is quite an accomplishment for the period and afterward.

The sequence with Fafnir occurs quite early in the running time and is the film's highlight. We first see Fafnir leaning over a stream taking a drink and it looks remarkably life-like.

5

If it weren't for the somewhat silly-looking face, one would almost take Fafnir for some sort of lizard with sharp fins running down its back. Actually a marvelously well-designed, full-sized construction, Fafnir is mobile enough to move its limbs up and down, duck its head, even exhale smoke and snort fire and it interacts amazingly well with Richter as the actor swings his sword at it. The only thing Fafnir can't do is open its mouth convincingly as it roars and snaps at Siegfried, but considering how effective it is, that's a quibble. Fafnir outacts other mechanical monsters in films made many decades later. As it dies, it gushes a veritable river of blood, the better for his slayer to bathe in.

The acting in *Siegfried* helps to keep one's interest in the human characters, with Richter both naive and boastful as the hero who is betrayed by those he's aided. Due to her lack of raving beauty, Margarete Schon has the unfortunate appearance of a man in drag, but this was apparently not the case; Schon had a long career in Germany. Hanna Ralph, who exudes a ferocious intensity as the equally betrayed Brunhilde, was for a time married to actor Emil Jannings. The modern-day soundtrack of the film employs themes from Wagner's operas — the famous Ring cycle — that treated the same subject matter. Even played on an organ, the melodies are evocative. Eventually Fafnir would be eclipsed by dragons created with more sophisticated optical effects, but for a brief time he was the dragon to beat.

The Secret of the Loch (UK, 1934) was one of the earliest films to deal with Nessie, the Loch Ness Monster, which has generally been considered some kind of sea serpent; for a long time it was popularly thought that Nessie was a long-necked prehistoric plesiosaur. Jimmy Anderson (Frederick Peisley), a reporter for the London *Daily Sun*, arrives in Loch Ness determined to get an interview with the peppery Professor Heggie (Seymour Hicks), who is convinced that the Loch Ness Monster is legitimate and aims to prove it before anyone else can. Not everyone in the village agrees with the professor; as local barmaid Maggie puts it, "the best descriptions [of the monster] always come from our best customers." Jimmy breaks into the professor's castle and winds up meeting the old coot's pretty granddaughter Angela (Nancy O'Neil). When a diver named Jack (Eric Hales) is killed while exploring a cave beneath the loch, an inquest holds the professor responsible, driving him nearly insane. Jimmy bravely descends into the depths of the loch to prove the monster's existence, and comes face to face with it, narrowly avoiding death. Nessie rises to the surface for all to see and the overjoyed professor's reputation is salvaged.

The Secret of the Loch is a pretty mediocre movie, with too much running time given over to the antics of the reporter and his run-ins with belligerent Angus, the professor's manservant and bodyguard (Gibson Gowland). The monster itself doesn't make any kind of appearance until over halfway through the movie, when we see its enormous shadow on the wall of the cavern as Jack explores, a scene which is creepy in a minor fashion. Jimmy later comes upon the diver's helmet, all that's left of the poor lad. (If this film had been made twenty or thirty years later, a head would have been inside the helmet.) When the monster comes to the surface (in long shot) at the end, there are some lyrical moon-lit shots of it swimming contentedly.

The special effects in the movie are largely unconvincing. Neither Jack nor Jimmy actually look as if they're under the surface in the "underwater" sequences; even the bubbles coming out of the suits do little to sustain the illusion. The monster itself is merely a big, stupid-looking iguana that's blended in with Jimmy in the climax via cheapjack process shots or by holding a doll representing the reporter in front of the not-very-curious reptile. The ultimate result probably didn't create too many thrills or scares even back when the picture was released.

If the monster's performance is inadequate, at least the human players are more on the mark, with Hicks really scoring as the professor. A scene in which the professor's crew tries to pull diver Jack up from the water only to come upon his torn air hose, reminds one of a sequence in a film made twenty years later, *The Beast from 20,000 Fathoms*, a sea serpent movie *par excellence*. David Lean, who would go on to greater things, such as directing *Lawrence of Arabia*, served as *Loch*'s editor. As director, Milton Rosmer adequately covers the action. The screenplay was written by Charles Bennett, who scripted several films for Hitchcock as well as *The Lost World* (1960) and *Curse of the Demon* (1958).

One Million B.C. (1940) fostered the insidious notion that dinosaurs and humans walked the Earth at the same time when in reality they were separated by hundreds of millions of years. Carole Landis and Victor Mature play Stone Age lovers in a story that is essentially a charming, wildly idealistic allegory showing how the kinder morals and values of one tribe eventually influence the more savage, callous and selfish characteristics of another. The film is half over before the monsters appear, the first being a laughable man-in-a-T-Rex-suit that attacks the camp. There are giant armadillos, woolly mammoths, and plenty of photographically blown-up lizards, one of which has a no-holds-barred battle with an alligator. This scene is fairly exciting due to a giant prop claw and process shots that make it look as if the creatures are having their struggle directly over a crevice in which our lovers have taken shelter. The climax has a huge lizard cornering some of the people in their cliffside caverns, eating one of them, while Mature and the other men toss boulders at it. Werner R. Heymann's score keeps things from getting too tedious.

Footage from *One Million B.C.* found its way into countless monster movies in the years to come. One clever shot of a woman falling before, and being covered by, a lava flow, was repeated even in movies that had no monsters. In 1961 a completely "new" movie was fashioned chiefly by using stock footage from *One Million B.C.*: *Valley of the Dragons* was a very loose adaptation of Jules Verne's novel *Career of a Comet*. An Irishman and a Frenchman are fighting a duel over a woman when a comet smashes into the Earth and drags along the section of land that they're standing on. Millions of years earlier the same comet smashed into the prehistoric Earth with the same result, so the two men (who eventually become friends) find themselves in a world of cavemen and monsters. Every highlight of the film is taken directly from *One Million B.C*, with actors Sean McClory and Cesare Danova (and the cave-babes they wind up with) cleverly substituted for Landis and Mature in some of the process shots, observing things that the former pair did in the previous film. In addition to the footage from *One Million*, there are also slithering salamander-like monsters, a quick shot of a pterodactyl taken from *Rodan*, and a fake prop spider-monster in a cave. There are also cave dwellers with hairy bodies, claws, fangs, and ugly mutated faces who resemble Morlocks. The movie gets points for some skillful editing and expert use of stock footage, if little else.

The Beast from 20,000 Fathoms (1953) was one of the most influential films ever made, ushering in the whole creature feature cycle of the fifties and beyond. Physicist Tom Nesbitt (Paul Christian), who is overseeing an atomic test in the Arctic, tries to rescue a colleague caught in a blizzard when he sees a prehistoric animal through the snow. After encountering much resistance, he and another man who saw the beast convince paleontologist Thurgood Elson (Cecil Kellaway) of the monster's existence. Elson identifies the "paleolithic survivor" as a "rhedosaurus" (a fictional dinosaur). Christian bonds with Elson's assistant Lee (Paula Raymond), especially after the professor dies while getting a look at the animal via a diving bell. The beast surfaces to rampage through Manhattan, its diseased blood causing sickness in the soldiers trying to kill it. Cornered at the Coney Island amusement park, the dinosaur is destroyed with a radioactive isotope fired into its body, a mighty titan defeated by modern science.

Hampered by a low budget, stop-motion expert Ray Harryhausen was still able to come up with several impressive sequences. Chief among these is the monster's bold trek through lower Manhattan, probably inspired by the big ape's rampage in *King Kong*. There is a wonderful shot of the monster's head rising up out of the harbor behind some stevedores enjoying a smoke on the docks. Smashing cars, snarling at people, toppling walls onto huddled pedestrians, the Beast cuts a formidable figure. Harryhausen didn't just use back projection to blend his actors with the monster. Sometimes the live footage would be shot first and projected on a much smaller screen behind the puppet-dinosaur. This live footage would be advanced frame by frame as the monster model was manipulated to interact with the projected actors behind it. When this method was combined with back projection, it was called a "reality sandwich."

There is no attempt to "humanize" the monster or make it sympathetic. It is a terrifying threat, ripped out of its proper time and place by atomic testing (which thawed it out, presumably), and mankind has to show it as little mercy as it does the people it crushes underfoot. This sequence includes a "shock" scene when a policeman fires at the dinosaur, only to have it bend down while he reloads his weapon and grab him up in its teeth. All these years later, the shot of the Beast pulling up the screaming man and engulfing him in his mouth, swallowing him like some kind of squiggling raisin, is still disturbing. Harryhausen himself pointed out that a modern-day filmmaker would probably show spattering blood and falling body parts, even though the beast's maw is large enough to swallow the cop whole. The beast's savagery is amply illustrated in the sequence when it tries to get at soldiers who are firing at it from behind a barricade; it's like an unleashed force of nature constantly on the verge of exploding.

In addition to the handsome stop-motion model, Harryhausen employed a mock-up of the beast's head for a couple of sequences: an attack on a fishing ketch and on a lighthouse. The head is well-designed, its mouth can open and close, but it doesn't perform as well as the model. For a couple of quick inserts — the beast seen through a rainy window or windshield by prospective victims — it serves its purpose.

Another outstanding sequence is when the beast attacks the lighthouse in Maine. The screenplay by Louis Morheim and Fred Freiberger presents not just lead characters who seem to be real people with back stories, it even gives us three-dimensional minor characters such

The *Rhedosaurus* of *The Beast from 20,000 Fathoms* (1953) rises up from the Hudson River and prepares to lay siege to New York City. It was animated by Ray Harryhausen.

as the two lighthouse keepers. One is an old man who talks about his frustration when he tried to play a song he liked in the tavern — "something about gin and wild women," he says — but the jukebox busted down. His much younger, poetically handsome assistant says, "I like the ballads, the old ones that warm you even when the fog is a foot thick." These two brief but incisive portraits add a touch of pathos to the scene when moments later the beast crawls out of the sea, jumps up on the lighthouse, and tears it apart, killing the two likable men we've just been introduced to. There is a sublime creepiness to this scene — something enormous and inexplicable sneaking out of the sea at night to wreak havoc on the completely unsuspecting.

The diving bell sequence is well-handled by director Eugène Lourié. Professor Elson excitedly describes the monster to assistant Lee through an intercom as he and the diving bell operator peer in awe at the beast through a porthole. He gives detail after detail to Lee as the rhedosaurus, spotting the bell, comes closer and closer to it, its maw widening ominously all the while. Finally Elson says, "but the most astounding thing about it is that...." The maw fills up the screen and we regrettably have to say goodbye to poor Professor Elson. This is followed by a tender scene between Nesbitt and Lee as he comforts her when she breaks down thinking about the professor's terrible and "futile" death. His final moments — like the cop's (and indeed the diving bell operator) — must have been horrendous.

The Coney Island climax — which was actually shot in California — has Nesbitt and a

9

corporal who's a crack rifleman (Lee Van Cleef) riding up the roller coaster to get the best shot at the beast. There is some splendidly fluid animation of the beast as it thrashes about destroying the roller coaster and then writhes in its death agonies, but there's only one shot showing the animal in the same frame as the two men, which minimizes the impact of the sequence. Later on we see the magnificent dead beast in the same frame as the many people who witnessed its demise.

One can suspend disbelief and momentarily accept that an atomic blast could resuscitate a prehistoric animal from many millions of years ago, but it's harder to accept the reactions of some of the human characters. The beast is first revealed in its full glory not to Tom Nesbitt, but to his colleague George, who sees it only a short distance away (in a striking process shot) without any obstructions. (This Arctic set with its chunks of ice and blowing snow is very realistic.) Nesbitt only catches a glimpse of the animal as it roars from *high overhead*— during a blizzard. Had George survived, it might have made sense for him to become obsessive on the existence of the beast, but it stretches credulity to have Nesbitt so absolutely convinced that he actually saw and heard a living prehistoric animal instead of, say, a bit of jagged wreckage carried away by the howling gale.

Worse is the fact that Elson decides to *stake his reputation* on the existence of the beast simply because two independent witnesses — Nesbitt and Jacob Bowman, who survived the monster's attack on a fishing ketch — identify the same dinosaur from sketches. Compelling, perhaps — but *proof*? Elson seems to throw out his commendable skepticism and logic just because the storyline requires him to. But this illogic doesn't hamper one's enjoyment of the film.

The Beast from 20,000 Fathoms is well served by an excellent cast. Paul Christian and Paula Raymond make an attractive couple and play with admirable conviction, an appealing earnestness of delivery that helps you believe what's happening. Their growing attraction to one another is obvious but never overpowers the focus of the film. Cecil Kellaway, one of our Grand Old Character Actors whose presence enhanced every film he was in, is delightful as the tragic Professor Elson. Well-known genre players such as Kenneth Tobey, King Donovan, Ross Elliott, and others also make strong contributions. The musical score by David Buttolph, with its dramatic four-note intro (the theme of the beast), is first class. Eugène Lourié's direction lifts the movie from what could have been a hack item to a classy and memorable production that works every step of the way. Lourié would make two more dinosaur-on-the-loose movies of descending quality.

The Beast from 20,000 Fathoms made millions of dollars for Warner Brothers, and Toho Studios in Japan took note. It was the success of *Beast* that engendered the creation of *Gojira* (1954), which also had a dinosaur–sea monster — it might be more accurate to call it a dragon — but one that was radioactive and of truly staggering proportions. The following year, a dubbed American version with new scenes came out, and *Godzilla, King of the Monsters!* was born.

In Japan, a series of ships have been obliterated by a mysterious "flash of fire" that on at least one occasion has been observed by the residents of Oda Island. The cause of the destruction turns out to be a 400-foot dinosaur that rises from the sea to destroy the island, then turns its wrath on Tokyo in a series of ever more devastating attacks. This is observed by American reporter Steve Martin (Raymond Burr), who is nearly killed by falling debris. Dr. Yamane (Takashi Shimura), a leading paleontologist, theorizes that the monster was resurrected by atomic bomb experiments. His daughter Emiko (Momoko Kochi) is in love with Marine officer Ogata (Akira Takarada) but married to another scientist, Serizawa (Akihiko Hirata), who uses a weapon he devised to destroy Godzilla. He also sacrifices his own life so that Emiko and Ogata can be together.

Whatever its flaws, *Godzilla* is an interesting, moody, absorbing film in any language, and it at least seems to have more on its mind than the average monster movie. Partly this is due to the grim tone of the film, the somber musical score, the believable performances of the rather intense actors, including Burr in the added sequences. One could quibble that the theory that Godzilla's rampage through Tokyo is essentially meant to be a reenactment of the bombings of Nagasaki and Hiroshima is pretentious, but there is simply no getting around it. The implication is not that it was *testing* that resuscitated the beast but the dropping of the atomic bomb itself. Godzilla is not so much the mythical dragon of the superstitious Oda Island natives but the living personification of an atomic nightmare. A great deal of understandable awe is worked up over the creature, who causes much more death and destruction than the much smaller rhedosaurus of *Beast from 20,000 Fathoms*.

Therefore it's a shame that Godzilla itself is such a letdown. It isn't just that the creature is only a man in a monster suit, but that the suit — especially the head — is so poorly designed. A lot of suspense is worked up over the supposed unseen approach of Godzilla to Oda Island at night, but he never actually appears until daytime, where his silly appearance can't even be disguised by shadows. With a dopey-looking face and a body like a flabby T-Rex, Godzilla is about as fearsome as a Muppet, even with his metallic-sounding roar. Not until *The Giant Claw* the following year would there come a monster so capable of sabotaging its own movie. The only thing that keeps Godzilla from completely wrecking the film is the quality of other aspects of the production, including some effective process shots.

With feet as big as subway cars, Godzilla smashes through Tokyo, shattering some excellent miniature buildings and vehicles. The action is rarely brought down to a human's eye level, but there are some scary interactions between Godzilla and people. Chief among these is when he attacks a tower upon which some reporters and cameramen are standing. Godzilla snaps out at and apparently eats the reporter describing the carnage (although this is in no way as effective as the beast-eats-cop scene in *Beast*). There is a very striking shot of a nearly deserted Tokyo burning, many fires lighting the sky in the background.

The scenes with Raymond Burr are cleverly integrated into the original film, although they may have caused continuity problems when some footage was cut. Dr. Yamane, the paleontologist, is called in long before Godzilla shows up, although there's no reason to consult with him simply because some ships are burning up in a flash of flame. This whole business is strange anyway because Godzilla doesn't even develop his famous fiery breath until he clutches some electrified cables (an unsuccessful attempt to kill him) and the charge brings out his heat beam. This happens a long time after those ships were destroyed.

Not that one would expect scientific accuracy in a film about a 400-foot-tall dinosaur, but the method of destroying Godzilla can only be described as poor science. Serizawa has developed an "oxygen destroyer" that removes oxygen from sea water. This might certainly kill marine life, but why does it *skeletonize* them as we see when he tests the device in a tank of fish in front of Emiko? Godzilla is also reduced to a skeleton—because there's no oxygen in the water? The "effect" used to show the oxygen destroyer at work is simply to fill up the screen with a lot of bubbles.

The ending of the film is strangely moving, and not because the big beastie is dead, but because of Akira Ifukube's decidedly downbeat musical score and the sacrifice of Serizawa after saving the world. Or maybe it's just a realization of what *Godzilla* is really about, in which case the poor appearance of the monster may be beside the point. Yet it must be remembered that *Godzilla* was produced chiefly to make money and deliver thrills—it should have delivered a more memorable looking monster, although the idea and concept of Godzilla is certainly terrifying and compelling. The film is well-directed by Ishiro Honda, with the American sequences supplied by Terry Morse. *Godzilla* was so successful that it became a franchise, with each film becoming sillier than the one before, a sad bowdlerization of its original premise. The later American version with Matthew Broderick dropped the theme entirely and was not in the least serious, to put it mildly.

King Dinosaur came out from Lippert Pictures in 1955, and is of special note as the first of prolific director-producer Bert I. Gordon's giant monster movies. The picture at least starts out with a novel, if inexplicable, premise—"Earth has a new neighbor." A new planet has suddenly appeared next to the Earth, orbiting the sun. This would result in probable planetary upheaval, but there is no mention of any cataclysm in the narration as the movie begins. The first few minutes consist mostly of dull stock footage—and an awful lot of it— as a team is assembled to man the first spaceship to the new planet Nova. The team consists of zoologist Dr. Richard Gordon (Douglas Henderson), geologist Dr. Nora Pierce (Patricia Gallagher); medical doctor Ralph Martin (Bill Bryant), and chemist Dr. Patricia Bennett (Wanda Curtis). Their rocket ship doesn't actually land on Nova, mind you—a see-through rocket is simply superimposed over the landscape. Once upon the ground, the rocket ship is only a cardboard cut-out with a ladder behind it standing in for the stairs.

The group soon discovers that Nova is still in the prehistoric era, with flora and fauna to match. They become fascinated by a volcanic island with strange vegetation lying some distance off the shoreline. (There are some highly atmospheric shots of this placid "sea.") The "thunder" they hear coming from the island turns out to be the roars of dinosaurs. However, the first creature they encounter is merely a normal-sized alligator that Ralph wrestles with after he trips and rolls into its lair. The first out-sized animal is a giant ant or bug of some kind that makes its presence shrilly known but doesn't take any especially aggressive action; it seems stuck in a web anyhow (the real ant, not the "giant" one). It's killed with a shot from Ralph. When Dick arrives back at the camp, neither he nor Ralph make any comment on the big dead bug even though there's a quick cut to it after Ralph asks Dick if he saw "anything unusual."

The second half of the short movie takes place on the strange island, where our heroes encounter the King Dinosaur, whom we first see standing up on its hind legs behind a rock in a mediocre process shot (one imagines the rock hid the arm of the lizard handler who was holding the poor thing upright). The scientists tell us that this creature—merely an ordinary earth lizard blown up to huge proportions — is a T-Rex, which, as one of them puts it, "dominates Nova as it did Earth's past" even though it seems limited to just one island on Nova. King Dinosaur traps two of the group in what appears to be the same Bronson Cavern that Gordon used for his later film *The Cyclops*. King Dinosaur has a certain amount of personality, and there is a good process shot of it sticking its head (and later its claw) into the cavern as it tries to get at the people inside. King Dinosaur is distracted from this by the approach of an alligator — giant-sized this time — and battles it to the death. Incredibly, the lizard emerges victorious from this duel with "bloodied" lips, although it's hard to see how a lizard could manage to survive the huge snapping jaws of an alligator. There is some suspense generated as the expeditioners flee from the cavern and breathlessly make their way to the island's shore as King Dinosaur chases after them. Along the way they also encounter a giant armadillo, a gargantuan mammoth that comes out of nowhere, and a strange, turtle-like weird thingie whose size isn't clear because it's never in the same frame as any of the actors. For no apparent reason, the scientists decide to blow up the entire island with an atomic bomb, as if afraid the dinosaurs would not only pursue them to the mainland but somehow fly back to Earth in the spaceship with them. "We've brought civilization to Planet Nova," Richard says ironically.

The actors in the film are professional and show realistic emotion at the various situations they find themselves in. "Little Joe," the Honey Bear who shows up to befriend the party, also gets a credit and gives a charming, if limited, performance. Gordon doesn't direct the movie so much as cobble it together. He would make much better films in the future. Mischa Terr's music features a lazy theme for flute and oboe that sounds like a poor man's *Bolero*. *King Dinosaur* is far from being a good movie, but it's just the thing for a rainy, lazy Sunday afternoon.

The Saga of the Viking Women and Their Voyage to the Waters of the Great Sea Serpent (popularly known as *Viking Women and the Sea Serpent*) was another slickly directed item from the prolific Roger Corman. In the 1957 fantasy-adventure, a group of Viking women vote on whether to not to stay in their village or set sail in search of the men who set off to find a more hospitable home years ago and who never returned. After some debate, they agree to build a ship and go in search of their lovers. Joining the women is Ottar (Jonathan Haze), who was presumably too young to join the other men when they left, although it is clear that he has been sailing before when he recognizes a whale that the women confuse with a sea monster. Before long, they encounter a legitimate sea serpent, "the Monster of the Vortex," who rises out of a whirlpool that destroys the Viking ship. Washed ashore on an island, the women discover that their menfolk have been enslaved by the evil king, Stark (Richard Devon). "Once you have a Grimholt warrior," he assures the women, "you'll forget the pale Viking slaves." After a series of misadventures involving the king's simpering son Senya (Jay Sayer) and the big brute Zarko (Mike Forrest) who engages Ottar in battle numerous times, the women and their men are reunited and set sail for home. The king and his soldiers, in hot pursuit, meet their fate at the fangs of the Monster of the Vortex.

The Monster of the Vortex was created by the FX team of Jack Rabin and Louis DeWitt. In closeup, the serpent is simply a puppet head with many rows of pointed teeth. It has a flat head with big round eyes and roars most convincingly. In long shot it is revealed as long, lean and slithery, with scales and fins. Fortunately, the monster is only seen in quick cuts and always in the middle of a tempest, so its patent phoniness is somewhat disguised and it comes off as an effective enough beastie. The whirlpool is created via use of a tank, wind machine, and back projection; these scenes are simplistic but reasonably convincing. There is an excellent matte painting depicting the king's castle seen in the distance, and a nice shot of the serpent's head rising out of the water far out at sea at the seeming command of the island's ruler.

Viking Women has a large cast of well-known Corman players and other actors who went on to greater or lesser fame. Athletic Jonathan Haze starred in the original *The Little Shop of Horrors*, among other Corman quickies, and in this takes on the formidable (6'3") Mike Forrest several times during the course of the film until he finally kills him. Forrest is given not a single line of dialogue, but a few years later — as Michael *Forest* — would prove his acting chops when he starred as Apollo in the classic *Star Trek* episode "Who Mourns for Adonais?" Gary Conway and Brad(ford) Johnson are two of the enslaved Viking men. Conway went on to appear in such TV shows as *Burke's Law* and *Land of the Giants*. As Vedric, Johnson's line readings are so flat that he comes off as little more than a hunky lunkhead.

The Viking women are led by Abby Dalton as Dasir and Susan Cabot as the scheming high priestess Enger, who eventually sacrifices herself for the others. Both play with conviction, and Cabot (who also played *The Wasp Woman*) is as authoritative as ever. June Kenny, who a year later would star in *Earth vs. the Spider*, also acquits herself nicely as brave, sweet Asmild. Richard Devon is on the money as the lecherous king who's simultaneously regal and barbaric, and Sayer is splendidly whiny as the weasel-like prince who gets struck by lightning. Albert Glasser turned in one of his very best scores; a particular highlight is a frenzied dance during a bacchanal halfway through the picture. As usual, Corman keeps things moving at a very rapid pace, although his Vikings are not always the swiftest. Desperately rushing to escape from the king's soldiers, they come upon canoes on the beach — *and stop dead in their tracks and yak* instead of piling into the boats and making their getaway! They finally take off a few minutes later, giving the soldiers plenty of time to catch up with them. *Duh!*

Viking Women and the Sea Serpent shouldn't work at all — and for many critics, who found it utterly lamentable, it doesn't — but the professional acting, solid musical score, brisk direction, and surprisingly interesting story make it much more watchable than other grade C products. And that briefly appearing sea serpent is an added bonus.

After years of toiling on low-budget if memorable movies, Ray Harryhausen moved up into the majors with the release in 1958 of the Technicolor *The 7th Voyage of Sinbad*, one of the finest fantasy films ever made. Sinbad (Kerwin Mathews) is sailing home to Bagdad with his bride-to-be Princess Parisa (Kathryn Grant) when they stop to rescue the wizard Sokurah (Torin Thatcher) from a Cyclops on the island of Colossa. During the escape from the angry monster, Sokurah loses his magic lantern and conspires to return to Colossa to retrieve it. When Sinbad's father, the caliph (Alec Mango), refuses to provide him with a ship, Sokurah uses his powers to shrink Parisa to the size of a doll. Importuned to help the princess, Sokurah agrees to do so but insists that he not only needs a piece of egg shell from a giant bird called the Roc, but other potions that he has in his castle on Colossa. Sinbad sets sail again, and after dealing with a mutiny, two enraged Cyclopes, a huge, two-headed roc, a fire-breathing dragon, and Sokurah's treachery, his beloved is returned to normal size and Baronni (Richard Eyer), a genie who has helped them, is transformed into a normal boy.

7th Voyage is a handsome, classy production with fast-paced direction from Nathan Juran, who had previously worked with Harrryhausen on *20 Million Miles to Earth*. (As Nathan Hertz, he also directed the infamous *Attack of the Fifty Foot Woman*.) Ken Kolb fashioned a screenplay that is full of thrills, wonder and amusement. Bernard Herrmann's score, beginning with the Rimsky-Korsakov–influenced opening credit theme, is consistently rich and exotic, embellishing every scene as Herrmann's scores generally do. And Harryhausen's special visual effects are of a very high order. His animation techniques were dubbed "Dynamation."

There is a host of curious creatures in *Voyage*. First is the petulant one-eyed, cloven hooved (like a satyr), one-horned Cyclops that Harryhausen imbues with lots of personality. There is a great scene when the Cyclops comes upon Sinbad's men trying to loot its treasure chamber, and it deposits them one by one in a cage. He ties one of the men to a spit over an open fire and starts to roast him. The movements of the stop-motion sailor are perfectly matched to those of the live actor. Although the sequence never becomes unnecessarily grisly, it has some of the gruesome flavoring of the original Sinbad stories, as does the scene when the monster crushes a few sailors under a huge tree trunk. In spite of this, you almost feel sorry for the Cyclops when it's killed, as in its eyes (eye?) it was only protecting his possessions and probably just wanted to be left alone. (There is an unintentionally hilarious moment when the shrunken princess climbs on top of the cage to free the prisoners. Sinbad *flings up* the now-unlocked trapdoor at the top of the cage without ever checking to see exactly where the little woman was standing. Good thing there wasn't a nasty accident.)

With the huge two-headed roc, Harryhausen had not only a pair of wings but two snapping beaks to keep track of as he moved the segments of the model up and down one frame at a time. In spite of this, the sequence is flawless. The dragon that guards Sakurah's castle is a bit cartoonish in appearance , but otherwise it is very well designed and animated, reminding one a bit of the rhedosaurus from *Beast from 20,000 Fathoms* (this would be the case for other monsters animated by Harryhausen et al.). When it battles Cyclops number two, the sequence reminds one of the battle between Kong and the T-Rex in *King Kong*.

Another excellent sequence occurs when Sokurah shows off his magical prowess by combining Parisa's lady-in-waiting Sadi (Nana De Herrera) with a big snake, turning her into a four-armed dancing serpent-woman who nearly strangles herself with her own tail! (When the film was re-released in the 1970's, this scene was inexplicably cut from some prints.) But the most outstanding scene may well be the duel between Sinbad and a sword-wielding skeleton brought to life through Sokurah's wizardry. Shot and executed with startling precision, the sequence has added impact due to the superb and lively "dance" music for castanet, xylophone and trumpet Herrmann composed as background for the savage roundelay.

Kerwin Mathews was no Olivier, but besides having the right look he knows how to play this material with the right touch and is properly heroic and commanding when he needs to be. Kathryn Grant may have been somewhat average-looking for a princess, but she is not without her charms. As the genie, Richard Eyer, a busy child actor of the period, is cute if adenoidal. Torin Thatcher steals the show as Sokurah, exuding oily, insincere charm, inwardly sneering, always a beat away from a leer (although he's more interested in the magic lantern than he is in Parisa), authoritative without ever going over the top. A highlight has Thatcher coming out of his cave with his dragon, urging the beast to "Kill! Kill!" Sokurah's cavern headquarters, partly a matte painting, has a darkly beautiful color scheme that reflects his strictly sinister intentions.

Naturally success begat imitation, and it wasn't long before a producer, in this case Edward Small, decided to make his own carbon copy of *7th Voyage*, with much less felicitous results. *Jack the Giant Killer* came out in 1962 and it featured the same lead actor, the same villain, the same director, and the same FX technique, borrowed from Harryhausen by an uncredited Jim Danforth. Danforth was second unit director and also led a team of animators which included Wah Chung, Gene Warren, and Tim Barr. Either Small could not meet Harryhausen's price or the master animator was busy on another project. Possibly he just felt he had already "been there, done that."

The screenplay by Orville H. Hampton and Nathan Juran is basically a re-working of the elements that comprised *7th Voyage*. Pendragon, the exiled king of witches (Torin Thatcher), disguises himself to give a gift of a dancing doll to the princess Elaine (Judi Meredith). The doll grows into the giant Cormoran and walks off with Elaine, but the brave farm boy Jack (Kerwin Mathews) rescues her and defeats the giant. The king has a knighted Jack set sail with Elaine for a place of safety, but Pendragon sends his witches to kidnap her. With the aid of a leprechaun in a bottle (Don Beddoe) and a cabin boy named Peter (Roger Mobley) — *Voyage*'s magic genie divided by two — as well as a Viking named Sigurd (Barry Kelley), Jack storms Pendragon's castle and again rescues Elaine after defeating a number of creatures, including Pendragon himself transformed into a dragon.

The little doll that grows into a giant somewhat resembles Thatcher. Like all of the monsters in *Jack the Giant Killer*, its design lacks that certain stolidity and quality of Harryhausen's models, and the animation throughout the film is more than adequate but never top-notch. It's as if the models are moved every fourth or fifth frame instead of every frame. None of this made a difference to children who in general were just as thrilled by the colorful situations as they had been with *Voyage*, but the difference is apparent to any discerning adult. To be fair, Cormoran's protracted battle with Jack in the mill house is exciting and well-done.

But the other animation sequences in the film are not as good. Designed to resemble the Cyclops in *Voyage*, the two-headed giant with cloven hooves that shows up later in the picture merely looks goofy with the two big fangs on either side of its mouths. Worse still is the laughable sea monster summoned by Pendragon with its unconvincingly slithering tentacles and silly popped-out white eyes. The battle between these two creatures is like a home movie version of the fight between the Cyclops and the dragon in *Voyage*. The dragon itself has a canine-like head and somewhat resembles a belligerent puppy with slick outspread wings. There are some nice shots of it flying over the water and dropping boulders on Sigurd's boat, and it looks a bit creepy in long shot. The dual between Jack and the dragon as the former strides the latter's back and lashes out with his sword is in no way comparable to the skeleton fight or anything else in *Voyage*. This is probably why Danforth left his name off the credits.

Other effects sequences are similarly disappointing. Pendragon creates some soldiers who appear in a puff of smoke to menace Jack but all they do is stand there marching in place—why don't they just attack the guy? Then there are a bunch of silly arms growing out of the walls of a corridor that pathetically strike out at Jack as he races by. The optical effect of witches descending in a carriage and the storm that heralds their approach are more on the mark, however, as is a superior matte painting of Pendragon's castle overlooking the sea. The musical score by Paul Sawtell and Bert Shefter is no match for anything by the great Bernard Herrmann. At least Nathan Juran generally keeps things moving as swiftly as he did in *Voyage*.

Kerwin Mathews is as effective as he was in *Voyage*, although there is absolutely no difference in his acting style considering in the first film he was playing a noted hero of royal blood and in this he is just a farm boy. Thatcher is as good as ever. Judi Meredith makes a fetching Elaine, who is turned evil by Pendragon's magic. (We can tell she's now "evil" because she instantly becomes sexier—and wears red lipstick!) When cabin boy Peter's father is killed, one can tell young Mobley was instructed to repeatedly blink his eyes to create tears. Anna Lee scores as Lady Constance, who is secretly working for Pendragon until she is exposed as a witch and brought out of her spell by smashing a mirror.

Although there are dull sections, *Jack the Giant Killer* is not a bad movie; it just isn't in the same league as its obvious inspiration.

"*And the Lord said behold now—The Behemoth!*" So intones a voice at the beginning of *The Giant Behemoth* (1959) against an ominous backdrop of a swelling seascape hiding some*thing* beneath the waves. *Behemoth* (known as *Behemoth the Sea Monster* in the U.K.) was Eugène Lourié's follow-up to *Beast from 20,000 Fathoms*. Originally it wasn't meant to be a dinosaur film at all, which is why the film has such a strange schizoid quality. Lourié remembered that the monster in the film was supposed to be "a blob of expanding radiation" but was changed to a prehistoric beast at the insistence of the British producers (the film was an U.S–U.K. co-production).

Working with Daniel Hyatt, Lourie (who received sole screen credit for the script) quickly threw together a screenplay simply in order to sign the contract, but there was no time to do any of the planned rewriting. Which is one of the reasons why *Behemoth* is so similar to *Beast*. And so different.

Steve Kearns (Gene Evans) is a marine biologist who warns attendees at a conference that because of atomic testing, sea life has been absorbing radiation, the amount of which increases exponentially the higher the life form is up the food chain. According to Kearns, this has resulted in "a geometrical progression of deadly menace." It is only a matter of time before some mutated something "strikes back at us." A fiery creature rises from the sea at Cornwall to burn to death a fisherman who talks about a "behemoth." There are other incidents which point to the existence of a marine animal of "tremendous size and strength."

The radioactive dinosaur in *The Giant Behemoth* (1959) strides past a bus, cars and pedestrians who are scrambling for their lives. This time the scene of devastation was London.

With Professor Bickford (Andre Morell) of the Atomic Energy Commission and Samson (Jack McGowran), the curator of the Natural History Museum, Kearns attempts to track down the creature. Samson identifies it as a paliosaurus, which is electric like an eel, enabling it to send out burning waves of the radiation it has absorbed. After rampaging through London, the monster is destroyed with a torpedo containing pure radium. Kearns and Bickford then discover that in all probability yet another monster is romping off the coast of America.

The effects for the film were designed and created by Willis (*King Kong*) O'Brien with the participation of Jack Rabin, Irving Block, Louis DeWitt and Pete Peterson. The first appearances of the behemoth are inauspicious because instead of a stop-motion model, a prop head and neck is employed. Reportedly, the wire-controlled head was capable of some movement but it broke down during the filming of a key sequence and could only flop around rather pathetically. This sequence has the behemoth attacking a ferry boat on the Thames. The cutting from the real ferry to the miniature is sabotaged by the fact that it is all too obvious that the ferry model is devoid of inhabitants. Tiny toy cars drop into the drink, intercut with real people splashing into the water, as the monster overturns the ferry with its neck. The prop head of the behemoth is well-designed but it just can't do anything; the neck looks as if it can barely hold up the creature's head. The worst effect in the movie, however, is when what appears to be a sock puppet that's supposed to be the behemoth's cranium nudges the mini-sub that's been chasing after it with a radium torpedo.

The stop-motion sequences are another matter. The film's highlight is when the behemoth treks through London, the loud thud of its footsteps and the intense music combining to create a feeling of dread. Many of the same shots are used again, sometimes against a differing background so the repetition isn't too obvious on first viewing. Still the sequence has almost as much power as the rhedosaurus' rampage in Manhattan. The stop-motion model with its glistening, wet, textured skin is beautiful, and the animation is often quite fluid. The behemoth looks this way and that, peers curiously up at buildings, its tongue wiggling in its mouth and letting out the occasional roar for good measure. In the underwater climax, the behemoth looks good as it swims, its legs furiously pumping up and down as the mini-sub pursues it. One of the best shots of the monster has it rising out of the Thames at night near a deserted park after the first attack, pulling up to its full height like a snarling, demonic fury.

The Giant Behemoth in general has a much nastier tone than *Beast from 20,000 Fathoms*, the devoured cop scene in the latter notwithstanding. There are numerous scenes of the behemoth exuding radioactive energy that fries a farm boy, soldiers, and a group of curious, mostly elderly pedestrians to a blackened crisp. (These grisly shots seem to be created by the simple method of doctoring still photographs.) When the behemoth's outsized foot comes down on one automobile, you can hear the frenzied scream of the (unseen) man inside before he's mushed to jelly. The rhedosaurus may have carried a virulent disease, but the behemoth's radioactive aura wipes out sea life for miles around. Even the ending has a downbeat tone to it with the implication that another behemoth may kill thousands more.

The behemoth is described as being 150 to 200 feet long. In a photograph that the police show to Kearns and Bickford, its footprint is about ten times the size of a police car. But as the monster tears through London, it's clear that its feet, while a bit out of proportion, aren't that much bigger than the cars it smashes flat. While the behemoth is a frightening monster, somehow it's disappointing that it's just a radioactive dinosaur and not the unknown malevolent mutated life form that Kearns suggests at the opening and the moody first half of the movie seems to be preparing us for. Not only is there absolutely no explanation for how the extinct paliosaurus survived to the 20th century, Kearns, Bickford, and even Samson don't even wonder about it. The somewhat airy Samson simply says that he always knew that dinosaurs were alive somewhere and the reports of sea monsters were just "the tall, graceful neck of paliosaurus." *Okay.*

In spite of its many script loopholes and other flaws, *The Giant Behemoth* is often tense and suspenseful, with creepy scenes such as when the behemoth first comes out of the sea in Cornwall to appear before the fisherman or when it is seen as a huge radiating mass behind a building at the farmhouse. An unusual feature of the film is that there is no love interest or secondary romance, no sexy lady scientist or assistant, to distract from — or add to — the proceedings. But perhaps there's just too many cheesy elements to the production for it to be a true classic, although it certainly has its admirers, this writer included.

19

As in *Beast*, the film is full of interesting characters and flavorful performances. Gene Evans and Andre Morell make a good team as the earnest, impatient American and the more laid-back Britisher who is at first amused by Kearns' insistence that something monstrous is hiding out there in the ocean. In Cornwall, where hundreds of dead fish have washed up on shore, Kearns looks out the window at the sea and talks portentously about the mysterious monster while Bickford seems to be trying hard not to laugh at him. Jack MacGowan, who years later played the murdered director in *The Exorcist*, is a hoot as the nerdy, likable scientist who searches for the monster by helicopter; a sudden wave of energy wipes it out of the sky.

Henry Vidon has a nice turn as the old fisherman, Trevethan, who first sees the behemoth, while Leigh Madison isn't bad as his daughter, though her crying over his body is so unconvincing that it often engenders laughter at screenings. John Turner is very effective as her boyfriend John, who inexplicably and stupidly shoves the back of his hand into the glowing stuff surrounding the old man's body and shyly says "I'm afraid it isn't very pretty" when Kearns asks to look at his injury. It's almost as if the scene where he shows off the burn was filmed before the scene when he gets injured. Since the makeup person didn't realize that John would more likely have had his fingertips burned if he touched the strange "stuff" (in itself not very smart), the only way they could get the burn on the back of his hand was for him to illogically kind of slap it against the material in a most unnatural manner.

The scenes of running pedestrians have some unintentionally humorous moments. There is the one odd-looking lady who walks along, unconcerned, with as much haste and fear as if she were having a Sunday stroll in the park or somebody told her she'd get, say, a donut if she just moved along with the rest of the crowd, only nobody told her a 200-foot-long monster was supposed to be right behind her. Then there's the nervous guy who beats feet and looks properly scared but uses one hand to hold his coat together throughout the entire scene as if he lost a button and the day were just too chilly to let go, giant behemoth or no giant behemoth. Funniest of all is one extra who flops his arms this way and that, dashes to the right and then the left, looks petrified to the point of stupefaction — as if he'd run over his own mother if she got in his way, his emoting commendable but just a trifle *too* dramatic. If this extra had been shown running next to a car right after it got crushed or something along those lines, his panicky hysteria wouldn't have seemed so overdone.

There is a slackness, a second-rate, cobbled-together quality to *Behemoth* that puts it several cuts below its predecessor, although many people find it more enjoyable than the better-made *Beast from 20,00 Fathoms*. Maybe it's the eerie tone, Edwin Astley's creepy musical score, that great big tongue of the behemoth, or those highly dramatic pedestrians.

Whatever it is, it somehow works.

Sir Arthur Conan Doyle's famous novel *The Lost World* had already been filmed during the silent era when Irwin Allen decided to produce and direct a new color version for Twentieth Century–Fox in 1960. Although Willis O'Brien, who did the animation effects for the original, was hired as effects technician, it's debatable how much he had to do with the film when real-life lizards were substituted for stop-motion models of dinosaurs. The movie suffers greatly because of it.

Jules Verne had been the first author to introduce prehistoric animals into a modern storyline in *Journey to the Center of the Earth*, and Conan Doyle elaborated on the theme in *The Lost World*. The 1925 silent film version set the standard for two types of monster films and was a combination of both. In the first type, people traveled to "lost worlds" (such as the isolated South American plateau in the movie) and encountered monsters, and in the second type, giant monsters crashed into modern civilization (such as the brontosaurus which attacks London at the end of the film).

The silent *Lost World* was also a trendsetter in the field of special effects by the wizard Willis O'Brien, who employed perhaps a cruder form of the stop-motion animation that he would use to bring King Kong to life eight years later. Although some of the early process shots are poor, others are first-rate, such as when Ed Malone spies on some stegosauri. The especially memorable scenes include the fight between a brontosaurus and an allosaurus which ends with the former falling off a cliff and landing in the mud far below, and an attack on the camp by another allosaurus in the middle of the night, the horrible glowing eyes of the creature the first clue that something scary is about to make its presence known. (O'Brien has the first allosaurus curl its lip in an almost campy kind of contemptuous sneer, and repeats this with the brontosaurus that rises from the lake in *King Kong*.) Many feel the best sequence in the movie, especially where effects are concerned, is when the huge brontosaurus runs wild through the streets of London. The dinosaur's movements are not dissimilar to those of *The Giant Behemoth* (1959), which is not a surprise as Willis also did the stop motion for that film. Like its 1950s descendant, the brontosaurus also accidentally crashes into the Thames.

In the remake, the blustery Professor Challenger (Claude Rains) heads an expedition into the Amazon to explore a plateau that he insists has been isolated from time and upon which dinosaurs still thrive. Other members of the party include Professor Summerlee (Richard Haydn), who hopes to prove Challenger wrong; adventurer Lord John Roxton (Michael Rennie); Ed Malone (David Hedison) of Global News; and Jennifer Holmes (Jill St. John), brash daughter of the publisher who is funding the expedition. In South America they are assisted by helicopter pilot Gomez (Fernando Lamas) and his simpering buddy Costa (Jay Novello). They do indeed find living dinosaurs on the plateau, as well as bad-tempered can-

The 1960 color remake of *The Lost World* (1960) featured Jay Novello, Claude Rains, Richard Haydn, Ray Stricklyn, David Hedison, Jill St. John.

21

nibals who wish to sacrifice the lot of them to their Fire God. With the aid of a pretty local girl who has taken a shine to Jennifer's brother David (Ray Stricklyn), the party makes its way through the Cave of Fire and emerges at the bottom of the plateau just before the whole shebang explodes.

Children at the time were fascinated by the whole Allen stew and saw nothing out of place—as many critics did—with Jennifer's shocking pink knee boots. Co-screenwriters Charles Bennett and Allen himself weren't content with all the action of Conan Doyle's original novel, so came up with time-consuming—and rather tedious—subplots involving a love triangle (between Roxton, Jennifer and Malone) and a secondary sort of romance between David and the unnamed local girl. (The business about Gomez holding Roxton responsible for the death of his brother was actually carried over from the novel.) They also decided to throw diamonds into the mix and turn the plateau into the legendary El Dorado for good measure.

Kids came to see the dinosaurs and Allen and company basically delivered, even if the dinosaurs were just lizards tricked up with neck pieces and fins on the back. One small gator who battles one of the lizards is made up to resemble a sailback reptile. They all come off more like dragons than dinosaurs. There's a decided creepiness of a minor sort when we first hear one of the beasts, barely seen, crashing through the trees as it comes near the camp and then chases the members of the party in circles. Our first full view of a dinosaur occurs when Frosty, Jennifer's toy poodle, bravely runs into a clearing where one is contentedly munching on leaves—dog versus dinosaur (the screenplay is littered with moments of similar "cuteness"). This is a split screen shot with the monster on the left of the screen, supposedly observing with dispassion the people and poodle on the right before it lets out a roar and frightens them all away.

A lizard poses as a rampaging dinosaur in *The Lost World* (1960).

The first "big" scene occurs when another lizard (well, probably the *same* lizard but a different "dinosaur," if you get the picture) chases Jennifer and Malone through the jungle and winds up in a fight with the aforementioned "sailback gator," who seems to be in a bit of a stupor. Nevertheless the two engage in a lively fight, and there is a genuinely striking process shot showing them battling on top of the cliff as the lizard's tail knocks the human couple onto an outcropping below, then swings back and nearly hits them again. If only every shot were of this inventive quality! More often we see dinosaurs making their way past gnarled "prehistoric" trees with big above-the-surface roots (the easier for the lizards to knock the trees over) or shots of dinosaurs growling in the foreground and Jill St. John lying helplessly in the background. For good measure there is a green superimposed spider that menaces the local girl on more than one occasion. There are also some unconvincing man-eating plants, one of which almost swallows up Summerlee.

The second "big" scene, alas, occurs at the end of the picture when the party escapes through the Cave of Fire. Like some of the jungle settings, the caverns have a nice, atmospheric look to them. When they arrive at the Graveyard, however, the actors are simply walking down the same steps that were used for the Atlantis sequence in *Journey to the Center of the Earth*, redressed with smoke and big dinosaur ribs in the foreground. One of the nicest effects in the picture — another split screen approach — has the party hugging the walls of a cliff on one side while there's a sheer drop into a river of molten lava on the other. One of the least impressive effects has to do with tentacles that inexplicably grow out of a wall at an entry point into the Graveyard. Arranged in a circle, these snake-like appendages seem about as threatening as flaccid, over-tooted New Year's Eve noisemakers.

The highlight of the long Cave of Fire sequence is the party's encounter with the Fire God, another big lizard of course, which awakens and eats poor Costa when Gomez tries to shoot Roxton. A soft doll was placed in the lizard's mouth to represent Costa. This particular specimen was an especially expressive, if not hammy, lizard with just the right kind of attitude and carriage to play a "God." Alas, it's soon drenched in lava from an overhead dam and hence failed to be nominated for an Oscar.

Talky and often slow-paced, *The Lost World* is not helped by Irwin Allen's direction, but some of the actors are another story. Claude Rains is very amusing as the hot-headed but lovable Challenger and manages to survive dinosaurs and Frosty with his dignity intact. Peppery Richard Haydn is the only one in the cast who is a match for him, with the exception of brilliant character actor Jay Novello. A highly versatile actor, Novello was so able to lose himself in his many characterizations that it's hard at first to imagine that the crafty, cowardly South American of *The Lost World* is the same man who enacted the geeky Mr. Meriweather on the classic "séance" episode of *I Love Lucy* ("Ethel to Tilly! Come in — Tilly!"). But it was.

Goliath and the Dragon (Italian, 1960) started life as *Hercules' Revenge* (or *La Vendetta di Ercole*) but when the film was acquired by American-International Pictures they had to change the hero's name to Goliath because another company owned the rights to Hercules. *La Vendetta* was another in a long line of mostly cheesy "sword and sandal" or "sword and sorcery" flicks churned out by the Italian studios and starring assorted muscle boys of various nationalities. The star of *Goliath and the Dragon*, Mark Forest (not to be confused with Michael Forest of *Viking Women*, who himself starred in some Italian flicks), was born in Brooklyn as Lou Degni. He used the money he made appearing in numerous sword and sorcery flicks to study opera, and became a vocal coach after retiring from films. Like other musclebound hunks of the period and as well as today, he has a well-oiled but utterly hair-less body.

Goliath and the Dragon concerns the efforts of evil ruler Eurito (Broderick Crawford) to destroy his hated opponent Goliath by any means at his disposal. He enlists the aid of pretty slave Alcinoe (Gaby André, who would later star in *The Cosmic Monsters*) in a scheme to pit Goliath against his sensitive brother Illo (Wandisa Guida). There is already a strain in the brothers' relationship because Illo has fallen for Thea (Federica Ranchi), whose parents were supposedly responsible for the deaths of the brothers' parents. Goliath wants to drive the two lovers apart but Alcinoe lies and tells Illo that Goliath really wants Thea for himself, which Illo passes on to Goliath's wife Dejanira (Eleonora Ruffo). Before it can all turn into a massive soap opera, Eurito tries to feed Dejanira to his pet dragon, which Goliath slays, but not before dispatching a host of other macabre creatures. Goliath tears apart Eurito's castle, a repentant Alcinoe sacrifices herself to save Dejanira, and Eurito falls into a bed of poisonous snakes. Illo and Thea are happily reunited, as are the two brothers.

The monsters in *Goliath and the Dragon* are not too impressive. A winged, man-sized bat creature swings over a creditable swamp set with flaming pools but in close-up it resembles a bad-tempered Muppet. A bear that attacks Alcinoe and is killed by Goliath simply looks as if a stunt man threw a bear-skin rug over his shoulders. A three-headed St. Bernard–sized fire-breathing monster with a canine snout, and one pair of flip-flopping legs, registers zero on the believability scale. Most disappointing is the dragon, who makes a brief appearance at the beginning of the film and turns up again at the climax. In long shot the creature is a silly-looking model not badly animated by stop motion expert Jim Danforth in a couple of brief inserts. When our hero interacts with the beast in live action shots, however, a phony life-size mock-up head is substituted and looks ridiculous. It's basically a big, laughable funhouse puppet with smoke streaming out of its nostrils and a red painted maw with colossal white teeth that unconvincingly tries to take bites out of Goliath. The whole sequence is a big bust. At least the caverns where these scenes take place are impressive if overly lit.

One of the movie's best scenes employs a large animal that is not an actual monster. Eurito takes great pleasure in executing men by having an elephant step forward and crush their heads beneath its foot. (The sequence is gruesome but not graphic; there are no spurts of blood or shots of mashed craniums.) Illo is about to be the next victim when Goliath races in and tackles the elephant himself. Forest is actually shown wrestling the presumably trained beast to its knees! What a performance!

Goliath and the Dragon is well-paced under the direction of Vittorio Cottafavi, and Les Baxter's score is flavorful if minor. The movie benefits from one of the best dubbing jobs ever done for this kind of movie (even Broderick Crawford's voice is dubbed, which was probably for the best), with the voice-over actors performing as if they themselves were up on the screen. The settings and costumes, while attractive, sometimes have a kind of shabby, second-rate look to them. With better special effects, *Goliath and the Dragon* might have been a contender.

In 1961 Eugène Lourié came out with his third and last dinosaur movie, *Gorgo*, which sort of brought everything full circle. Just as *Godzilla* had been inspired by the success of

Beast from 20,000 Fathoms, *Gorgo* was in a sense an imitation of *Godzilla*. Like Godzilla, the monsters of *Gorgo* walked upright and were much taller than the typical dinosaur. At approximately 200 feet, the mother monster in *Gorgo* is about half the size of Godzilla — while still quite formidable — while the baby, christened Gorgo, is 40 or 50 feet tall.

Off the Irish coast, deep sea salvagers Joe Ryan (Bill Travers) and Sam Slade (William Sylvester) encounter underground volcanic activity off the Irish coast which causes extinct creatures to rise to the surface. One of these creatures is a huge dinosaur that they manage to capture and bring back to London, exhibiting it in a circus. They are unaware that the creature's mother — four times the size of the baby — is coming after the animal. When she makes her presence known, the authorities arrogantly predict that they can quickly dispose of her. Unfortunately the mother proves too much for the armed forces and she smashes through London, causing massive death and destruction, and retrieves her infant. The two creatures make their way back to the sea and disappear into the mist.

Both the baby and mother monster are better designed than Godzilla. They have big clawed feet, glowing red eyes (especially the mother) and huge hands that also end in curved claws. Their eyes and mouths open — although as with Godzilla, the maw doesn't open in a convincing manner — and their ears wiggle a bit. They look exactly alike because only one rubber suit was built; the scene showing the two of them going off together at the end was a process shot. Unfortunately, the illusion of life is never really created the way it could have been with a stop-motion model. A smart decision on Lourie's part was to have just about everything happen at night or in fog to help disguise the beasts' phoniness. Gorgo first rises out of the sea in a moody sequence where men in rowboats with torches glide through the mist searching for a comrade who disappeared. The film has good miniatures and most of the process shots are effective, although you can often see right through the falling debris.

As in *Giant Behemoth* there is no love interest. The two heroes befriend a small orphan boy named Sean (Vincent Winter) who bonds with Gorgo and stows away on their boat. Frankly, Sean's identification with the beast makes him seem demented, and one of the men even calls him a "little nuthead" at one point. While Sean is indeed prescient in suggesting that capturing Gorgo will lead to disaster, his smile at the conclusion — after witnessing the gruesome deaths of hundreds — simply because baby Gorgo is returning home makes him a serious candidate for psychological analysis. Sean is meant to be a touching, wise figure but his dopey admiration for the monsters makes him only come off as a fool.

The problem with *Gorgo* is that it's the kind of monster movie — like *King Kong* (especially the Peter Jackson remake), which it also resembles — that unfairly expects the viewer to sympathize with the monster instead of the innocent people that are crushed and mangled underfoot. Yet the scenes of mayhem in *Gorgo* are particularly terrible and intense, especially when the ceiling of an underground station collapses on hundreds of men, women, and children who have taken refuge there. What's worse, the greedy instigators who brought Gorgo to London survive unharmed while other people pay the price of their folly. True, Gorgo and her mother did not ask for the baby dinosaur to be kidnapped, but — as amazing as they are — they're still just monsters.

John Loring and Daniel Hyatt's screenplay, whatever its deficiencies, follows the lead

Gorgo (1961) was the third dinosaur-on-a-rampage movie directed by Eugène Lourié. Gorgo and his even bigger mother, played by actors in monster suits, tore big chunks out of London.

of Lourié's previous two dino thrillers in that the characters generally seem like real people. Sam is the more sensitive of the two men, disturbed and guilt-wracked by each new death at the hands of Gorgo (who breaks free at one point before Mama shows up) and trying to act like a father to the boy. Joe is the more rough-hewn and expedient of the two, willing to overlook everything in the name of money, but even he eventually comes around — although far too late.

Gorgo is not named after the actual dinosaur Gorgosaurus but after the mythical Gorgon, who turned men to stone with its gaze. Dorkin (Martin Benson), the circus owner who puts Gorgo on display, implies that Gorgo's appearance is so frightening that the beast could have the same figurative effect on anyone who looks at it. People at the circus seem more amused by the animal than anything else, however. In fact, never is there any particular awe worked up over the beast and no one ever seems to wonder where it exactly came from or how it survived since the Cretaceous period. The mother eventually causes awe but only after the military realize she's a hell of a lot mightier than anyone ever imagined.

In vivid color, *Gorgo* is much more intense than *Beast* or *Behemoth* and perhaps for that reason isn't nearly as much fun. The panicking crowd scenes are truly disturbing (the city isn't evacuated because of the military's arrogance), with the devastation described by one reporter as "worse than the blitz!" The special effects are not good enough to make the production that interesting. The actors are all professional, the music by Angelo Lavagnino is serviceable (the movie ends with the attractive, somewhat sappy theme for sappy Sean), and Lourie keeps things moving as always. But *Gorgo* doesn't really stand out in the annals of films about sea monsters and dragons.

Bert I. Gordon came out with one of his most entertaining films when United Artists released *The Magic Sword* in 1962. The sorcerer Lodak (Basil Rathbone) kidnaps Princess Helene (Anne Helm) and tells her father that she will be fed to his dragon unless he turns his kingdom over to Lodak. Young Sir George (Gary Lockwood), who has loved Helene from afar, volunteers to save her with the aid of a magic sword, Aikalon, and a host of international knights. Sir Branton (Liam Sullivan), who wants Helene for himself and is secretly aiding Lodak, objects to his participation. The knights face death and doom at the hands of seven curses laid down by Lodak across the path to his castle. With the help of his foster mother Sybil (Estelle Winwood), George saves Helene and defeats the terrible dragon. Transformed into a panther, Sybil takes care of Lodak.

The mostly low-tech but enthusiastic effects were done by Bert and Flora Gordon. The first curse the knights encounter is an economy-sized ogre that stands about twenty feet tall, with a hairy body, and a mask with grizzled teeth and fright wig that fits over the actor's head. He interacts with the knights via process and forced perspective shots. There are heat waves, death pools, and floating heads that are serviceably done. One knight encounters a sexy babe who turns out to be a hideous sharp-toothed hag in disguise. (Maila Nurma, aka Vampira, who appeared in *Plan Nine from Outer Space,* plays the hag but not the babe.)

Inside Lodak's castle we are introduced to cackling midgets who enter Helene's cell to torment her, "coneheads" with pointy, bald craniums, and six-inch people who are kept in a cage and wind up in the stew. A highlight has them cutting the ropes that bind George and freeing him to save Helene. A nifty bit has Lodak mounting traitorous Sir Branton's head on his wall with a contemptuous flick of his finger, and there's a simple but effective touch of having the statue of a monster seem alive by giving it a real moving eyeball. For her part, his nemesis Sybil is attended not only by an adorable chimp in a red tunic, but by a two-headed bald housekeeper played winningly by twin actors.

The best effect in the film is the impressive, two-headed, fire-breathing dragon that shows up at the climax. It was built full-size, and process shots make it appear to be even larger. Beautifully designed, the mechanical construct has fangs, flaring nostrils, immobile eyes, a sweeping tail (which does not move too convincingly), and bumpy mottled skin with decorative fins and scales. The fire comes from the dragon's nose and not its mouth. The creature's roars seem to have been borrowed from the sound track of Irwin Allen's *Lost World.* It is the best thing in the movie and one of the best mechanical monsters of its type.

The Magic Sword, which many consider Gordon's best movie, is a winning combination of gruesomeness *à la* Grimm's Fairy tales and a lot of fun and whimsy. Basil Rathbone is as superb as ever as Lodak, and Estelle Winwood plays with just the right touch as Sybil. Gary Lockwood displays boyish charm as the hero although it is never explained why he is called *Sir* George when there is nothing to indicate that he has been officially knighted by the king, who is completely unaware of his existence. Richard Markowitz's music is full of ominous expectancy, and Franz Bachelin's art direction gives the picture a generally handsome look. Gordon's direction ensures that the action never flags long enough for the film to bore.

Jason and the Argonauts (British, 1963) is generally considered the high-water mark in the career of top special effects artist and stop-motion expert Ray Harryhausen. Indeed, forty-five years after its release it remains one of the finest fantasy films ever made. Fearing that Jason (Todd Armstrong) will fulfill a prophecy and slay him, Pelias sends him off on a voyage from which he hopes he will never return. (Oddly, Pelias also sends his son, Acastus, played by Gary Raymond, with Jason to keep an eye on him.) Jason and his "Argonauts"— so called because they set sail on a ship built by Argos (Laurence Naismith)— are to capture the mystical Golden Fleece from the land of Colchis at the end of the world. Although occasionally aided by Hera, Queen of the Gods (Honor Blackman), the Argonauts have their hands full with such menaces as Talos, a gargantuan bronze statue come to life; two flying, chittering harpies; and huge, clashing rocks that nearly crush them and their ship before the giant-sized sea god Triton comes to their rescue. On Colchis, Jason must contend with a seven-headed hydra that guards the fleece, as well as an army of living skeletons. Triumphing over all odds, Jason sets sail with Medea (Nancy Kovack), who has betrayed her country out of love for him.

Jason and the Argonauts has first-rate production values, including beautiful settings — such as Mount Olympus and the altar room of Hecate — and exquisite costumes, including the handsome uniforms worn by Jason and his crew. The effects, of course, are of a high order, even in the "lesser" scenes, such as when Jason is summoned to Mount Olympus and stands on a tabletop with the gigantic Gods before him, a puff of gentle mist playing across the checkered floor. The long sequence with Talos, who is several hundred feet high, is one of the most noteworthy, beginning with Hercules and his young friend Hylas' entry into a sinister valley full of huge statues on pedestals and ending with the death of Hylas under the crushing weight of Talos' shattered body. Clunky and creaking as an animated statue would be, Talos is one of Harryhausen's most awe-inspiring creations. (Not to nitpick, but the manner of defeating Talos — via a convenient "Achilles' heel" or bolt in his ankle which once opened releases "blood"— is a mite convenient. Also, the continuity as Hercules and Hylas walk toward the statue of Talos in the valley is a bit careless. Although we see them walking closer and closer to the statue in long shot, the medium shots continue to show the two of them standing in the same patch of grass.)

The scene with Talos on the Island of Bronze is only the first of several marvelous set-pieces in the movie. Some scenes have as a backdrop what remains of an actual 5000-year-old temple. There is a wonderful shot when one of the Harpies grabs the cloth belt in Phineas' outfit and pulls on it, causing the old man to roll across the ground, the movements of the live-action actor matching perfectly with the taunting motions of the witch-like flying harpie.

The sequence with the *Argo* attempting to pass through the aptly named clashing rocks is very suspenseful and harrowing. Harryhausen saved some time by using an actor to play the giant Triton instead of a stop-motion model, but this proves more effective than expected, largely because the effects work is still excellent and the uncredited actor has just the right

The colossal bronze statue of Talos comes to life and attacks the sailors in a splendid scene from *Jason and the Argonauts* (1963).

look and attitude (Harryhausen told him to stick out his lower lip). Perhaps all these afore-mentioned great sequences take a back seat to the two major battles that climax the film: Jason versus the Hydra, and the Argonauts versus the Children of the Hydra's teeth. With seven snapping heads and long necks, the hydra was undoubtedly a challenge for Harryhausen to animate. There is also a puppet Jason and a prop hydra tail that grabs up the live actor in its coils.

The sequence that follows took the longest to shoot. After the hydra is slain, King Aeetes calls down a fireball to roast it and has his men collect the teeth from the blackened corpse. Throwing the teeth onto the ground, he calls forth the skeletal remains of men murdered by the hydra, who battle Jason and his crew in an elaborate, protracted, and eye-popping sequence that takes the same concept as the Sinbad vs. skeleton climax of *7th Voyage of Sinbad* to a higher power and then some. The somewhat tongue-in-cheek quality of the sequence doesn't detract from it at all.

Not all of the memorable scenes in the movie have to do with FX. As Jason is collecting his crew for the *Argo*, a skinny latecomer named Hylas appears to challenge Hercules for a spot on board via a discus-throwing competition. Everyone is convinced that the manly Hercules will win over the man-boy, but Hylas uses his brain and has his discus skipping across the water to land farther out at sea than the one thrown by Hercules. Hylas' death on the Isle of Bronze is undeniably tragic. A guilty Hercules, who stole a brooch from the treasure chamber of Talos against Hylas' advice, refuses to accept the lad's death and remains on the island to search for him. There is also much amusing and interesting banter between Zeus and Hera as they watch the events unfolding from their lofty perch atop Mount Olympus.

Harryhausen always directs his special effects scenes, but director of record Don Chaffey does a good job with everything else, including the opening scenes depicting the forces of Pelias attacking Thessaly and Pelias himself murdering Jason's mother in the temple of Hera. Although it may not bear up under close scrutiny, the screenplay by Beverley Cross and Jan Read makes lively and intelligent use of classic tales of mythology. Wilkie Cooper's photography brings everything to life in bold and vivid hues. Bernard Herrmann's score grabs you by the throat from the dramatic opening notes of the theme and, as usual, enhances every scene, especially the brilliant fight with the skeletal warriors.

Because it is obvious that his voice is dubbed, some may have assumed that Todd Armstrong was an Americanized name ("Armstrong," no less!) of some Italian actor chosen to play Jason because of his looks. Very handsome and bearded, although not muscle-bound, Armstrong undoubtedly ignited a few schoolgirl — and schoolboy — crushes when *Jason* was released. But the actor was actually born John Harris Armstrong in Missouri in 1937. He had already had small roles in a couple of American films before being cast as Jason, and he did a few more films and some television work afterward (he died in 1992). The producers of *Jason* presumably felt that Armstrong's voice didn't sound European or noble enough for Jason. It was the same thing with Nancy Kovack as Medea, who was also dubbed so she would sound more patrician and continental. (British actors Tim Turner and Eva Haddon did the honors, respectively.)

The cast was rounded out with some well-chosen and unusually talented British players, including Laurence Naismith, who would later appear in *The Valley of Gwangi*. Naismith manages to maintain his dignity despite the fact that he spends much of the movie wearing what looks like a large diaper and nothing else. Gary Raymond, oily and smirking as Acastus, had had a triumph in the title role of *Playboy of the Western World* (1962) and also appeared in *Suddenly Last Summer* (1959). Some felt Nigel Green was not enough of a muscleman to play Hercules, but he is excellent and heroic in the part, and perfectly beefy to boot. Jack Gwillim comes right up to the edge of campy madness as King Aeetes of Colchis, but never quite crosses the line. Douglas Wilmer is appropriately sinister as Pelias, and Honor Blackman — "Pussy Galore" of *Goldfinger* and the forerunner of Mrs. Peel on *The Avengers*— makes a fetching and more than competent Hera. John Cairney is an appealing Hylas. Niall MacGinnis, perfect as Zeus, appeared in many other genre films of the period.

Some of Harryhausen's films have been criticized because all they seem to have going for them is the wonderful stop-motion effects, but this is certainly not true of *Jason and the Argonauts*. It does not just contain great animation but is, in a word, *splendid* on virtually all levels.

In 1966 Hammer Films came out with a remake of the Hollywood dinosaur movie

One Million B.C. adding the word *Years* to the title to differentiate it from the earlier version. Instead of blown-up lizards and other creatures, the movie boasted the stop-motion animation work of Ray Harryhausen. *One Million Years B.C.* essentially uses the same storyline as the original film (with a new screenplay by the film's producer, Michael Carreras), with Raquel Welch and John Richardson playing the two lovers (Luana and Tumak) from different tribes. Tumak's people are cruel, brunette, and barbaric while Luana's tribe is blond, nurturing and delicate, but not terribly brave. It is Tumak who rushes to assist a man being chewed on by a dinosaur while the members of Launa's tribe initially flee, only coming together to combat the fearsome beast after Tumak has taken the lead.

Stodgily directed by Don Chaffey (who might have been much less interested in the material than he was with *Jason and the Argonauts*), the movie is pretty slow-going between the dinosaur scenes. This was the first of several Harryhausen flicks that prompted critics to complain that while the effects were wonderful, everything else was comparatively forgettable. Even the dinosaur scenes are uneven in effectiveness, although much of the stop-motion work is outstanding. There is also a credible climactic earthquake and eruption, well-done but for a few tacky process shots.

The first dinosaur to appear *is* actually a blown-up lizard, a hungry-looking iguana that tries to make a meal out of Tumak. Great sound effects as the thing hisses and drags itself after the tiny man add to its ferocity, while the process shots blending man with monster make the beast seem almost of Godzillian proportions. At one point the lizard pauses dramatically and lets out a kind of petulant wheeze or whiny growl as it stares down at its continually evasive prey, making the whole sequence strangely amusing.

With the exception of a big spider feasting on a beetle, the other animals are of the stop-motion variety. A brontosaurus that crosses the valley in the distance is a bit disappointing, but the humongous turtle that shows up next is more on the mark. The feisty turtle doesn't do much of anything; it just seems on its way to the ocean. The people throw spears at it but let it go by, although they certainly could have eaten the thing and used its shell, etc., for other purposes. The battle between a triceratops and a kind of T-Rex (with a horn on its snout) goes on too long but is otherwise well-done.

The two best sequences have to do with a pterodactyl and an allosaurus. The former flies down to the beach and grabs up Luana in its claws; there's a great shot of Raquel Welch hanging helplessly over the hungry pterodactyl babies in the nest with the sea far below them. This is followed by an excellent scene with the first monster fighting another pterodactyl for its supper. By far the best animated sequence in the movie presents a hyper-active, vicious allosaurus as it attacks the camp of Luana's tribe. The beast arrives at just the right moment; immediately following a bucolic scene when the tribe is laughing and relaxing. Snapping at a terrified child in a tree, crunching on a poor man, lashing out at the tribespeople, diving on top of Tumak only to impale itself on his weapon, the allosaurus is an expert and memorable performer and the scene presents Harryhausen at his most magical.

The human actors do better than you might expect in this material. Raquel Welch, promoted to superstar and sex symbol supreme because of the film's poster (on which she appears as a cave woman of the type that hardly ever trod the Earth), is decidedly attractive and competent. John Richardson gives off the proper air as her lover. Exotic, earthy

Martine Beswick, who took part in a deadly gypsy "cat fight" in *From Russia with Love,* gets in another violent tussle with Welch in this. The character actors who comprise the rest of the cast were all clearly chosen for their expressive faces and ability at pantomiming. The scene when Tumak tries to spear a fish as Luana and her women friends do, only to fall on his face as the others laugh at him good-naturedly, is genuinely charming. Almost in spite of himself, he winds up with a fish on his spear, engendering a fresh flood of gentle laughter. There are some expansive, striking settings photographed by Wilkie Cooper, but Mario Nascimbene's musical score, which tries to be "otherworldly" in the hoariest sense possible, is sappy and third-rate.

Hammer decided to do a sequel of sorts to *One Million Years B.C.* with *When Dinosaurs Ruled the Earth* in 1970. *Jack the Giant Killer* proved that you couldn't do a Harryhausen movie without Harryhausen and expect to have something in the same league. But *Dinosaurs* was a different story. Harryhausen was not associated with the film — he was busy working on other projects — but the effects turned out better than expected. And other elements of the film made it — surprise — actually superior to its forerunner in many ways. The chief difference was a better script and direction, both courtesy of Val Guest.

In *Dinosaurs* we again have two star-crossed lovers from different tribes, Sanna (Victoria Vetri) and Tara (Robin Hawdon). Sanna is one of several blond women who are to be sacrificed by her tribe (who wear alligator head masks), but she falls into the sea and is rescued by another tribe. Tara is instantly smitten with her, to the dismay of his lady friend. Lost in the jungle, Sanna hides out in an empty egg shell, and winds up being adopted by the mother dinosaur after befriending its baby. As in *One Million Years B.C.* Tara believes that Sanna has been killed. His people tie him to a raft and set it on fire, but he escapes to be reunited with Sanna just as the creation of the moon causes a cataclysm on Earth.

This time Jim Danforth took full credit for the stop-motion work and it's easy to see why. It was almost as if he were waiting until his work was of a Harryhausen-like quality before he would put his name to it. In truth, the animation in *Dinosaurs* is perhaps a cut below that of the best of Harryhausen, but it is still of a higher grade than that of most of the master's competitors. First of all, there is the handsomely designed and very smoothly animated plesiosaur with its massive flippers that breaks loose and threatens the tribespeople until they cover it with a type of oil and set it afire, effectively cooking the creature. There is a well-animated triceratops that punctures a couple of people with its horn, then chases one along a ledge until it tumbles right off of the cliff to its death. There is a scuttling spider-crab that reminds one of the trapdoor spider in the O'Brien-animated *The Black Scorpion* (see Chapter Two), and some other busy man-sized crabs with outsized pincers. The baby dinosaur that befriends Sanna is of the cuddly variety while its mother, even more handsome than the plesiosaur, reminds one somewhat of Harryhausen's rhedosaurus. There is very fluid animation in all of these scenes, as well as superior process work.

Other effects include a man-eating mushroom-plant that envelopes Sanna and basically resembles a big turd. There are two unnecessary clips inserted from *The Lost World* (1960), a lizard crashing through the forest, and a brief shot of the two big monsters in the midst of battle. The effects for the cataclysmic final sequence are excellent, especially when the raft holding the lovers is washed onto a cliff overlooking the sea. The final shot — with the lovers on one side of the frame while the new moon glistens over the sea on the other side — is a stunner. There is more variety in the scenic locales than there was in *One Million Years B.C.* Much of this scenic splendor is on view during the film's suspenseful final quarter, when the lovers are chased by the tribe and are constantly thrown from one danger into another against a backdrop of striking landscapes. For another type of landscape, the producers did not forget to hire some busty stunt women for the obligatory cat fights.

Hero Tara may seem like a complete stinker the way he immediately dumps his loving brunette girlfriend for the blond Sanna ("typical male!" some women in the audience may have snorted), but during the climax when his ex is swallowed up by mud he does try to save her and is visibly distressed by her death. A jerk maybe, but not a completely insensitive one. For her part, Sanna seems unaware of the brunette's existence ("typical bimbo," others may have snickered).

The actors in the film emote believably and Mario Nascimbene's musical score is a big improvement over the one he did for *One Million,* with a memorable main theme and a charming motif for the mother and baby dinosaur. Val Guest was a much more experienced and creative director than Don Chaffey, the latter's good work on *Jason* notwithstanding, and *When Dinosaurs Ruled the Earth* emerged as a much more entertaining movie than its predecessor. But while Danforth was shooting *Dinosaurs* Harryhausen was working on a project that would not only eclipse *Dinosaurs* but prove that he was the undisputed master of stop-motion effects. That project was *The Valley of Gwangi* (1969).

The Valley of Gwangi, the story of a lost valley in Mexico filled with prehistoric monsters, had been a dream project for Willis O'Brien, who never realized it in his lifetime. T. J. Breckinridge (Gila Golan) is owner of a small circus in turn-of-the-century Mexico. Carlos (Gustavo Rojo) brings her a new attraction, a tiny prehistoric horse called an eohippus. An aged gypsy lady, Tia Zorina (Freda Jackson), believes the animal is cursed and wants it returned to the Forbidden Valley that it came from. When the little horse is stolen, T. J. wrongly blames the theft on her ex-lover Tuck Kirby (James Franciscus). Tuck and the others pursue the horse to the valley where they discover many different prehistoric animals, including an allosaurus (similar to a T-Rex) that they capture and put on exhibit. Tia Zorina's associate, a dwarf, releases the beast, who wreaks havoc in the town and enters the huge cathedral. Tuck destroys the monster by setting fire to the building.

With *Valley of Gwangi* Harryhausen not only did an obvious homage to *King Kong,* but also created one of his liveliest creations. Chewing on the dwarf who set it free, battling a hapless elephant, stalking people in the cathedral, striding malevolently through the town, snapping at other dinosaurs in its home territory, Gwangi — as the monster is known — is a truly spectacular performer. There are other well-realized monsters in *Gwangi,* but the title beast is truly the main attraction.

The little horse that we first see on a tabletop at the circus — it later runs through the desert as the humans give chase — is a charming creature, as is the five foot or so ornithomimus that becomes a meal for the suddenly appearing Gwangi as it springs out of nowhere in an dramatic introduction. The pterodactyl that almost flies off with the little orphan boy Lope (Curtis Arden) is excellent, although it's filmed primarily in long shot. It seems unlikely that Lope would be too heavy for it to carry, so we can only assume it drops to the ground with its squirming burden because the kid was much too likable to kill off. For live action closeups as it wrestles with armed men, a big prop is substituted for the stop-motion model. Although well-designed, it's obvious that all of its movements come from the actors making it wiggle. Harryhausen had previously animated an elephant for *20 Million Miles to Earth* for a battle with the movie's giant Ymir, and does the same for *Gwangi*'s allosaurus-vs.-elephant sequence with highly felicitous results.

Valley of Gwangi has two knock-out sequences that are better than anything in *When Dinosaurs Ruled the Earth*. The first is a battle between Gwangi and a Triceratops-like styracosaur. This takes place in a huge dusty plain in the Forbidden Valley, in front of an open cavern in which the humans have taken refuge. Tuck and the other cowboys try to rope the animals, and almost succeed in snaring Gwangi before it snaps the ropes with its teeth. The interaction between the two dinosaurs and the men on horses, the lassos whirling through the air and encircling the beast's neck, are all executed flawlessly by Harryhausen. The combination of beautifully detailed models with exacting animation make for a thrilling sequence. Even in these days of computer images, the effects in *Gwangi* still look great. (Unfortunately the big prop of Gwangi that we see after it crashes through the tunnel from the Forbidden Valley and is knocked unconscious by a rockslide doesn't quite work even with the eyes rolling up in its head.)

In the superb sequence in which (as *The New York Times* put it) the "monster goes to church," Gwangi pursues Tuck, T.J. and little Lope inside the cathedral, its loud footsteps echoing in the supernal quiet of the building, a primeval, ferocious, outdoor life form in an enclosed (if coliseum-sized) space. The sequence makes the most of the bizarre incongruous juxtaposition of this snarling, terrifying, almost mindless beast on the loose inside this hushed place which is so sacred to the villagers. Since some of the superstitious townsfolk see the dinosaur as a "demon," it seems fitting that it's destroyed in the church, although Gwangi gets the last laugh in a sense by taking the whole cathedral with it. A particularly good shot has Tuck trying to spear the monster from a balcony as Gwangi snarls and snaps at him, but the entire protracted sequence is state-of-the-art.

William Bast fashioned a screenplay that is full of familiar elements blended in an amusing and exciting fashion. It could not exactly be considered pro-feminist, however. We learn that Tuck ran out on T.J. without a word because of commitment-phobia and wanderlust. Nevertheless, she falls for the not-terribly-likable guy all over again. Tuck has a dream of settling down on a ranch in Wyoming, but when T.J. expresses her own ambitions and what she hopes to achieve by exhibiting the eohippus, Tuck is infuriated by her attitude. He expects her to help him pursue *his* dream — the ranch — but God forbid she should pursue a dream of her own. Even Lope, the little boy they've befriended, tells T.J. that Tuck "is a very proud man." One can only hope that T.J. comes to her senses and sends Tuck packing. In any case, the love story doesn't intrude too much on the dino-action everyone paid to see. The film's conclusion, with tears streaming down Lope's face, is moving but Lope isn't crying for the death of Gwangi — rather for the loss of the cathedral around which all of the villagers' lives revolved. To these simple-minded peasants, the destruction of their church is much worse than losing their homes or their lives.

Whenever "lost world" movies contain pterodactyls, it's always tempting to ask why these flying monsters didn't fly out of the valley, mesa, island, what-have-you that contained them and wind up in the real world (in fact the pterodactyl in *Gwangi* is first spotted flying *outside* the Forbidden Valley, if not too far away). The answer, although it's never expressed in any of these movies, is that the creatures would naturally stay close to their nests and to their home environment, as would any other flying animal, prehistoric or not. However, it's no surprise that in movies of this nature, it's almost always the pterodactyls that are spotted before any other animal.

The human animals of *Gwangi* are almost as effective as the monsters. Israeli actress Gila Golan is cute, feisty, and very appealing; her accent isn't exactly Mexican but neither is her name, so we can assume she, like the cowboys, is from the States. The talents of James Franciscus, who started out as a "serious" actor but was never in the front ranks of thespians, is capable of handling the somewhat strutting part of Tuck without working up a sweat. Richard Carlson, who appeared in many dramas as well as genre items, is fine as T.J.'s associate and surrogate papa, Champ. Laurence Naismith, who also appeared in *Jason and the Argonauts*, is as professional as ever as Professor Bromley, the paleontologist who hopes for a knighthood for the discovery of eohippus but gets crushed by Gwangi instead. Curtis Arden as the charming boy hustler Lope was not just a cute kid but a genuinely talented actor, and Gustavo Rojo bristles in manly fashion as Carlos, who wants T.J. for himself but becomes a snack for Gwangi. Freda Jackson is suitably creepy and commanding as the old one-eyed gypsy woman. One could argue that the dwarf (Jose Burgos) who sets Gwangi free at her direction and winds up an appetizer for the beast is in reality a sacrificial offering for those in the audience who hate and fear anyone who is "different," especially since the dwarf is made especially "evil" and unattractive. But then Tia Zorina herself is hardly a "positive" portrait of a gypsy.

Jerome Moross, a "serious" composer of Broadway and light operatic works, contributed the score, with its derivative if rousing credit theme. The score is nice, although the music when Tuck, T.J. and the others first enter the Forbidden Valley is sprightly when it should be sinister and suspenseful. The film was produced by Harryhausen's long-time collaborator, Charles H. Schneer. James O'Connolly's direction is workmanlike and competent and the film is well-paced; the major FX scenes were, as usual, directed by Harryhausen himself.

The fantasy worlds of dragons and sorcerers made a memorable return in *Dragonslayer* (1981), which takes place when paganism is giving way to Christianity. A contingent from a small village in medieval times importunes the aged wizard Ulrich (Ralph Richardson) to help rid them of a dragon (one of the last of its kind), "Vermithrax Pejorative." Instead the task falls to his apprentice Galen (Peter McNicol), who winds up imprisoned by the king when the latter believes him to be a faker. Galen discovers that Valerian (Caitlin Clarke), a young man he befriends, is actually a young *woman* who pretends to be male in order to avoid the lottery by which the dragon's virginal sacrifices are chosen. She reveals her true sex after everyone mistakenly believes that Galen has buried and vanquished the dragon. When the Princess Elspeth (Chloe Salaman) discovers that her name was purposefully left out of each lottery, she decides to sacrifice herself to Vermithrax. Galen fails to save Elspeth, but with the help of Ulrich, who's come back from the dead, does manage to destroy the dragon.

35

The amusingly named Vermithrax has a ridged, bony face with a tapering snout, a body covered with scales, and assorted curlicues or such under the neck and elsewhere. Quite ancient, the dragon resembles a wizened, wise-looking beastie with chin whiskers. To bring the dragon to life, *Dragonslayer* employed a variation of stop-motion called go-motion. Instead of the model of the dragon being perfectly still as each shot was taken, it would be in motion (accomplished with a computer), creating a blurred effect that supposedly created more realistic-looking movement; the results aren't bad.

Although the effects in the film seemed marvelous at the time of its release, and are still quite good, they don't have the quality of the best of Harryhausen, go-motion or no go-motion. For better or worse, it was in a sense the beginning of using computers to bring monsters to life. Dennis Muren, of Industrial Light and Magic, later worked on *Jurassic Park*, as did Phil Tippett, who animated the dragon, along with Ken Ralston.

That being said, Vermithrax *is* very lifelike in certain shots. Well-designed, movable prop claws and tail, as well as a full-sized head and neck, are used in close-up shots involving actors. The baby dragons that kill Elspeth are puppets that are poorly designed and never look alive. However some of the animation shots, such as when Vermithrax squeezes through the tunnels in his lair in search of Galen, are very impressive. The sequence when the dragon slowly rises from the lake behind Galen and then lashes out at the young man with its fiery breath, is a stunner. The dragon also looks splendid when it soars magnificently through the sky. Other effects, such as when a landslide caused by Galen covers the entrance to the dragon's cavern, and the landscape collapses during an "earthquake" when the beast re-emerges, are first-rate. The atmospheric lair of Vermithrax with its narrow tunnels and fiery lake is another plus. (The production design was by Elliot Scott.)

In one of the best and most disturbing scenes, most of the dragon is unseen: One of the young female sacrifices manages to get out of her chains and runs off from the stockade that has been erected outside the dragon's cave. But before she can get too far, an enormous foot comes stomping down, cutting off her escape. She turns to run in the other direction and is confronted with an enormous tail. The chilling cat-and-mouse game comes to a cruelly abrupt finale when a rain of red-hot fire showers down on the girl, blasting her out of existence. Incredibly, Vermithrax can subsist on only two virgins a year, so one has to wonder why he'd want to eat ashes. He later uses his heat breath on a priest who comes to confront "Satan" and is boiled and charred for his trouble. Galen sleeps with Valerian to keep her out of the lottery — remember, only virgins need apply — which makes you wonder why all the other girls in the village don't run about getting happily laid — or why everyone doesn't just move to another town.

American Peter McNichol, who went on to appear on sitcoms and such shows as *Ally McBeal*, *Numbers*, and *24*, is very charming as the brave if out-classed hero of *Dragonslayer*. Ralph Richardson classes up the whole production as the rather vague but still powerful Ulrich, while Sydney Bromley scores as Ulrich's even older assistant Hodge; ditto for John Hallam as Tyrian, the dishonorable knight who murders Hodge. Director Matthew Robbins, who received a co-screenplay credit with Hal Barwood, fails to keep things moving at a brisk enough pace, however, the film's biggest deficit.

Best-selling novelist Michael Crichton took an idea that was similar to the one used in British author Harry Adam Knight's novel *Carnosaur*—dinosaurs brought into the modern world and put on exhibition—and wound up with another literary blockbuster. The 1993 film version of his book *Jurassic Park* was another huge success. Entrepreneur John Hammond (Richard Attenborough) has built a park in which living dinosaurs will be on display for millions to see. The dinosaurs were recreated by extracting blood from ancient mosquitoes caught in amber—the blood was sucked from dinosaurs and hence contains their DNA. Hammond invites paleontologist Alan Grant (Sam Neill), paleobotanist Ellie Sattler (Laura Dern), mathematician Ian Malcolm (Jeff Goldblum) and lawyer Donald Gennaro (Martin Ferrero) to the island to see that everything is shipshape before opening the zoo to visitors. A series of events proves that the park isn't quite ready to deal with its dinosaurs, and the visitors and others are soon fighting for their lives against all manner of prehistoric wildlife. The result is several deaths and the virtual destruction of Jurassic Park.

Fifteen years after its release, *Jurassic Park*'s computerized special effects—which once seemed so seamless and marvelous—aren't nearly as impressive (this is not to say in any way that they are *bad*). Our first sight of the huge brachiosaurus (or brontosaur or apatosaur) has less impact because it doesn't look quite real—less real than a Harryhausen creation, in fact. Just as the initiated can sometimes spot the different "layers" in a stop-motion film, the layers in this shot—separating the dinosaur from Grant and Ellie as they approach, wide-eyed with wonder—seem obvious. It just doesn't have the impact that it once did, although Sam Neill and Laura Dern help to get across that certain sense of wonder with their performances and reactions to the hulking creature so high above them.

In addition to computer effects, "live action" props and mechanical models were also used. Sometimes these are forgettable, such as the baby dinosaurs that hatch out of the eggs in the lab and which don't look remotely alive. However, the full-scale triceratops which lies ill on its side is very well constructed and rather lifelike. The savage T-Rex that figures in much of the action is a combination of computer wizardry and live action. Beautifully designed—and its first appearance is genuinely frightening—the T-Rex looks startlingly alive until the mechanical dinosaur is substituted, generally in scenes when the beast's big head comes close to the human actors. The flock of small galloping dinosaurs that nearly run over Grant and Hammond's grandchildren, Lex and Tim, look good if a touch cartoonish, but the lively computer-generated velociraptors are excellent.

Jurassic Park has many exciting scenes, such as when a car thrown by the T-Rex plunges down a tree after Grant and Tim as they race down the branches ahead of it. There's a clever bit with Grant and the children climbing over a switched-off electrified fence not knowing that elsewhere on the island Ellie is at that moment about to switch the electricity back on. The dinosaurs have some good scenes as well, including an amusing sequence that turns creepy when Dennis Nedry (Wayne Knight), who hopes to sell dinosaur DNA for big bucks, gets cornered by a man-sized spitting dinosaur that blinds and devours him. And there's a thrilling sequence when the T-Rex chases after a Jeep at an alarming pace and even butts it with its lowered head. Yet the movie doesn't really have that breakneck *Perils of Pauline* quality because there are too many slack, even dull sequences between these memorable moments. The pace could definitely be tighter at times.

As in the novel, Hammond's young grandchildren get involved in the action, but it

The *Tyrannosaurus rex* escapes from its enclosure in *Jurassic Park* (1993).

lessens the fun considerably to constantly see kids in terrible danger. The ending, when the children try to hang on to some dinosaur bones as the T-Rex skeleton in the grand hall falls apart (because the real T-Rex and some raptors have gotten in) reminds one of a scene out of a particularly bad Walt Disney movie. The lawyer Gennaro runs off and leaves the kids in the car when the T-Rex attacks, but Grant and Malcolm do absolutely nothing to help the children for what seems *like an eternity*, making them seem just as "cowardly." (In the novel it's Malcolm who runs for his life.) The business with the petrified Gennaro being attacked by the T-Rex as he hides in a toilet stall borders on camp, but it's not the only scene which skirts dangerously near black comedy or even parody.

For a paleobotanist, Ellie seems to know an awful lot about animal ailments, suddenly turning into a zoologist or even a vet as she examines the ailing triceratops with Grant. Grant stupidly takes the kids with him into the park to see the triceratops, oblivious to whatever danger they may face. Later, when he and the kids are in the branches of a tall tree, he calls over one of the brachiosaurs because, as he tells the children, it's a herbivore and won't harm them. It never occurs to the idiot that elephants are "herbivores" but they can be pretty dangerous under certain conditions!

Wayne Knight and Jeff Goldblum give the best and most flavorful performances. The two children, Joseph Mazzello and Ariana Richards, prove quite adept and talented. Richard Attenborough is solid as Hammond, and the two leads, Neill and Dern, are adequate but a bit bland by comparison. Dern hardly registers enough disgust or shock when she comes upon one piece of the lawyer's body — she's not playing a member of *CSI*, after all — but she's a bit better reacting to a severed arm that falls on her during a later sequence. John Williams composed a majestic theme for the dinosaurs (which is too muted in the film to be effective) but otherwise his score isn't so special. Director Steven Spielberg seems to have let everyone else, including all of the FX technicians, throw together his movie.

Dennis Muren was responsible for the full motion dinosaurs, while Stan Winston came up with the live-action beasties. Although stop-motion was not used in the film, animator Phil Tippett was hired as Dinosaur Supervisor, as the computer specialists apparently followed his lead in "animating" the monsters.

Overlong and overrated despite its merits, *Jurassic Park* is not as much fun — and frankly not as eye-popping — as such movies as *Jason and the Argonauts* and *The Valley of Gwangi*, maybe because an army of technicians, no matter how skilled, can never deliver that personal touch that distinguished the Harryhausen product. *Jurassic Park* engendered two sequels, with a third set for release in 2008. (*Carnosaur* was also filmed and begat two sequels, but none of these films are memorable.)

The Lost World: Jurassic Park (1997) is even more bloated and matter-of-fact than the original, with a veritable army of characters invading another island where engineered dinosaurs roam. The attempts at characterization are admirable, but you get impatient waiting for the monsters to appear. Some of the dinosaur scenes certainly deliver (some men trying to rope a baby T-Rex, for instance), and the Mama T-Rex looks absolutely magnificent escaping from the boat in San Diego. But the best scenes have little to do with dinosaurs: a harrowing business with a trailer dangling precariously over a cliff; and an unmanned boat smashing into the dock in San Diego. One might suggest that the finale with the mother T-Rex tearing up San Diego is a homage to the brontosaurus rampage in London at the end of the 1925 *Lost World* but there's no sense of respect for the past in this movie or the novel upon which it was based. (Crichton doesn't even acknowledge Conan Doyle or his seminal book!) The San Diego epilogue features such borderline campy and crude scenes as the T-Rex invading a backyard to drink water from the pool and swallowing the family's dog as a tacky sight gag.

Although some fans of the first two movies excoriated *Jurassic Park III* (2001), it may be the simplest and best entry in the series and it got some unexpected raves in critical quarters. With a more manageable running time and no bloat, it deposited its smaller cast of characters on the same island as *LW:JP* and brought on a formidable array of frightening dinosaur adversaries such as a huge, finned spinosaurus, and pterodactyls who were just as threatening simply walking across a bridge toward the actors as they were diving down out of the air to fly off with them. Fans were surprised to learn that Ellie (Laura Dern) from the first film did not marry her sweetheart Alan (Sam Neill)—the two were only friends in Crichton's novel—but was happily domesticated with another fellow. An edgier movie might have made more of the fact that Alan has no new female love interest in the film but seems rather close to a handsome younger assistant named Billy (Alessandro Nivola). *Jurassic Park III* was well-paced under the direction of Joe Johnston.

Good, old-fashioned, evil dragons came back with a vengeance in *Reign of Fire* (2002). The young son of a (woman) railway tunnel project engineer is one of the only survivors when the crew comes upon an ancient dragon that awakens beneath the earth and burns everyone alive. Over a period of many years, a scourge of dragons ravages most of the world. The young man, Quinn Abercromby (Christian Bale), is now head of a ragtag community of humans living in a castle compound in the English countryside. Along comes a group of American dragon-fighters headed by Denton Van Zan (Matthew McConaughey) and Alexandra Jensen (Izabella Scorupco). After a series of dragon attacks, as well as much tension between Abercromby and Van Zan, they decide to team up to destroy the only male dragon in existence. Van Zan is killed during the effort, but Abercromby succeeds in his mission, giving the human race another chance at life.

The dragons, "who burned the dinosaurs to dust," remind one a bit of Vermithrax Pejorative in *Dragonslayer*. They are beautiful, sleek creatures but until the climax we only get quick glimpses of them as they soar in, roast people or landscapes, and then disappear just as swiftly. A dead prop dragon with a blackened body and a red, twisted tongue looks very realistic. When Quinn faces off against the Daddy Dragon in the big finale, the creature looks good but frankly a bit less "real" than a stop-motion model would have due to the insufficiencies, at least in this film, of computer imagery. Another difference, as previously indicated, may be that stop-motion artists like Ray Harryhausen either worked alone or with one or two colleagues, giving their films a personal touch that whole teams of FX people can hardly emulate. For instance, *Reign of Fire* has a crew of 25 effects people and 89 *visual* effects people! That number would increase with each new monster movie. (Richard Hoover supervised the effects work on the film.)

The lively dragons figure in many exciting sequences, beginning with the first dragon climbing up the shaft after the elevator cage that Quinn and his mother are trying to escape in. When a group of people decide to leave the compound and try their luck elsewhere, there's a harrowing business with a dragon cornering them in a greenhouse. This amply illustrates the sheer terror of coming up against a huge creature than can kill you from yards away just by opening its mouth and *breathing*. The dragon fighters use copters to go after their prey and, when the copters crash, fly through the atmosphere in rocket packs with the dragons "hot" on their heels; this makes for a thrilling sequence. After the dragons lay siege to the castle compound there's a moving scene when the frightened children, who were feared dead, come out of hiding into the shattered, burned ruins of their former home. There's another powerful moment when the English people hold a celebration after Van Zan and his men kill several dragons, with Van Zan having to angrily remind them that three of his men were lost as well.

Reign of Fire is one of those movies that grows on you. Its strengths were lost on most movie critics and even creature feature fans when it was released, and it unfairly faded away rather quickly. There were those who saw it as more of an action film than a monster movie, complete with "macho" McConaughey as anti-hero (the main character is actually Quinn). Some people didn't like it because it wasn't dumb and campy, or more of a black comedy; it just wasn't "fun" enough. True, the movie is a bit depressing — as most apocalyptic movies are — but it also contains many likable characters and has a message of hope. The excellent screenplay by Gregg Chabot, Kevin Peterka, and Matt Greenberg presents an interesting conflict between those who simply want to survive, and those who want to make a difference, even at great cost. The characters are better-developed than you might expect in a movie that boasts fearsome monsters as its main attraction.

Reign of Fire has a great look to it, due to Adrian Biddle's superior photography, Simon Wakefield's set decoration, and Wolf Kroeger's absolutely spectacular production design. Edward Shearmur contributed a first-rate musical score. The movie has hardly a dull moment under the helm of director Rob Bowman. The enthusiastic and talented cast also helps to make this one of the more memorable of modern-day creature features.

TWO

Into the Ant Hole

Warner Brothers had such a hit with *The Beast from 20,000 Fathoms* that they wanted an even more monstrous follow-up for the following year and hence *Them!* (1954) was born. The title came from a scene when a little girl, snapped out of a trauma by the smell of formic acid, screams out "Them!" in reference to the creatures that killed her parents. Although today there would be nothing at all unique about the monsters of *Them!*, in 1954 it was a different story. *Them!* was the very first giant insect movie, and it was so successful that it engendered dozens of similar features of varying quality that continue even to this day.

In White Sands, New Mexico, site of the first atomic tests, radiation in the sand has created a mutant breed of ants that grow to anywhere from nine to fifteen feet in length (they are about the size of automobiles). They inject their victims with formic acid, then drag them off to eat them. FBI agent Robert Graham (James Arness), cop Ben Peterson (James Whitmore), and scientists Harold Medford (Edmund Gwenn) and his daughter Patricia (Joan Weldon) team up to wipe out the monsters before they can multiply. Their first nest, a cavernous ant hole, is wiped out, but they discover too late that the flying queens have escaped. One queen lays eggs on a ship, and the other begins a new colony in the miles of storm drains under Los Angeles. The Army comes in and wipes out this new nest, including the queens.

There is an excellent, suspenseful build-up to the first appearance of the ants; up until this point we only hear them and see the results of their carnage. But once they show up, much of the tension is temporarily dissipated. The trouble is that the monsters are full-size mechanical props that are very well-designed but have limited mobility. As the first ant we see hovers over Joan Weldon, its limp, wiggling antennae draws giggles. As the picture progresses, one gets used to the lumbering ants and their appearance is even effective in certain sequences, but *Them!* would have been an even better movie had the menaces been brought to life via special opticals of real ants or stop-motion animation. Even on a low budget, Ray Harryhausen could have done a lot for this picture. (To be honest, even Bert I. Gordon's optical effects for *Empire of the Ants* might have worked better.) Other props, such as large egg casings and the like, are more realistic.

The sound department came up with some creepy chirping noises for the ants — one of them even roars as it dies — and Bronislau Kaper's musical score embellishes every scene with real dread. There are indications that Warner Brothers considered the film somewhat more of a prestige item than it did *Beast from 20,000 Fathoms*, perhaps because they now

An ant grown large from atomic testing lurches across the desert toward some potential victims in *Them!* (1954).

fully realized the money-making potential of this type of picture. There are more elaborate
sets than in *Beast,* for one thing. There were also carry-overs from *Beast* such as the lovable
absent-minded professor (in this case played by Gwenn instead of Cecil Kellaway) and his
pretty assistant (in this case his daughter). As usual, all the men are gratified that the lady
scientist is so attractive; she's introduced climbing down out of a plane, temporarily caught
on something so they everyone can spend several moments admiring her legs.

There are several memorable sequences in the film, beginning with the off-screen death
of Whitmore's partner, who steps outside of and passes by the window of a store he's guarding and screams in terror as the ant noises intensify, followed only by silence as the wind
and dust rush by. What must have been a major gross-out moment for the 1950s occurs
when the group searches by helicopter for the ants' nest, and comes across a pit from which
emerges an ant holding a human's rib cage. The ant drops the rib cage and it rolls down a
hill to join a collection of other human bones and chewed-up clothing. "You've just found
your missing persons," Patricia tells Ben.

The descent into the ant hole after most of the ants have been gassed is eerie and effective as the team traverses smoky tunnels and climbs down through a series of pits until they

reach the egg chamber. The climax, in which Whitmore, Arness and soldiers engage the ants in the storm drains as they search for two missing children, is quite exciting. Whitmore's death after he heroically saves the children is tragic, and the shot of the queen ants in their half-demolished underground chamber almost makes you forget you're looking at phony beasties brought to life through hydraulics. The children look very realistically terrified, probably because they were young enough that the rather large mechanical monsters undoubtedly scared the bejesus out of them. The idea of giant ants crawling around through the 700 miles of storm drains under the city of Los Angeles can create a certain *frisson*, especially in locals.

There is also a quick sequence with the ants breaking out of the hold on the aforementioned ship and attacking the sailors, as well as a documentary (shown by Gwenn) which relates fascinating statistics about the ant population, such as that they are the only species to engage in warfare besides man. This type of scene would be repeated in many of the big bug movies that followed *Them!*, along with the sexy lady scientist and the shots of bones of the victims picked clean.

Gordon Douglas' direction is generally taut and fast-paced, although the problem with the movie is that the very seriousness of its approach makes it a little dull at times. The efficacy of the film is greatly bolstered by the presence of Edmund Gwenn, one of Hollywood's grand old character actors, and James Whitmore, one of the country's finest actors, who bring conviction to their every scene. James Arness is solid if in a different league as the FBI man. Joan Weldon's function seems mostly decorative, as she reads her lines with a certain listlessness. Olin Howlin scores as Jensen the drunk who sees the giant ants in the storm drain from his window in the alcoholic ward. Leonard Nimoy has a bit part as an Air Force sergeant who reads a report he has received of strange occurrences to an operator who contacts the authorities.

While *Them!* may not have much shock value anymore, it is still a good movie, and it certainly opened the floodgates for all manner of colossal creepy-crawlies to come raging out of the woodwork and everywhere else.

Despite the occasional ludicrous moment, *Tarantula* (1955), the next major "big bug" movie, emerged as one of the best creature features ever made, largely due to the swell "acting" of its stupendous spider. Leo G. Carroll plays a scientist, Professor Deemer, who has come up with a nutrient that he hopes will become a rich, new food supply. Unfortunately, he uses a radioactive isotope — no surprise there — to bond the solution together, which creates unexpected results (for Deemer, not the audience). Carroll doesn't seem the least concerned that a side effect of being fed only the nutrient is that his test animals — which include the usual white rats and guinea pigs and for inexplicable reasons a tarantula — greatly increase in size. Which makes it even crazier that Deemer's two assistants inject themselves with the nutrient. Instead of turning into Bert I. Gordon–style Colossal Men, they instead develop rapidly evolving acromegaly, which makes them horribly deformed and eventually kills them — but not before one attacks and injects Deemer, and also smashes the case holding the tarantula, which escapes into the Arizona desert and continues growing despite the fact that it's eating only cows and people.

Dr. Matt Hastings (John Agar, whose taut smile almost makes him look evil) gets involved when he questions how anyone could have developed acromegaly so quickly, and because he has the hots for the professor's sexy new assistant "Steve" Clayton (Mara Corday). When the sheriff scoffs at Hastings' notion that Deemer's diagnosis of the dead men is wrong, Hastings replies that "there's nothing like the safety of prestige." Hastings leads the investigation into what's eating animals and humans and leaving only bones and big white pools of venom behind. (These shots of pieces of skeletonized remains combined with bits of chewed clothing are still gruesome today.)

The monster at the heart of *Tarantula* is an actual spider photographically "blown up" and inserted into the live action via process shots of varying quality. When the tarantula calmly walks out of Deemer's lab, you can clearly see the web it was photographed in. At times it pops up over a mountain and some of its legs simply disappear. But most of the shots are highly effective and enormously creepy. For one thing, the spider has a great flair for dramatic pauses, such as when it stops at the top of a hill and seems to ponder its actions before descending to munch on a corral full of horses and the hapless rancher who comes out to shoot at it. A great sense of somewhat comic dread is achieved by having the monster, continuously growing bigger until it's nearly the size of a mountain, slowly approaching from the background as its victims go obliviously about their business until they finally spot the critter — moving a lot faster the closer it gets.

A special type of nutrient has had the alarming effect of turning a spider into a monster the size of a mountain in *Tarantula* (1955).

In addition to the aforementioned corral scene, there are two other splendid sequences: when the spider goes after two prospectors; and when it attacks Deemer's house. The prospectors are clearly long-time friends, and there is something almost touching in the way one of them runs back to pick up the other after he's fallen into the spider's path twice, and the way they huddle together in terror as the monster's fangs ultimately descend upon them. (Two prop fangs were superimposed over the live-action in these sequences.) By the time the spider attacks Deemer's lab it has become as big as the formidable mansion that houses it, and there's a scream-out-loud sequence when we see its eyes peeking into the bedroom where Mara Corday is getting ready for bed. Another shot of its fangs clicking as it hungrily eyes Corday makes it clear that it's interested in her flesh for very different reasons than Dr. Hastings. This marvelous sequence is capped by a startling shot of Corday running down the driveway towards a waiting Agar while the spider demolishes the manor behind her.

Director Jack Arnold summons up a lot of suspense once the gargantuan spider makes its appearance — in the second half of the film the action rarely flags — and the actors are generally professional. In their romantic scenes, Agar and Corday merely seem to be reciting lines while giving each other coy looks, but Carroll (especially as he begins to suffer the affects of acromegaly), Nestor Paiva as the sheriff, and Ross Elliott as the newspaper reporter, are convincing. Hank Patterson scores as Josh, the hotel clerk and comedy relief. After Agar meets Corday in the lobby he asks them "Aren't you going to introduce yourselves?" to which they reply, "No!" "Gettin' to be a fast world," says Josh. Clint Eastwood shows up briefly as the leader of a squadron of jets that fire napalm at the spider and burn it up.

The final sequence, as the townspeople watch the conflagration engulfing the truly massive arachnid in the background, is impressive although one could quibble that the proportions and measurements are a bit off. The uncredited musical score adds a lot to the atmosphere of crawling menace that permeates the movie.

An unintentionally funny moment occurs when Deemer shows up to claim the twisted body of one of his assistants. He tells Agar and the sheriff that when he last saw the man, he was running off crazed into the desert, where his body was found. When Agar says he wants to do an autopsy, Deemer says, "I was in attendance [at his death] and signed the death certificate." *Before the man even died!* Neither Agar nor the sheriff wonder why Deemer would have signed a death certificate when he just finished saying that the dead man was running off into the desert when he last saw him.

Like *The Giant Behemoth*, *The Black Scorpion* (1957) features stop-motion effects work by Willis O' Brien, some of which had been put together years before for projects that were never completed. A volcanic eruption in Mexico unleashes gigantic prehistoric scorpions that emerge from under the Earth and cause death and panic. They destroy Mira Flores, the ranch of Teresa Alvarez (Mara Corday, fresh from *Tarantula*), which was being used as a base by two geologists, Hank Scott (Richard Denning) and Arturo Ramos (Carlos Rivas). Together with scientist Dr. Velasco, they contrive to destroy the creatures before they can tear apart Mexico City. A truly gargantuan black scorpion kills off all the others, and is itself destroyed by an electrified harpoon fired into the unprotected area under its neck.

The Black Scorpion is an atmospheric chiller that begins like *Them!*, with our heroes coming across crushed buildings and automobiles, a bawling infant, and a corpse of a sher-iff while the monsters' particularly horrifying noises —fiendish roars combined with a kind of chirping sound — are heard periodically in the distance. The scorpions apparently don't eat their victims — although we do see a shot of a torn-up steer — but do somehow man-age to suck the blood out of them. We first get a look at the big critters when they attack some telephone linemen working just outside Mira Flores, then swarm into the ranch itself. Scuttling, speeding horrors whose size does little to slow them down, they make for very formidable monsters.

Black Scorpion benefits enormously from the contribution of O'Brien, whose three-dimensional, expertly designed scorpions rivet attention (and give us an idea of what *Them!* might have been like with stop-motion effects). Less successful, although hardly in the cheap Roger Corman *Attack of the Crab Monsters* class, are mechanical props which are used for close-ups. These are still very gruesome sights to behold, with mobile eyes, fangs and claws, and mouths that drip saliva as they lick their chops in anticipation of snagging a vic-tim. A large prop of a claw was also used for live-action scenes in which actors are picked up off the ground by the scorpions.

Another technique used to bring the creatures to life involves superimposing a some-what transparent (still animated) scorpion onto streets full of running people; this is espe-cially used in the climax when the "granddaddy of them all," the black scorpion, rampages through Mexico City. (Inserting monsters into live action is done via use of what is called a "traveling matte," into which footage of the monster is placed. Before that is done, all that can be seen is a *silhouette* of the monster on top of the live action. It's generally held that the producers ran out of money and couldn't afford to insert the monster footage into these scenes — hence the use of the silhouette — but it's also possible that they thought the silhouette of what was meant to be the biggest and *blackest* scorpion of all was effective enough on its own, further differentiating this scorpion from the others. Also, this "silhou-ette" isn't completely featureless.)

If there's any problem with the multiplicity of techniques, it's that the switching back and forth from one to another becomes distracting, and close ups of the scorpion faces are not well integrated into the long shots of them running amok. The same essential close-up is used over and over again regardless of whether the scorpion it's meant to represent is fac-ing in one direction or another or has its head up or down, and so on. Some animated shots are also repeated throughout the film: a march of several scorpions in a cavern is used again when they attack a train, for instance.

Still, some of the FX work is spectacular, especially in the climax when the black scor-pion enters an arena and does battle with tanks, trucks and helicopters, a couple of which it grabs in its pincers and smashes to the ground (the same shot used twice, actually). The attack on the train is nightmarish, a scene out of Hell, as the scorpions move in like grotesque demons to pick among the passengers, lifting several up in their claws, and fighting over the tiny morsels screaming in abject terror. The sequence has a graphic intensity that prob-ably kept many children — and not a few of their parents — wide awake on the night they saw the film.

A lengthy sequence takes place in the huge underground caverns in which the scorpions have their nest. In addition to those horrors, the cave is also home to a weird thirty-foot-long worm creature with arm-like appendages up front and spiny outgrowths on the tail. This creature gets into a fight with a scorpion and loses. There is also a comparatively small trapdoor spider that pops out from under a stony slab and pursues the little boy, Juanito, who stowed away in the small open cab which Hank and Arturo used to descend into the cavern. The cab is supported by a thick wire attached to a crane high above. A highlight of the cave sequence is when one scorpion grabs up the cab in its pincers and has an almost disastrous tug of war with the crane. The film also benefits from other good locations, such as the boulder-strewn fields (with fissures issuing smoke) that surround Mira Flores. There is a striking shot of the hacienda with the volcano spewing smoke behind it, an excellent matte painting.

Like *Giant Behemoth*, there's a kind of sadistic streak to the film that you don't find in most of the other big bug movies. Some of this has to do with the brutality in the animation sequences — the attack on the train, for instance — which reminds one of King Kong smashing in the elevated subway car and crushing all those innocent people. Then there's the scene in the arena when a soldier fires the harpoon at the scorpion and misses. He pulls it back so he can shoot it again, but in the confusion he forgets that it's still electrified, picks it up in his hands, and is apparently instantly killed. Whether he got careless or it's the fault of the soldier in charge of turning the current on and off, or maybe overseer Hank's fault, it's still a disturbing moment. Hank then fires the shot that kills the monster. The dead soldier is forgotten as Hank goes off with Teresa for some R and R at the end.

The performances by the three leads are competent, with Corday as attractive and spirited as ever, and Denning and Rivas proving to be more animated heroes than, say, James Arness or William Hopper. Denning always had a laid-back kind of charm that worked perfectly well for him on all kinds of different assignments. Paul Sawtell's musical score is serviceable, while director Edward Ludwig sustains suspense and keeps things moving. The screenplay by David Duncan and Robert Blees goes *Them!* one better by giving the busy monsters in *The Black Scorpion* much more to do. In general, they do it well.

The Deadly Mantis (1957) not only features one of the best mechanical monsters ever put on film, but makes the most of its by now familiar premise — really big bug (only one this time) menaces mankind — with a plethora of intriguing situations. Several military men have disappeared in the Arctic, including two from the wreck of a small plane, and Colonel Joseph Parkman (Craig Stevens) finds only strange tracks in the snow and a three-foot piece of unidentified material that seems to come from a living creature. Parkman calls in Ned Jackson (William Hopper) from the Museum of Natural History — Marjorie Blaine (Alix Talton), the editor of the museum's magazine tags along — to identify the material. After much deliberation, Jackson tells them that it is a spur off the leg of what has to be one of the biggest things that ever lived, a prehistoric preying mantis that atomic testing must have thawed out of the Arctic ice that imprisoned it. "You're making a lot of assumptions," Marjorie tells Ned — to put it mildly! As Jackson tells them, there was indeed a two-foot dragonfly in prehistoric times but there has never been a record of any insect as large as the one in *Deadly Mantis*— which is part of the fun of the movie. Since it's obligatory in these pictures for the monster to be the most deadly thing that ever lived — at least since the last bug movie — Jackson intones, "In all the kingdom of the living, there is no more deadly or voracious creature!" (It's amusing that he's actually referring to the ordinary praying mantis, not the monster.) Of course, as always, Jackson is dead-on in his assertions and before long the mantis is flying toward civilization where it devours more people, causes general havoc, and is finally cornered in the Holland Tunnel and killed.

The screenwriters decided to let their imaginations and sense of humor run riot and make their monster one of the most audacious bugs in the movies. One great scene has the creature literally sneaking up on the military base where Jackson, Marge and Parkman are conferring. Inside the building, Jackson says, "I'm trying to figure out just how big this thing is" just as the insect rises to its full height and towers magnificently over the edifice. Following the lead of the spider in *Tarantula*, it peeks in the window at the heroine, who naturally lets out a scream that could be heard back in Washington, D.C. Speaking of which, the mantis later has the unmitigated gall to land with a thud on the side of the Washington Monument — scaring the life out of two guards who huddle together in terror as they observe its body through the window — and crawl its way up to the top. It derails trains, knocks a bus over on its side, but never smashes into any airliners, which you think would have been the military's first concern.

The mantis makes an impression from its first dramatic appearance, attacking an Eskimo

The giant praying mantis looks most unwell after its defeat in the Holland Tunnel in Manhattan in *The Deadly Mantis* (1957).

village in a scene mostly made up of stock footage. Unlike the ants in *Them!*, the mantis looks reasonably creditable due to a particularly excellent design and an added mobility that makes it at times seem very lifelike. The monster was not life-size, of course, but process shots made it seem much bigger than it was. Its lumbering pace on the ground seems realistically due more to its massive size than to any mechanical flaw. Although the noise it makes is described as sounding like a "squadron of heavy bombers," it sounds more like a swarm of bees. When it flies it looks like a blurry indistinct bug-like blob. Unlike other bugs, the mantis is very fastidious, eating every part of its victims (probably swallowing them whole due to its size) and never leaving behind any bones or bits of clothing. (Somehow this is even more horrifying, innocent men and women gone into its gullet in one gulp.) Jackson theorizes that because the man-sized bugs it ate in prehistoric days are all extinct, "it's doing the best it can." William Hopper delivers the line with a certain air of black comedy.

The climax of the movie takes place in the tunnel into which the bug, after being hit by Parkman in his plane, takes refuge, overturning cars and squealing in a panic. The tunnel is filled with smoke or fog to hide the movements of the advancing soldiers who polish it off. It's a very atmospheric sequence greatly abetted by the believability of the monster. The movie has one last joke when Marjorie raises her camera to photograph the dead insect; its claw, behind her, rises up in the air as if it's about to snatch her up and pop her into its maw. "Just an auto reflex mechanism," says Jackson. The process shots blending Marjorie with the huge creature in front of her are very effective.

Despite some instances of padding with dull stock footage, the film moves at a pretty brisk pace under Nathan Juran's direction. William Hopper and Craig Stevens are suitably stalwart as the man of science and the man of action, respectively; of course it's the latter who gets the girl. Alix Talton is perfectly competent as Marjorie and plays it with a certain degree of charm and humor that never descends into out-and-out parody. Donald Randolph is fine as General Mark Ford, who tells the public that the big bug is not a hoax, as a Congressman has, understandably, charged. Paul Smith is amusing as a horny corporal who is instantly love-smitten when Marjorie walks into the all-male Arctic military base. Starved for female companionship, the men all act as if the attractive but not-that-sexy Talton were Marilyn Monroe! William Lava's musical score, featuring a dramatically rising five-note theme, is on the money.

In *Monster from Green Hell* (1957) the monsters are wasps that have grown to tremendous size due to forty hours' exposure to cosmic rays after being shot into space by a group of scientists. Bailey (Jim Davis) has seen how a much shorter exposure can double the size of other test animals, such as crabs, so he's convinced the wasps will turn out to be gigantic monsters. He and his associate Dan travel to Africa, where the space capsule holding the wasps has landed, to investigate and, if necessary, destroy the creatures with Gelignite grenades. As the two trek across the jungle via a lot of stock footage from *Stanley and Livingstone* and other older movies — the production never actually left California Studios in Hollywood — the wasps go on the rampage in a territory that the native people call "Green Hell." (This is not due to the giant wasps, however.)

After encountering hostile humans and wildlife and nearly dying of dehydration, the two scientists and their goods bearers arrive at the conclave of the elderly Professor Lawrence and his daughter Lorna (Barbara Turner). The professor is killed but the others set out into Green Hell to get rid of the monsters. When the Gelignite fails, it is up to a volcano to slay the beasties.

Monster from Green Hell is slow in spots and is padded with stock footage, but at least these scenes are genuinely well-done and entertaining. The film is unusual in that we get our first look at one of the monsters less than ten minutes into the running time. It appears positively gargantuan as it comes over a mountain in pursuit of some screaming people, but its fellows turn out to be on a much smaller scale. It is likely that the big one was supposed to be the queen mother, who shows up at the climax, rising out of the crater in double negative to rush — well, not exactly rush — after the heroes.

Throughout the film a life-size (on a giant scale, of course) wasp mock-up is used for scenes in which the monsters interact with live actors, somehow lifting them off the ground or impaling them with their stingers. The mechanical beast — one suspects there was only one built — has metal beaded eyes that revolve in their sockets. It doesn't resemble a wasp that much, but that point is taken care of in dialogue which mentions that the wasps have "mutated" and are different in appearance as well as larger. The mock-up is not as effective as the life-size ants in *Them!*

The wasps are also brought to life via several small stop-motion models with rapidly fluttering wings, but the animation is quite crude compared to the Harryhausen brand. Nevertheless this method provides the film's liveliest sequence, when a stop motion snake inexplicably decides to wrap itself around a much bigger wasp, which shakes it off and stings it, drawing a milky fluid. In the somewhat eerie sequence that follows, a whole bunch of the wasps surround the scientists' campfire but stay back because of the flames. In the climax, when the scientists and their party approach the crater where the wasps have settled, the humans are shown in an effective long-shot which emphasizes their relative puniness compared to the giant bugs. The monsters squeal like baby humpback whales as they are roasted by the lava.

Star Jim Davis was in between career high points when he made *Monster from Green Hell*. Nine years earlier he'd been Bette Davis' leading man in *Winter Meeting*, playing a war hero who frustrates Davis by his desire to enter the priesthood, and years afterward he played the patriarch in the hit TV series *Dallas*. Say what you will about his acting, he at least pretends to be sincerely interested in getting to Green Hell and wiping out the wasps. Eduardo Ciannelli, Mysterious Doctor Satan himself, has little to do as the leader of the porters. Joel Fluellen is effective as Arobi, who works for Professor Lawrence. The other actors are all perfectly professional.

And then we come to leading lady Barbara Turner, who is an enigma. Is she one of the worst actors to disgrace a screen, or is she simply a naturalistic talent who would appear brilliant were she cast in a bit of Italian neoclassicism with subtitles? Not long after her first appearance, she learns that her father has been killed, which certainly explains her hang-dog look throughout the rest of the movie. But while she doesn't lack emotion, she is consistently expressionless and ill-at-ease. Although not without appeal, Turner is far from the typical blond starlet-bimbo usually cast in these pictures, so it seems a bit grotesque when

Davis practically leers at her from his sick bed when he first sets eyes on her: "And *who* are *you*?" he asks her as he lazily smokes a cigarette. Admittedly, some of the actresses in these films are entirely too perky considering the horrors that surround them, but Turner goes to the other extreme, eschewing "animation" completely. Yet at the same time, like the snake vs. the wasp, she's one of the elements that makes *Monster from Green Hell* more interesting than it deserves to be. (Turner also appeared in the black comedy *Wink of an Eye* and appeared on many TV shows. She later became a writer and director and is the mother of actress Jennifer Jason Leigh. Turner was married to Vic Morrow from 1957 to 1964.)

Director Kenneth G. Crane covers the action in adequate fashion.

Beginning of the End (1957), another Bert I. Gordon production, has been one of the most excoriated creature features ever, in spite of the fact that it is fast-paced, suspenseful, and highly entertaining. The title is a reference to the biblical plague of locusts, reproduced here to a grotesque degree. Audrey Ames (Peggie Castle) of the National Wire Service is pursuing one story when she comes across a bigger one: The town of Ludlow, Illinois, has been demolished, and all of its 150 inhabitants (which doesn't make up much of a "town") have disappeared without a trace. Wondering if radiation could be responsible — why not? — Audrey follows a lead to a nearby experimental lab run by the Department of Agriculture. There she meets the project director Ed Wainwright (Peter Graves) and his deaf-mute assistant Frank. Wainwright has managed to grow giant-sized — if inedible — tomatoes and strawberries by using a radioactive isotope that creates an "artificial sun that never sets," making things grow as if photosynthesis lasted 24 hours. Unfortunately, grasshoppers have gotten into the food supply as well as eaten some of the big vegetables, so naturally they have grown into monstrosities as big as buses. After the bugs hiding in the forest have wiped out some National Guardsmen and destroyed one adjacent town, they advance on Chicago where Wainwright lures them to their deaths in the lake by use of a special sonar frequency.

Using real bugs instead of mechanical models gives the film a shuddery veracity. Only rarely are the locusts transparent (given the second-rate nature of process shots in most Gordon films). In fact, photographed in extreme close-up and in high resolution they look disgusting and very frightening, and are better actors than the ant models in *Them!* Most of the process work is quite effective, such as an impressive shot when a big locust crosses the foreground in front of some soldiers who are firing at the bugs in the background. Not as successful are the long shots showing a grasshopper imprisoned in a cage in the skyscraper laboratory set up by Wainwright. The tops of the bars just disappear into space. However, the closer shots, showing the big bug beating against the corrugated side of the cage, are a little unnerving. (Eventually the bug breaks out as expected and kills a helpless soldier.) Unlike their normal-sized counterparts, these locusts can't fly (probably because Gordon, who did the effects himself, had enough on his hands just dealing with bugs that more or less stayed put). When the grasshoppers converge on the lake and drown, all they look like is some poor dead tiny grasshoppers in a bowl of water.

This is the film that has the notorious "photograph" shots in which locusts are simply placed on a photo of a skyscraper and left to do their thing, supposedly climbing up the sides of the building. It is not true that the bugs walk off into space in these shots, which actually work just fine, considering the budget. However, one of the bugs does blithely walk past a jutting terrace as if the building's walls were perfectly flat. The sounds made by the bugs resemble cricket noises pumped up in volume. The more frenzied these sounds become, the more likely the locusts are to attack. (Not enough is done with this interesting idea.) Like the Deadly Mantis, the locusts leave absolutely nothing of their victims behind, not even a shred of clothing.

Which is why it's odd that a soldier tells Audrey she better "have a strong stomach" when he takes her on a tour of Ludlow. Their drive through town is intercut with shots of buildings that have been torn to the ground. There is nothing especially gruesome to see, certainly not the rib cages of *Them!* or the tattered bones of *Tarantula*. As in *Deadly Mantis*, the *complete* disappearance of the victims is especially chilling, as is the notion of 150 men, women and children being devoured overnight while in their beds. This aspect is like something out of Lovecraft, although it is not exploited as well as it could have been.

Still the screenplay by Fred Freiberger and Lester Gorn is rather good, all told, providing a chilling opening and plenty of scenes that take advantage of the terrifying monsters. There are the obligatory scenes, such as Wainwright showing a documentary on locusts to military brass, and a bit when a grasshopper climbs up a building to peek in at a sexy woman in a bath towel, mouth parts working. The first appearance of one of the locusts, as it advances on Frank from a field behind a shattered warehouse, is disturbing, as we watch Frank, who couldn't hear the warning chirping of its approach, back up in terror only to fall prey to its mandibles (this last is left to our imagination). Another exciting scene has an especially large locust running after and nearly overtaking a truck full of soldiers who are desperately firing at it.

The film has some humanistic touches, such as the banter between two soldiers as they walk into the woods near Ludlow to rout out the insects. A younger soldier is clearly terrified of what they may find — this is something out of his wildest nightmares — while his older, cynical buddy makes jokes to keep up his own courage as well as his friend's. Both are presumed killed in the following onslaught. At the climax, the soldier guarding the lab says, "I'm 37 and just beginning to realize that life can't be taken for granted." Only moments later the grasshopper breaks loose from its cage and kills him.

The film is abetted by the professionalism of the lead actors. Peter Graves, brother of James Arness of *Them!* fame, probably wasn't a much better actor than Arness, but in this he plays as if he believes everything he's saying. (This is one time that a scientist *admits* that he's at least indirectly responsible for the disaster.) Peggie Castle, another one of those hard-bitten blondes churned out by Hollywood during this period, almost makes you believe she's a real person. Morris Ankrum and Thomas Browne Henry as the military men are as reliable as ever. Albert Glasser's music is suitably dramatic. At the helm, Gordon keeps things moving at a very brisk pace that doesn't leave you too much time to ponder the absurdity of it all. It's just pure nonsensical fun.

"It must eat you to live" ran the ad copy for the penultimate big bug feature of the 1950s. AIP's *Earth vs. the Spider* (1958), another "BIG" movie from Bert I. Gordon, was an imitation of *Tarantula*, only geared to an even younger — and heartier — audience. The very first scene offered something that was not on view in *Tarantula*—a lot of repellent squirting blood. The film begins with a truck driver encountering a huge web stretched across the highway; when he crashes into the web, the blood splashes across his face as he screams in horror. The victim, Jack Flynn, is the father of the film's heroine, Carol (June Kenney), who attends high school with her boyfriend Mike Simpson (Gene Persson) in the "isolated mountain community" of River Falls. Searching for her father in a cave outside of town, they discover a giant spider that is eventually gassed with large amounts of bug spray and presumably killed. But at an inopportune moment it wakes up in the school gymnasium where it was put on exhibit and proceeds to rampage across town. Maneuvered back into the cave where Carol and Mike are trapped, the spider is electrocuted and the world is safe again.

Admittedly one of the lesser big bug movies, it is nevertheless fast-paced and entertaining, as are all of Gordon's creature features. The very uneven effects work is problematic, although it isn't bad considering the budget. The giant "bird spider" was poked and prodded by an animal trainer and blown up to monstrous proportions, although shots blending it with the actors are rare. While the shot of the sleeping monster in the gymnasium on one side of the screen and the gawking people staring at it on the other is effective, other split screen shots, the blend of differing elements, are awkwardly done and unconvincing. (It is generally assumed that the music played by the band rehearsing in the gym wakes the spider up, but it's more likely that it simply came out of its DDT-induced coma at that point.)

As it chases after the hero of the film, the science teacher Mr. Kingman (Ed Kemmer) — who believes in the existence of the spider awfully quickly — the spider briefly appears translucent (something that happened in most of Gordon's films, as he and his wife did all of the effects) but at least its feet touch the ground. When the spider enters one neighborhood and attacks the science teacher's home — wouldn't you know it? — where his wife and baby are sitting ducks, a very fake-looking "leg" is thrust into the room to make it seem as if the spider is enveloping the whole house. A shot when it looks into the window at the woman and child does not give one the shivers the way the similar shot in *Tarantula* does. The spider squeals like a demented pig whenever it appears. In the climax, a terrible spider mock-up is substituted for the real spider, probably because they couldn't figure out a way to get the real thing to hang down from the rocky ceiling of the cavern on cue. However, this mock-up wriggles its legs with conviction. We never learn the spider's origin and no one seems to care where it came from or why or if there are any others.

When the girl's father's body is found in the cave, all the juices sucked out of him by the spider, the body more resembles a wizened alien than it does the shriveled-up corpse of a man. However, when the deputy Dave receives the same treatment from the monster, his sucked-out husk is more on the mark. The "isolated mountain community" looks much more like a small city — or a suburb of Los Angeles — when the monster spider goes on the attack. Some gruesome moments — a crying, blood-spattered baby in the middle of the road; a woman whose skirt is caught in a car door and who screams in terror as the spider approaches — are effective bits of horror. The film's credits shrink in size and disappear into a drawing of a spiderweb, a nice touch.

Throughout the movie the high school couple, the science teacher, the cops and exterminators all walk around the cavern that is home to the spider without the aid of a single flashlight or torch. Even considering that light might filter into the recesses of the cave from the large opening in front, this is still incredible. Much too late in the film we are told that the walls are coated with "luminous algae," which doesn't quite explain why the young couple practically jump right into the spider's web at one point because they can't see where they're going. (This web consists of thick ropes that aren't very sticky and most people have no trouble wriggling out of them.) The movie greatly benefits from some shots filmed by a second unit in New Mexico's Carlsbad Caverns with its deep, impressive interiors; they offer the film its only extra-special "production value" (most of the cave scenes were actually filmed in Bronson Caverns or in the studio). Another plus is Albert Glasser's eerie music, which is sometimes hokey but somehow fitting.

The high school students in the film are all played by actors who aren't much younger than the handsome hero, Ed Kemmer, who was thirty-seven at the time. (One supporting player, Troy Patterson, a "high school student" who leads the band that plays in the gym, was thirty-five!) Kemmer starred on TV's *Space Patrol* and did much work on soap operas and other series in later years. Kemmer is competent but little else. June Kenney, who was not a bad actress, was also in Gordon's *Attack of the Puppet People* and Corman's *Viking Women and the Sea Serpent*. Gene Persson, who is also effective, played young Willie Kettle in some of the Ma and Pa Kettle films. Gene Roth, who plays the laconic Sheriff Cagel, was a very busy character actor of the period, as was Hank Patterson (of *Tarantula* fame), who appears briefly as the janitor Hugo and is best known for his portrayal of Mr. Ziffel, owner of the pig Arnold, on *Green Acres*. He also appeared in several other Gordon productions, as did June Jocelyn (playing Carol's mother). Sally Fraser, who plays Kemmer's wife, starred in Gordon's *War of the Colossal Beast*.

Whatever its flaws, *Earth vs. the Spider* isn't bad at all.

From the United Kingdom, where it was originally entitled *The Strange World of Planet X*, came *The Cosmic Monsters* (1958), an oddball big bug feature that nearly talks itself to death before delivering some gruesome and shuddery goods. (In most sources the title is singular, but the title in the film itself is *Monsters* with an s at the end.) Gil Graham (Forrest Tucker) is a Canadian researcher helping out British scientist Dr. Laird (Alec Mango) in his government-sponsored experiments in a quaint village. Laird's device can realign the molecules of metals and turn them brittle, useful in warfare against enemy planes and so on. Unfortunately, the field of Laird's apparatus is widening, which the villagers could have told him as his device interferes with TV reception at the local pub. The magnetic field the device creates is disrupting the ionosphere (this was years before we worried about spray cans and the ozone layer) and letting in dangerous cosmic radiation.

This radiation drives some of the villagers mad, turning one into a psychotic killer, and also has the highly dubious and unexpected effect of mutating all the "quick breeders" — such as insects — so that all the bugs in the nearby forest grow into giant monstrosities practically overnight. With the help of a friendly alien — more on him later — and the military, the bugs are all destroyed along with Dr. Laird and his infernal machine.

Much of the film's 74-minute running time is taken up with dull scenes of bureaucrats discussing Laird and Laird and his associates discussing the bureaucrats and the problems with the device. The film is enlivened a bit by the arrival of Michele Dupont (Gaby

André), a healthy-looking Frenchwoman and computer expert who has come to replace an injured assistant. The reaction of Graham and Laird to the news that the new assistant is female is reactionary even for the period. Graham insists that she'll be a "frustrated, angular spinster" and is pleasantly surprised at her appearance, revealing himself to be an aging make-out artist; he eventually gets her motor racing after another colleague strikes out. Andre is very pleasing and convincing in the part, a welcome respite from all the pencil pushers yakking.

Much weirder than Ms. Dupont, if not as sexy, is a strange man who simply calls himself "Smith" (Martin Benson). There have been reports of flying saucers in the news and Smith did indeed come to Earth from "Planet X" in a saucer which we see at the end and which he uses to destroy Laird's laboratory. (He also uses a zap gun on some of the big bugs.) Benson may be an authoritative player, but it is astonishing how he is able to convince Graham and Michele of his theories so very quickly. He *only* says that insects may be affected in any number of ways — "*Insects*! Mon dieu!" says Michele — but Graham almost immediately comes to the conclusion that giant bugs are busy munching on the populace. On the other hand, one can't say that he accepts "Smith" being from outer space too readily because once you've seen giant bugs you'll probably believe just about anything.

The first bug doesn't even make a cameo until 42 minutes into the running time, by which time most of the audience must have been pretty bug-eyed. However, the film is infamous for a sequence that had kids in this writer's neighborhood agog when it was shown on TV's *Chiller Theater*. Learning that the new schoolteacher Miss Forsythe (Patricia Sinclair) has gone to the bug-infested school house in the woods, Michele bravely makes her way there to warn her. (She's very brave because a mother has just shown her the huge egg that her bug-loving daughter has brought home from these very woods. "Boil it!" commands Michele.) Unfortunately, by the time she arrives, big beetles and cockroaches and other disgusting vermin have surrounded the schoolhouse to the hysterical teacher's horror. Understandably, Michele retraces her steps, bugs snapping out at her, until she accidentally steps into a giant spiderweb and is ensnared. She watches in terror as the spider battles a beetle, knowing all the while that once the spider wins the fight she'll undoubtedly be next on the menu. Michele then does what any sensible person would do and passes out. Both women are eventually rescued by the Army, Graham, and Smith with his trusty zapper. This is one of the rare old movies that doubles the damsel-in-distress formula for a very satisfying episode. Since heroines were somehow sacrosanct in these movies, the idea that two of them would be menaced with a fate literally worse than death — eaten alive by big bugs! — at the same time fascinated kids of both sexes who saw the film.

Alas, the special effects of *The Cosmic Monsters* are fourth-rate at best. There are many close-up shots of bugs staring out of bushes, but that's all these shots look like — little bugs staring out of bushes. With the exception of the aforementioned forest scene, there are no process shots blending people with bugs. Sometimes it looks as if someone is simply holding up a bug in front of a photograph or a bug is poorly superimposed over a scene of Gaby André screaming and running, or a backdrop of the forest. We do see a shot of Michele trapped in the web as the critters struggle high above her in the same frame, and there's also an effective bit when a bug peeks in the window at Miss Forsythe. One grisly moment

Gaby André is trapped in the web of a giant, voracious spider in *The Cosmic Monsters* (1958).

that is often cut from TV airings has a bug stripping away the flesh from the face of a wounded soldier. Since a toy doll of the soldier would have to be ridiculously minuscule to seem life-size compared to a real bug, one assumes the effect was created by using a live man, a close-up of a real bug, then a bug prop on top of easily peeled "flesh" over a white skull. However the shot was achieved, it's suitably gross.

If the optical effects department was not working at an optimal level, the same cannot be said for the sound department, who cooked up some chilling noises to portray the eating and crunching sounds of the bugs, as well as the fearful snapping as the bugs eat through the walls and doors of the school house in an attempt to get at pretty Miss Forsythe. Robert Sharpless' musical score adds nothing to the movie, however.

The performances in *The Cosmic Monsters* are all at least competent, which can barely be said about Gilbert Gunn's uninspired and stodgy direction.

Attack of the Giant Leeches (1959) pretty much put an end to the big bug cycle of the 1950s, although it is not without its charms. In this, the "proximity of Cape Canaveral" and its radiation is given as an explanation for the mutation of the leeches in the swamp. Big-bellied Dave Walker (Bruno Ve Sota), who owns the general store, discovers that his trampy wife Liz (Yvette Vickers) is carrying on with local stud Cal (Michael Emmet). Trying to scare them, he forces them into the swamp at gunpoint where they are promptly carried away by odd-looking giant leeches with arm-like appendages (the arms of the stunt divers who played them). Arrested for their deaths, Dave commits suicide in jail. Game warden Steven Benton (craggy pretty-boy Ken Clark) goes off on what he sees as a wild goose chase when his girlfriend Nan's father, the local doctor, insists that strange creatures are responsible for several disappearances and the death of one man. There is no reason for Doc Grayson (Tyler McVey) to leap to such a conclusion — especially with gators about — but although he's right about the monsters, the good doctor isn't right about much else. For instance, he suggests the creatures are nocturnal, even though they attack several people in broad daylight. Steve and the doc figure out that the missing victims may still be alive in air-filled underground caves. Explosives put paid to what appear to be only a couple of giant leeches in the swamp.

Attack of the Giant Leeches, written by Leo Gordon, is not by any means a good movie, but it exudes a cheesy fascination. The monsters — divers in black wetsuits dotted with white "suckers" of varying sizes — only look moderately convincing in long shots. The arm-like appendages make them look more like leech-*men*. This may explain why the doctor — although this is before he has actually seen them — attributes them with human-like intelligence. He is convinced that they tracked down and killed the man who fired at them in the pre-credit sequence. As was often the case in these cheapies, the monsters sound better than they look. Alexander Laszlo's musical score — sensual, kind of lazy, "bayou"-type music — adds a bit of eeriness to some sequences.

Some of the human characters are more interesting than the leeches. Yvette Vickers' portrayal of Liz is somewhat different from the skank, Honey, that she plays in *Attack of the 50 Foot Woman*; she's certainly bitchy and horrible to Dave, but she also displays vulnerability in her scenes with Cal. We know Liz is a complete loser for the simple reason that she wound up with Ve Sota, a very lower case Pagliacci. Cal is so craven that he turns on Liz and blames her entirely for their indiscretion when Dave discovers them in each other's arms. (This is only minutes after telling her: "You [can] tell me you killed your ma and pa and whole family, [and] I'd fight to protect you.") Steve initially seems like a big stiff, but he proves to be not so dull after all when he smooches with Nan (Jan Shepard). Steve gives perfectly valid reasons why he doesn't want her father to go about dynamiting the swamp but Nan is so rigid in refusing to see his side of it that she almost seems demented.

The most shuddery business in the movie has to do with the leeches bringing their victims to the underground dens (similar to those used by alligators) to "let them ripen" for a bit. Slowly being drained of blood, the people are too weak to fight off their attackers. After dynamite charges knock most of these people off the ledge and bring them to the surface, the doc does an autopsy and says that they had been dead for at least three or four hours before being dragged out of the water. Since we clearly see these people writhing about alive in the cave only *seconds* before the explosion, either the doctor is making yet another mistake or there was a really big goof in continuity. In any case, the various shots of the victims slowly rising up through the murky water, arms extended in a ghost-like way, their faces and bodies covered with wounds from suckers, are macabre.

Ve Sota has an expressive face and is credible if unsubtle as Dave. Vickers as is vivid and snappy as ever. Gene Roth makes an impression as the sheriff, who hasn't much use for

Steve or the doctor. Clark and Shepard are adequate but a cut below the assortment of fla-vorful character actors who play Dave's buddies at the store, some of whom become vic-tims of the leeches. Michael Emmet makes a more than credible Cal. Under the direction of Bernard L. Kowalski, *Attack of the Giant Leeches* proceeds at a deliberate although not leaden pace. A no-doubt campy remake of the film directed by Brett Kelly is to be released in 2008.

The Giant Spider Invasion (1975) is a far cry from *Them!* and *Tarantula*. Filmed on location in Wisconsin on a very low budget, it made little impression when it opened and disappeared quickly. The lives of the residents of the small town of Harton are disrupted when meteors crash in their backyard in an explosive display that gets attention from NASA. Inside some of the meteors is an element that is similar to industrial diamond, along with spiders of varying sizes. Ev Kester (Leslie Parrish) and her husband (Robert Easton) dis-cover that something has been chewing on their cattle even as some of the townspeople go missing. While Mr. Kester tries to find out how much money he can get for the diamond-like substance, local scientist Jenny Langer (Barbara Hale, "Della Street" from *Perry Mason*) and a man from NASA named Vance (Steve Brodie) team up to investigate whatever it was that fell from space. The pair come up with some kind of "neutron gadget" that is used to blow the one really huge spider (fifty feet) out of existence and destroy all the other smaller ones before they, too, can grow into giants.

If Bert I. Gordon had directed *Giant Spider Invasion*, it might have been fun. The story is workable, and there are plenty of gruesome situations to be exploited. Under the ama-teurish direction of Bill Rebane, however, the atrocious picture moves at a snail's pace and has almost zero entertainment value. The giant full-size prop spider doesn't look too bad from a distance as it crosses a field, but in close-up it's simply ludicrous. The prop has a "mouth" or opening in the bottom through which assorted actors are pulled as they scream, and unseen techies work the mobile fangs and drip "saliva" out of the hole. Big white pop-up globular eyes that glow in the dark make the monster seem even more fake, if such a thing is possible. It also emits high-pitched squeaking noises. This kind of phony mon-strosity might have worked in one of those briskly edited and directed Roger Corman films such as *Attack of the Crab Monsters* but in a film as dull as this it's just another nail in the coffin.

Steve Brodie and (especially) Barbara Hale play their parts with conviction but their professional level performances are completely wasted. The same can be said for the very good performances of Leslie Parrish and Robert Easton as the dysfunctional Kesters. They are given the film's big gross-out moment when Parrish fixes up a Bloody Mary, unaware that one of the spiders crawled into the blender just before she poured in the ingredients. Her husband never does get around to drinking any of the concoction, but the audience during one showing squirmed when Parrish took a sip and then shouted when she swal-lowed the mess and grimaced in disgust. Hale's real-life husband Bill Williams appears briefly as the bartender, Dutch. Kevin Brodie and Dianne Lee Hart are quite good as, respectively, Ev's younger sister and her boyfriend. (Kevin Brodie is the son of Steve Brodie and would become a director in later years, helming the second remake of *A Dog of Flan-ders* in 1999.)

While Bert I. Gordon may not have directed *Giant Spider Invasion*, he did helm *Empire of the Ants* (1977), which — while no worldbeater — was a considerable improvement over the former. Marilyn (Joan Collins) invites a group of potential investors — most of whom just want the free booze — to take a tour of Dreamland Shores, which is stuck together with spit and chewing gum. Even worse, some ants that have been nibbling at radioactive waste dribbling from barrels that washed ashore, have grown into tremendous giants. The ants attack some of the party and herd the others to a small town nearby, where it turns out they have brainwashed the inhabitants into becoming their slaves. About to be hypnotized by a puff of pheromones from the queen ant, Marilyn's employee (and boat captain) David (Robert Lansing) sets fire to the queen while another "investor," Joe (John David Carson), rams a gasoline truck into the sugar refinery where the rest of the ants are roasted alive.

Gordon had directed *Food of the Gods*, a very loose adaptation of H. G. Wells' novel, the previous year; benefitting from an effective ad campaign, that film did quite well for AIP. *Empire of the Ants* had even less to do with the short story by H. G. Wells, but his name was again invoked for whatever value or class it may have imparted to the fairly cheesy production. In her memoirs Joan Collins wrote amusingly of the lack of amenities she had while making the film, not to mention the indignity and discomfort of slogging through Florida swamps for days at a time. Films like *Empire of the Ants* had her fleeing to television in record time.

Gordon himself, as usual, did the film's effects, but the crudity of some of the process shots are more glaring in color than in his old black-and-white creature features. Nonetheless, some of the optical work is effective, such as a shot of the big black ants marching along a dock towards David's little boat. The clusters of ants crawling all over themselves and through the trees in the forest are convincingly creepy, and there's an excellent shot of them busily working in the foreground as we see the rowboat with the surviving members of the party traveling up river through the swamp in the background. When real live actors are included in shots of the ants playing in the sugar inside the refinery, the illusion is workable, but close-ups of the ants — like the close-ups of drowning locusts in *Beginning of the End* finale — just look like cute little ants in your sugar bowl.

Generally the real ants, enlarged through trick work, prove able enough performers, but Gordon really didn't help himself by including shots of phony prop ants that have little if any mobility, are poorly designed, and don't seem to actually do anything. Held by unseen prop people, these ants just seem to bump against the actors as they scream in terror. Shaky hand-held shots with the camera turned every which way don't disguise the flimsiness of these props but only make these sequences look even worse, and if possible, cheesier. If Gordon had relied on very quick cutting or eliminated these shots altogether, his opus would have been much improved. It was as if Gordon had forgotten the rudimentary rules of low-budget film-making that should have been imprinted on his brain since the 1950s. His "classic" creature features are much better than the ones he did twenty years later.

Although Gordon came in for criticism because of the aforementioned shots of bugs crawling over pictures in *Beginning of the End*, he does worse in *Empire of the Ants*. As the big ants head for the open door of the refinery, some of them begin climbing the building — where there is no building. To be charitable, one could suggest that the ants were merely standing on their hind legs, but of course it makes no sense that they would scratch their legs against open air. To represent the ant's-eye view of things, Gordon simply places a plate with several circles cut out of it over the lens. Needless to say, this is not too impressive.

One thing the movie has going for it is that the plot heads in an unexpected direction. Instead of the ants rampaging through Miami, they exert mind control via their queen on the townspeople. Each week, we are told, the town's inhabitants must report to the refinery where they enter a booth with the queen ant and inhale the mist she exudes. But right here we encounter a serious continuity problem. The ants are shown nibbling at the waste material at the very start of the picture. Somehow they manage to grow to huge size, take over a town, and begin their very own society in the space of a few hours — yet the townspeople have to *report to the refinery every week*? Not even a single day has gone by! Previous big bug movies made it clear that the monsters were at least second generation mutations, but the ants in this movie seem to grow instantaneously. If this is not the case, the movie fails to make it clear.

Most of the actors give the movie more than it deserves. Joan Collins had perfected her sexy bitch routine by this point, and she's never less than riveting and professional. Robert Lansing and Jacqueline Scott are very effective as, respectively, the captain and lonely woman who bond during the crisis. John David Carson is unintentionally amusing when he reacts to the sight of chewed-up bodies as if they were dead rabbits when everyone else around him is in shock, but otherwise proves competent, as does Pamela Shoop, who is perhaps a bit too overwrought at times even considering the circumstances. The best that can be said about Dana Kaproff's musical score, which apes *Jaws'* to a certain degree, is that it is no help at all.

For every good scene in the movie — an elderly couple hiding in the shack in the forest think they are safe only to come out and find themselves surrounded by hundreds of ants — there are two ludicrous ones (Joan Collins fending off the silly mock-up of the queen ant), making *Empire of the Ants* more of a travesty than anything else. And not nearly as much fun as *Beginning of the End.*

There were a few more minor big bug movies in the '80s and '90s. *Blue Monkey* (1987) somehow metamorphosed from a movie about a monster simian to a latter-day big bug feature. An elderly man brushes against an imported plant and develops a rash. It's bad enough that a weird larvae crawls out of the poor fellow's mouth, but this creature accidentally comes across some genetic growth stimulant and turns into a very large, even weirder, mutant bug comprised of several different species. In the meantime, people in the hospital are coming down with insect-related diseases that force the authorities to put one wing under quarantine. Detective Jim Bishop (Steve Railsback) comes to see an afflicted buddy and winds up leading the fight against several monsters who have taken up residence in the cellars and tunnels beneath the hospital.

The film's effects are mediocre. When they're seen quickly through shadows, the monster mock-ups are serviceable, but in close-up and out in the open they are silly-looking and patently phony. Any tension or fright that might have been generated by the film — and there isn't much — is completely dissipated by the sight of these creatures. A climactic battle in a lab where a laser beam is used against the big mother "blue monkey" is just full of messy, shake-it-from-side-to-side-to-cover-up-the-crappy-monster camerawork and is about as exciting as watching a fly beat itself against a window pane for hour after hour; less exciting, in fact.

Much of the picture's running time is taken up with the annoying adventures of several patients in the hospital. The two old ladies who proceed to get drunk aren't too bad, but the whiny married couple who are about to have a baby should have been the "monkey's" first victims. Director William Fruet was also responsible for the snake film *Spasms* (aka *Death Bite*) which was much better — and couldn't have been much worse.

In Gary Jones' *Mosquito* (1995) a meteor falls to earth and enlarges the size of mosquitoes which munch on campers and the like and suck them dry of blood. The lively monsters are about the size of humans, and are well-designed (if phony-looking) flapping rubber mock-ups. They look good but have limited movement, although their wings do flap very rapidly. There is some really excellent stop motion of flying bugs (no well-known stop motion artists were responsible, however) and cartoon animation is used for shots of hordes of flying bugs. *Mosquito* has a very workable script, at least in terms of action, with some very effective scenes, but there's way too much bad acting — one young couple at the opening barely react to the sheer size of a crushed mosquito they find on the highway — and too many disagreeably nerdy supporting characters, especially a bunch of irritating bank robbers and a rather amateurish park assistant. (Gunnar Hanson, "Leatherface" of *Texas Chain Saw Massacre*, is the heavyset bank robber, Earl.)

The best actor, Steve Dixon, plays a "meteorologist" who is not a weatherman but actually investigates meteors. One scene has a mosquito attacking a guy on a boat and thrusting its proboscis right through his eye. There's an exciting bit when the assorted characters attempt to outrace the bugs in their van, and the heroine nearly falls out as it careens down the road. Overall, the movie was not awful, but not nearly as good as it could have been.

In Tony Randel's *Ticks* (1993) a group of troubled inner city kids go off for a camp outing and run into ticks about six inches long. Apparently the ticks grew large because they fed on marijuana plants full of herbal steroids. The effects are generally quite good and the ticks themselves are excellent, except for a less effective man-sized tick at the finale that slowly gushes out from one poor victim's body. The actors are able to pull the ticks off of their skin much too easily — what about those tenacious mouthparts, for Pete's sake? Peter Scolari, the only name actor, plays one half of an adult couple accompanying the kids into the wilderness. Otherwise, both the characters (especially a couple of backwoods creeps) and actors in the film are obnoxious. Clint Howard is painfully obvious in a "character turn" as a young/old man and victim of the ticks. The scene when a heavy block falls down on him and pins him to the floor as the critters attack (eventually they infest his still living body) is well-handled. *Ticks* is second-rate all the way (except for some effects work) but undeniably fun, with some humorous moments.

One of the best and most unusual "big bug" movies of all time was *Mimic* (1997), which was based on a story by Donald A. Wollheim. New York City is in the midst of an epidemic of Strickler's Disease that is carried by roaches and is killing off many children. Susan Tyler (Mira Sorvino), a professor of entomology, creates a special "Judas Breed" bug that infects and kills off the roaches . Although the Judas bugs were designed to die after performing their task, it turns out they they've actually been breeding, and in three years have evolved into six-foot-tall, intelligent bugs who can walk upright and even disguise themselves as people! (They have also developed lungs.) Tyler, her husband Dr. Peter Mann (Jeremy Northam), and a cop named Leonard (Charles S. Dutton) descend into the subways where the roaches are breeding to try and put an end to the deadly infestation. Afer many harrowing incidents, they manage to obliterate the female roaches in their nest, while the one fertile male is crushed by a subway car.

The FX work in *Mimic* is excellent. Rob Bottin was responsible for the creature design. The big roaches are sometimes live-action mechanical devices or even sophisticated "puppets" and at other times (particularly when they spread their wings and fly) the result of computer imagery. The bugs can stand tall on two feet (disguised as people), fly, hop and run quite fast when they want to. One of the most interesting — and chilling — aspects of their design is the way their outer carapaces form a kind of humanoid face. When one is dissected it reveals highly realistic internal organs. Just as realistic — and disgusting — is a underground chamber in the subway that is full of slimy egg casings several feet in length. The effects work at the climax when a series of underground explosions and fires wracks the surface of the city is also superior.

Mimic meanders at times, as its characters do (wandering distractedly in and out of the subways and abandoned buildings), but it holds the attention with a series of creepy tableaus. There is the eerie moment when Susan is observed by one of the silent, unseen bugs as she works in her lab, and a scary bit when she is chased by one of the roach-men in the subway; he appears at first to be a homeless person, then opens his chest, spreads his wings, pursues her through the station, and flies off with her. There is a scene when the likable kids who bring bugs they find to Susan for cash are killed by a barely seen creature with wings and claws that corners them in a darkened underground chamber. (While disturbing because of the youth of its victims, it has a sad inevitability to it that doesn't make it seem an expression of child-hatred, often the case with similar scenes.)

In one highlight, most of the main characters enter an abandoned station and are trapped in a subway car with the bugs trying to smash their way in. The humans rub themselves in insect goo to try to fool the bugs into thinking they're fellow roaches. The climax with the lone male bug chasing Susan down the tunnel as a train approaches is thrilling even if the creature's manner of death is a bit convenient. Since the fate of the world is so dependent on this creature being killed, it seems an awfully simple solution that it is merely run over by a train.

The characters are interesting if somewhat underdeveloped. It is never explained why the bugs kill some of the people they come across, but simply drag others into the subway. One explanation could be their state of hunger at the time, but why kill the shoeshine man, Manny (Giancarlo Giannini), just as he finds his missing son? If the bug was hungry he would have eaten the boy, no? It's interesting that there's only one fertile male bug, just as there was only one male dragon in the later *Reign of Fire*. The business with the insects breeding when they're not supposed to reminds one of a similar situation with the dinosaurs of *Jurassic Park*.

In movies like this, the actors pretty much have to take a back seat to the bugs, but they are all strong enough to make an impression. Sorvino and Northam are an appealing heroic couple, just as Giannini and Alexander Goodwin (as his boy Chuy) make you care about the father and his son. Charles S. Dutton is solid as the cop Leonard, and F. Murray Abraham, although given little to do as Dr. Gates, provides a little extra class. Although the film could have been tightened up in spots, Guillermo del Toro provides some stylish and atmospheric direction. Don Laustsen's photography is first-rate. The "New York City" locations are actually Toronto, however, which often turns out to be the case these days.

Starship Troopers (1997) was based on a novel by Robert A. Heinlein. The Earth is at war with a race of Arachnids from the planet Klendathu. Johnny Rico (Casper Van Dien) joins the service to be with his lady love Carmen Ibanez (Denise Richards), but they're immediately separated when she decides to train to be a pilot. After he receives a (literal) "Dear John" video from her, Johnny resigns in disgust — only to re-enlist after his home land of Buenos Aires is obliterated by missiles from Klendathu. Johnny becomes an infantryman fighting giant spiders and other huge bugs on Klendathu, where the Arachnids commit wholesale slaughter. The tide seems to turn when humans capture the "big brain" mind-bug that controls the others. Perhaps there's hope for an Earth victory after all....

With over 200 visual effects people on staff (including Phil Tippett), it is no wonder that the FX work lacks the personal touch of a Ray Harryhausen. The Arachnids themselves — sleek, stylized, scorpion-like critters about the size of a tank — usually resemble something out of a more elaborate form of computer game animation. A giant acid- and flame-spewing beetle doesn't really look alive except in some shots that at least resemble stop-motion. However, one of the best scenes has Johnny jumping on the beetle's back and attacking it in bravura fashion, and there are many striking shots, such as a scary one depicting a swarm of hundreds of Arachnids rushing across the desert towards an abandoned Army base where many of the soldiers have taken shelter.

Other creatures include giant dragonflies that slice off soldiers' heads with their razor-sharp wings, lice-like baby Arachnids, and the massively repulsive brain-bug that figures in the climax. This creature has a gelatinous, phallic-like mushroom head, with black globules inside a red maw and pincers that suck out brains. The big prop bugs used in the anatomy class scene have very realistic internal organs, and the other FX throughout the film — explosions, ship crashes, conflagrations — are all impeccably handled.

Starship Troopers has serious problems, however. It takes a full hour for there to be any real action in this lengthy film, and the first half often comes off like some kind of awful teen comedy. One assumes Edward Neumeier's script is deliberately constructed to resemble, or to be a parody of, 1940s war films (only here the women do as much fighting as the men). Presented not as a straightforward "big bug" movie, *Troopers* has gruesome moments interspersed with what can only be called campy scenes, such as when two people on television debate on whether or not the bugs have brains and various recruitment messages. The movie never seems to have a point or even a real point of view — frankly, it doesn't seem intelligent enough — although it is hinted that the Earthlings may have asked for their troubles by invading the bug universe *first*. As the film proceeds and the body count rises to appalling proportions, the ages of the soldiers get younger and younger.

Starship Troopers (1997) brought together humans and big bugs in a much more graphic style than before.

Starship Troopers could have been a moving film — and it does inevitably have one or two briefly stirring moments — but it's way too preoccupied with grossing out the audience with one flying limb after another and with macho posturing among both the male and female players. The film is so relentlessly determined to be graphic in its depiction of mutilation-by-bug that after awhile it not only becomes repetitious but tedious. You're not shocked — after all, most people can figure out what happens to a human body when it's attacked by a giant spider; it doesn't have to be spelled out for you — just numbed or even bored.

Casper Van Dien is one of those square-jawed, minimally talented, good-looking actors who can deliver lines without tripping over their tongues, but heaven help them if they have to do any actual acting. Van Dien has an almost comically weak reaction to learning that his family and everyone and everything he knows has been wiped out by the Arachnids. He summons up the same level of anguish he might feel upon going to the drugstore and learning they're out of his favorite flavor of Chapstick. He and romantic interest Denise Richards are supposed to be from Buenos Aires, but they are about as South American as Dutch cocoa. However, the scene when a bare-backed Van Dien is whipped within an inch of his life for carelessness has a flamboyantly sadomasochistic tone that probably raised a few eyebrows in certain quarters. It is never explained how Johnny survives his first encounter with an Arachnid.

Dina Meyer, who plays soldier "Dizzy" Flores (and who also starred in *Bats*), is another story, displaying genuine acting ability, especially during her affecting death scene. Michael Ironside is good as a grizzled teacher called back into service, although he does tend to play it one-note at times. Patrick Muldoon exhibits an appealing insolence as Johnny's rival Zander. Neil Patrick Harris scores as Johnny's friend Carl, and Rue McClanahan offers a quirky moment or two as a zesty biology professor. By this time the promising director Paul Verhoeven, gone Hollywood, had completed his transformation from potential serious artist into an interesting, competent hack, but a hack nonetheless.

A sequel, *Starship Troopers 2: Hero of the Federation* (2004), went directly to video. As of this writing Edward Neumeier is helming a third film, *Starship Troopers: Marauder*, working from his own script, in which Casper Van Dien now plays a general called in to head the fight against a new plague of big terrible bug monsters.

THREE

Humongous

One particular breed of creature feature that has always fascinated the devotee is the giant monster movie, as gigantism has gripped the public imagination for centuries. Giant men and creatures of all kinds dominate our world's folklore and fairy tales. H. G. Wells brought gigantism to the forefront of popular fiction in his novel *The Food of the Gods*. Films of gigantic monsters can be sub-divided into several categories. In this chapter, we look at mostly ordinary animals who are of an extraordinary size, either freaks of nature or creatures that have been blown up to huge proportions by inadvertent scientific tampering or deliberate and sinister experimentation.

Jules Verne's fantastic novels have been good bets for filmic adaptation since the silent era. The first version of *The Mysterious Island* came out in 1929. It was originally planned as a silent feature, but some sound dialogue sequences were quickly filmed, and many sound effects were added before release. (A two-strip Technicolor sequence was also filmed, but subsequently lost.) The movie takes some concepts from Verne's *20,000 Leagues Under the Sea* and its sequel *Mysterious Island*, but otherwise has little to do with the books. Lionel Barrymore plays Count Andre Dakkar of the mythical nation of Hetvia. The mysterious island is simply his headquarters off the mainland, a submerged volcano. Dakkar wants to use his amazing new submarine, which can descend to undreamt of depths, for peaceful exploration, but the evil Baron Falon (Montagu Love) envisions it as an instrument of war. When Falon's forces attack the island, taking Dakkar's sister Sonia (Jane Daly) prisoner, Dakkar's assistant Nikolai (Lloyd Hughes) and their men are testing the sub underwater. Nikolai manages to rescue Dakkar, and Falon and his men, with Sonia in tow, pursue in another of Dakkar's submarines. On the sea bottom they encounter a strange race of sea people, as well as a series of monsters. Returning to the surface, a dying Dakkar makes his sister and her lover Nikolai promise to use his inventions only for peaceful purposes.

Much of *The Mysterious Island* is quite dull, but 1929 audiences must have found the picture's second half quite enthralling. Although the submarine looks like a toy you might find in a bathtub, some of the underwater sequences, employing credible process shots, are well done. The sea people resemble tiny mole men with big eyes, bald heads, and snow-white skin; they were undoubtedly played by midgets or children. One striking shot shows hundreds of the tiny sea people dragging the submarine toward their lair with ropes. During the sub's voyage to the sea bottom, a giant centipede is briefly glimpsed, as well as a giant, mud-encrusted crab-creature. An enormous monster which threatens the sea people, and which Nicolai drives away with the sub's weaponry, is an alligator tricked up with a big horn on its snout and an appliance on its back that makes it resemble a sailback reptile, or perhaps a stegosaurus, of the prehistoric era. The ungrateful sea people then unleash their own monster, an octopus that is larger than the submarine (although nowhere nears as big as the "alligator"). An interesting sequence has the octopus sending its tentacles in through the air lock to wrap around and crush the men inside the sub. The sub manages to get out of the beast's grip and make its way to the surface and safety. Despite these sequences, *The Mysterious Island* is not especially memorable and does *not* feature one of Lionel Barrymore's better performances. It took thirty-two years for Hollywood to make another version of *The Mysterious Island*, this time with the a deliberate emphasis on colossal creatures. More on this later.

King Kong (1933) really was the "Eighth Wonder of the World." Although it could be classified as a "lost world" fantasy or dinosaur/dragon movie, for our purposes we'll focus on the fact that it features an extremely large—indeed humongous—ape. Carl Denham (Robert Armstrong), who makes moving pictures about wild animals, needs a girl to appear in his next picture and winds up hiring a starving waif named Ann Darrow (Fay Wray). They travel to an island where there have been persistent rumors of a strange creature called Kong. The native people are fascinated by Ann's blond hair and kidnap her to sacrifice to Kong, who turns out to be a giant gorilla. Denham, his first mate Jack Driscoll (Bruce Cabot), and the other sailors pursue Kong and many meet their deaths at the teeth of assorted dinosaurs. Driscoll manages to save Ann, and Denham uses gas bombs to capture the ape. On exhibition in Manhattan, Kong breaks free, re-captures Ann, and breathes his last at the top of the Empire State Building, where bi-planes shoot him down.

King Kong was brought to life via stop-motion photography. An 18-inch model (24-inches for the Manhattan rampage scenes) of Kong was moved one frame at a time; when these many individual frames were run together, they created the illusion of movement. The human characters were blended in with the big ape via the use of back projection, with the monster footage projected on a screen behind the live actors. On some occasions a full-sized head and hand of Kong was employed, such as when Kong has screaming people between his teeth and chews them a bit, and when he lifts Ann Darrow off the ground. These full-scale props are quite well-done; the head can open and close its mouth and move its eyes a little, while the hand can curl its fingers around its prey. Any way you slice it, Kong is a remarkable creation, full of life, personality, curiosity, humanity, and all manner of vivid emotions. In some shots, however, he resembles a very big Teddy bear.

Stop-motion specialist Willis O'Brien took everything he had learned while making the silent *The Lost World* and ran with it, coming up with sequences that are still impressive today, especially when one considers the time-consuming, personal approach that he employed (a handful of men as opposed to literally *hundreds* of technicians hovering over computer screens). If one really *looks at* and *understands* and *appreciates* what O'Brien was doing, the effects do not look antiquated or quaint but quite startling and wonderful.

Yes, there is a "primitive" quality to some aspects of the effects, but these "old-fashioned" sequences can also be enjoyed on a certain level. For instance, when the men come across the stegosaurus, first seen in the background at the far end of a path through the jungle, the obvious back projection upon which the dinosaur is viewed almost looks like a

The big ape battles a *Tyrannosaurus rex* to the death in the classic *King Kong* (1993).

movie within a movie. But it still *works*, especially when the monster comes charging up the path towards the men in the foreground. Even more effective is the shot that shows Denham and the sailors traversing the length of the dead beast from left to right, with the creature's tail rising and falling sinuously in the background and giving the hardened seamen a nervous jolt.

Then there's the snarling brontosaur that sizes up the tasty man-morsel in the tree; the scene is a combination of back projection (live actor, projected monster) with excellent model work, both of the dinosaur and of the sailor as the latter is snatched off his perch by the teeth of the brontosaurus. The animation in this sequence, especially as the beast roars at the sailor clinging precariously to his branch, is especially smooth. In comparison, the lizard that sneaks up a vine and tries to attack Driscoll is forgettable. The primeval forest setting is expertly recreated with real plants and trees, prop plants, matte paintings — a multi-layered approach that creates a rich and distinctive atmosphere.

Once the characters get to Kong's island, the picture proceeds at such a breakneck pace that it seems to consist of one highlight after another. The suspenseful business of the tribespeople preparing Ann for her terrible fate leads into the powerful approach of the terrifying Kong through the crashing trees (one would imagine most of the trees in his path would have long since been torn out, however). The sequence with the brontosaur rising out of a foggy lake to snatch men off the raft has the quality of a nightmare. (In some shots a prop head of the monster is employed; in its comparative immobility it reminds one of the ferry-attacking prop monster in *The Giant Behemoth*— also worked on by O'Brien.) Even more hellish and grotesque is the scene when Kong shakes the rest of the sailors off of the log spanning the crevice. The "spider pit" scene was supposedly removed for being too graphic (as were other scenes, temporarily) and then lost, but one can't imagine how any of the men who fell off the log and plunged that great distance into the pit could have possibly survived to run afoul of giant insects.

King Kong battling the T-Rex remains one of the finest stop-motion dinosaur battle scenes ever put on film, capped by the amusing business of the big ape playing with the dead dinosaur's flapping jaw after tearing it apart. Kong pulling up that awfully convenient vine to which Driscoll and Ann desperately cling is thrilling, as is the scene with Kong pounding on the big wooden gate and pushing the door open despite the sailors' and locals' best efforts to stop him. One can only assume that in his maddened frenzy Kong wasn't intelligent or calm enough to simply climb over the wall, nor that he had any particular reason to do so before his blond pet was spirited away from him.

Some of the censored scenes in the movie were eventually re-inserted. These include shots of Kong grinding two tribesmen into the mud (if it were hard ground instead of mud, the scene would have been *too* distasteful, although it's unlikely the victims survived in either case); putting tribesmen and one New Yorker into his mouth (he chews on them but does not eat them); and the charming business with Kong tearing off strips of Ann's clothing and sniffing them. Another scene — a particularly disturbing one — has Kong pulling a terrified woman out of her bed in the hotel where Driscoll has taken Ann after the gorilla's escape from the theater. Realizing that the woman isn't Ann, he drops her many stories to her death. The hellish, phobic nature of the death combined with its suddenness — and the complete innocence and utter stupefaction of the victim — taps into the average viewer's deepest psychic fears. Perhaps the most disturbing scene of all was never cut out of the movie: Kong attacking the elevated subway train full of ordinary, tired New Yorkers coming home from work and expecting nothing but the usual dull routine. With Kong not only pulling the cars off of the track but smashing repeatedly at them as well, it's unlikely there were many survivors. Although one could certainly argue that Kong is just a dumb animal doing what comes naturally, and Carl Denham is ultimately to blame for these tragedies, it's kind of hard to feel sorry for the big ape when so many perfectly harmless human beings have been killed and mutilated.

Over the years, critics have subjected the film to all manner of often bizarre interpretation. One theory has it that Kong is violent out of sexual frustration (his inability to have intercourse with the doll-like Ann). This might make sense if it hadn't already been made clear that Kong is very violent, and has to be, if he wants to remain king of his island — or just survive among so many hungry predators. It is more likely that Kong sees Ann as a pretty bauble, a pet, one of his belongings, one that he won't give up until he's ready to; the "beauty" that killed the beast is a beautiful toy. Another theory, that Kong represents the anger of the black race, is inherently and appallingly racist. We never learn what happens to the local women who become "brides" of Kong — one assumes they are eaten (by

Kong or other predators once Kong loses interest in them) or simply die of terror or starvation. The film isn't concerned with their fate because it doesn't really see them as people (although it's equally tough on some New Yorkers).

Fay Wray is very pretty and appealing as Ann. Robert Armstrong and Bruce Cabot are both in "macho" mode, neither showing much emotion over the terrible deaths of their friends and colleagues, with Cabot being a somewhat better performer than the generally wooden Armstrong. Max Steiner, who often worked on pictures that were romantic in the more traditional sense of the word, contributed an excellent score. Of special note are the dance music for the tribal ceremony, and the music as the witch doctor approaches Denham's shore party, the music matching him step by step as he gets closer and closer to the curious onlookers.

Still the best of the three versions of the story, *King Kong* remains one of the finest creature features ever made. The 1976 *King* with its campy, bloated approach, man in a gorilla suit (or robot Kong), subway cars that clearly have no people inside them, fake mechanical giant snakes (and not a single dinosaur), and unmemorable performances, is hardly worth mentioning. Jessica Lange shows a certain presence as the irritatingly ditzy "Dwan" and the scene when Kong blow-dries her with his breath is kind of charming. The sequel, *King Kong Lives*, (1986), was a bad "animal rights" monster movie with little to recommend it.

Peter Jackson's version seems to have been influenced by the remake as much as by the original. We have plenty of dinosaurs, some very good FX work and exciting, harrowing, admittedly eye-popping sequences (especially involving the T-Rex), but the fatal miscasting of Jack Black as Denham (Robert Armstrong may not have been a great actor but he was much more suitable) only adds to the camp quotient of the picture. Like the 1976 version, Ann has way too much sympathy for Kong, as does the film itself, trying to come off like an epic tragedy about a murderous big gorilla instead of a darn good monster movie. In the original, Ann didn't care if the big monkey were offed, she just wanted to *escape* from him, a much more realistic and sensible attitude. In the original, Denham gives out the ironic last line about beauty killing the beast — and that's it. Jackson's version takes forever to get going, is perhaps even more bloated than the first remake, commits the almost sacrilegious act of completely muffing the dramatic potential of Kong's first appearance as he comes to get Ann, and takes itself much, much too seriously at the wind-up. Frankly, the original *King Kong* puts the Jackson version in the shade.

In PRC's *The Devil Bat* (1940), Bela Lugosi plays Dr. Paul Carruthers, a cosmetics firm chemical researcher who is beloved by the entire town of Heathville and is believed to be a virtual saint. In reality, Carruthers is embittered because he sold a highly successful formula he developed to the cosmetics company co-owned by the Heath and Morton families for an outright ten thousand dollars and they got rich off of it. Now a mere employee of the firm, he seethes at the injustice (although he was given the option of taking an interest in the company and refused it) and is determined to get back at everyone. To this end he has developed a monstrous killer bat (he used electrical impulses to make the creature grow to five times its normal size; it is never explained how he got the expertise for this nor why he chose this bizarre form of revenge). The bat is attracted by a special shaving lotion

The first remake of *King Kong* in 1976 was a campy disaster with mediocre effects.

(with a "strange Oriental fragrance") formulated by Carruthers which he easily manipulates his victims into wearing; he then sics the bat on them, and their jugular veins are severed. A clever reporter solves the mystery and Carruthers falls victim to a second killer bat that he produced after the first one was killed.

The Devil Bat is watchable primarily for the presence of Lugosi, who is, as was often the case, far superior to his material. Often wrongly dismissed as a ham, Lugosi could do more with a simple look than other actors could do with entire monologues. He simmers with repressed passion as he makes pleasant small talk with people he despises and then nurses his grudges when alone in his house. Whether he is being affectionate with his monster bat or dismissing a hare-brained photographer with a withering gesture, he is marvelous. Treating a nosy reporter to some aftershave, he says "Goodbye, Mr. Layton" with consummate understatement. Later he rails at a scientist on the radio who has confused his atom-age creation with a survivor from the neolithic or stone age. "Imbecile," he hisses. "Bombastic ignoramus."

Alas, Lugosi's supporting cast is not in his league. The nominal heroine, Suzanne Kaaren, seems to think she's appearing in a drawing room comedy. Two of her young brothers are horribly murdered in as many days, as well as a friend she's known since childhood, but except for a gasp over one of the corpses, she never reacts with any fear or sorrow. This is true of the other actors, who seem incapable of displaying more than one emotion at a time. If the particular scene calls for them to make pleasant banter, this is what they do, completing forgetting that in the previous scene their son or brother was found with his throat torn out. Of course cheap movies like *Devil Bat* were filmed very quickly and, like most movies, out of sequence, but that's no excuse. At least Dave O'Brien as the reporter Johnny Layton exhibits a certain degree of charm, although his photographer-assistant "One Shot" McGuire (Donald Kerr) is only an irritant as the comedy relief. With the exception of old man Morton (Guy Usher), the victims are young men of good looks and limited acting ability (Alan Baldwin, John Ellis, Gene O'Donnell).

The monster bat is a prop which hangs in a lab in Lugosi's house and is also seen flying on a wire in long shots. For close-ups, a real bat is substituted. Otherwise there are no special effects to speak of. A shot of the big bat flapping its wings as it tries to get through Mary Heath's window is fairly eerie. Early in the film the authorities claim that the wounds look like they were made by the beak of a bird, which is odd considering that bats don't have beaks, and are mammals, not birds, as more than one character in John Thomas Neville's script explains. But the stupidest aspect of the story is the way Lugosi shakes hands with the victims after pouring lotion into their palms. When second victim Tommy Heath (Alan Baldwin) playfully flicks some of the aftershave at Lugosi's face, he recoils in horror — but again he grasps his hand in his own as if completely unaware there would certainly be residue in the palm even after the younger man applied most of the lotion to his face.

At one point Layton and McGuire, who have seen the bat, decide to cook up a fake photograph and send it in to their paper. When a scientist uses a magnifying glass on the picture he sees a made in Japan label on the alleged monster's wing. The two men are fired by the paper, but when it turns out that there really *is* a giant bat, their editor rehires them. Why? The picture was still a phony and it was still an embarrassment to the paper.

Director Jean Yarbrough keeps things moving, but the picture is devoid of style and tension. It is also known as *Killer Bats*, especially when shown on television. A sequel entitled *Devil Bat's Daughter* came out in 1946 from PRC, directed by Frank Wisbar. The only giant bats that appear in the sequel, unfortunately, are seen in flashbacks that form the nightmares of Dr. Carruthers' pretty daughter Nina (Rosemary LaPlanche). Nina is tormented by the stories of her father's murders and is just ripe to be used by a sinister psychiatrist in a plot to kill off his wealthy wife, but his stepson uncovers the truth. This basic premise was also used in *Daughter of Dr. Jekyll* (1957). At the end of the film we're told that Dr. Carruthers was only a well-meaning researcher whose bats, tragically, escaped from his lab and killed people! Although *Devil Bat's Daughter* is well-acted, especially by pretty LaPlanche, it isn't of much interest.

Five years later a movie came out that had such similarities to *The Devil Bat*, as well as a screenplay by John T. Neville, that it is generally considered a semi-remake. In PRC's *The Flying Serpent* (1946) George Zucco is an ornithologist, Prof. Andrew Forbes, who has discovered a strange and large animal — half-bird, half-reptile — in a cavern near Aztec ruins in San Juan, New Mexico. The flying beast is the "feathered serpent" and Aztec god Quetzalcoatl, and it is guarding the treasure of the Aztecs, which is also inside the cavern. Forbes wants the riches for himself, so he uses the bird to kill off anyone who might learn of the treasure's existence. Plucking feathers from the weird creature's body, he plants them on his victims, who are then attacked by the beast who wants to retrieve its feathers. The bird also makes a snack of each victim, tearing out their throats and — this was an addition to *Devil Bat*— draining their bodies of blood. Forbes' stepdaughter Mary (Hope Kramer) and mystery writer and radio reporter Richard Thorpe (Ralph Lewis) uncover the truth and Forbes himself is killed by the demon bird.

The Flying Serpent is a bit more watchable than *The Devil Bat*— it's fast-paced and fun if decidedly minor — with a monster that's slightly more complex, interesting ingredients to its plot, and the crisp and commanding performance of George Zucco, who is almost as good as Lugosi. Almost as in love with the serpent as Lugosi was with his bat, Zucco intones with admiration, "They would think you were some monstrous leftover from a prehistoric age." The creature is a fairly convincing prop with wings, a long slithery tail, and a potent screech. It also hisses and roars, has fangs — and is almost as big as a man. As serpents go, it's just a pup, but for a bird it's rather large. The attack scenes are more effective than in *Devil Bat*. In two scenes the prop bird is sent soaring down a wire toward the camera and its victim, and it's pulled up and out of the hole in the roof of its cage with amazing swiftness.

Another ornithologist is murdered by the bird just before he is to be interviewed on Thorpe's radio program (unlike the Devil Bat, the Serpent does not limit its attacks to the evening). In a brief bit that vaguely reminds one of *C.S.I.,* Thorpe wonders why there's no blood around the victim. "Is it possible the blood was drained off into the ground?" The sheriff tells him: "No, we did an analysis of the soil." Thorpe has a bumbling colleague whose comedy relief routine is a bore. Using the name "Sherman Scott," director Sam Newfield keeps things moving but does very little else for the picture.

In 1953, RKO came out with a nominal monster movie, *Port Sinister*, that has a very interesting premise. Tony Ferris (James Warren) is convinced that a certain island, which appears on the ocean surface only every two hundred years or so, is once again due to rise up from the sea bottom. This island contains the ruins of a sunken city known as Port Royal. Ferris has understandable trouble convincing the scientific community of his beliefs, but Dr. Joan Elliot (Lynn Roberts) agrees to go see for herself. Ferris is waylaid by the evil John Kolvac (Paul Cavanagh), who steals a map which he hopes will lead him to the lost city's treasure. Cavanagh manages to get a job as bosun on the steamer heading for the island, and replaces the captain with one of his own men. After recovering from Kolvac's attack, Ferris makes his way to the island by plane. Ferris and the pilot rescue Dr. Elliot from the cutthroat sailors, who are killed when the island sinks back down to the bottom of the ocean.

For our purposes, the main point of interest is the island's sole indigenous life form: giant crabs. These hostile, man-eating horrors are man-size, spider-like props with clacking legs that have unconvincing puppet-like movements as they chase—without great haste—anyone luckless enough to cross their path. They kill one sailor, and menace Dr. Elliot after she's tied up by the villains. We actually only see one crab at a time, but it is assumed that there are a whole host of them on the island. While the crabs don't have the almost cartoonish appearance of the giant crustaceans in *Attack of the Crab Monsters* (1957), which was made four years later, they are not nearly as lively. The characters are grossed out by the big crabs, but register no real sense of wonder over them or anything else on the island, including the mostly unseen ruins of the sunken city. There is much more emphasis on the skullduggery of Cavanagh and his gang of thugs, and their attempts to capture anyone who can alert the authorities to their theft of the treasure.

Port Sinister has atmosphere to spare and a certain degree of suspense (somehow Ferris knows that the island will only stay on the surface for a few hours at best). But despite some exciting elements, fast pace, and short running time, barely over an hour, it becomes tedious rather quickly. This is despite the fact that there are plenty of dangers on the island besides the giant crabs: the walls and ground are constantly crumbling, there are explosions, lava flows and rock slides, and countless fire pits which emit heat, smoke, and six-foot-high flames. One sequence has Ferris, the pilot and Dr. Elliot being chased by the villains through an area which has a thin lava crust over a bed of quicksand and fog that comes up to everyone's knees. Strangely, instead of treading gingerly over the thin crust, all of the actors walk as if they're going from rock to rock in a stream, even though they can't possibly see anything on the ground.

The sight of the island rising from the sea is exciting, partly because of Albert Glasser's effective scoring. Director Harold Daniels keeps things moving but isn't able to sustain interest even with all that's going on the island. With the exception of busy and proficient character actors Paul Cavanagh and William Schallert, who plays one of Kolvac's henchmen, the actors are only competent at best.

Monster from the Ocean Floor (1954) is best-remembered as the first picture produced by the prolific Roger Corman. The movie was directed by Wyott Ordung, who also portrays Pablo. The story takes place in a small village on the Pacific coastline. Although the exact location is never specified, the Spanish names of the villagers would indicate Mexico.

While vacationing, a commercial illustrator named Julie Blair (Anne Kimball) literally runs into a one-man submarine driven by marine biologist Steve Dunning (Stuart Wade). Strange things have been happening in the village: A man's empty diving suit is found in the water but the man himself has disappeared; a dog has also disappeared, snatched right out of his chain and collar. Discovering that there have been disappearances and rumors of a sea beast off the shore since the end of World War II, Julie decides to investigate, but the patronizing Dunning is skeptical. "Lovely girls just don't run around worrying about non-existing sea monsters," he tells her. After surviving two attempts by a superstitious villager, Pablo, to sacrifice her to the monster, Julie finally encounters the creature — a giant amoeba — and is rescued by Dunning and his trusty mini-sub.

The cheap filming almost works to the advantage of the movie, which is atmospheric, with an almost *cinéma vérité* approach. Unfortunately Ordung hasn't any style or special expertise as a director, and the movie has many long takes which considerably slow down the pace. The story, although it takes place far away from New England, has a Lovecraftian feel to it with its talk of strange beasts, missing people, and human sacrifices. Bill Danch's screenplay is workable if imperfect, with some clumsy attempts at character development and cliché-ridden dialogue. Composer Andre Brumer provides some elegiac piano music for the underwater scenes, a type of drum roll for the appearances by the monster, and some effective suspense music for the climax.

The acting is pretty terrible. Anne Kimball is perky to a fault as Julie, and never quite seems like a real person. Stuart Wade as Steve is equally poor, giving all of his lines that earnest, "cute" delivery, similar to Kimball's, that marks the untalented amateur. Even worse is Dick Pinner, a serious non-actor, as his colleague, Dr. Baldwin, who claims to have found a non-fossilized pteranodon egg on a previous adventure. When conversing together on specious scientific matters — they think the world's future food supply will come from growing crops on the bottom of the sea — Wade and Pinner speak their dialogue with comically slow solemnity, as if they think it's supposed to be profound. Steve sings a song for Julie at one point; he was a much better singer than actor. Wyott Ordung is a much better actor than his leads, playing the villager who is persuaded by a witch-like resident to sacrifice Julie to the monster. After first leaving her in a cove into which he's dripped his own blood in hopes of attracting a shark, and then letting the air out of her scuba tank, Pablo subsequently tells a strangely and stupidly forgiving Julie: "Forgive me, senorita, I would not harm you!" (This after two murder attempts!) Jonathan Haze, who would become a regular in Corman films and star in the original *Little Shop of Horrors,* hasn't a chance to make much of an impression in the tiny role of another villager, Joe. Some sources list Roger Corman himself as one of the (uncredited) actors, but his presence in the film is not readily apparent.

Much of the picture takes place underwater. When we first see the mini-sub employed by Steve, it looks like something that belongs in the deep end of a Beverly Hills swimming pool, but in underwater shots it is capable of diving deeper than you might expect. Kimball (or a stand-in) seems to be interacting with a real shark in one underwater sequence and almost swims into what she describes as "a giant octopus" in another. (The octopus is of normal size.) The monster itself—a phony-looking mock-up with a searchlight for its one "big red eye"— resembles an octopus and is about as big, with a rounded head and several tentacles. Every shot of the giant amoeba, (presumably created by atomic radiation) is out of focus, an attempt to disguise its cheesy appearance. The one-man sub rams the beast, which dissolved its human and animal victims and consumed them, and kills it. All of the effects are "live" or mechanical; there are no process shots in the movie.

Monster from the Ocean Floor could easily be dismissed as grade–D cinema were it not for the atmospheric approach and air of mystery. One shot of the monster rising from the sea to terrify Julie and snatch a cow from the shore (it's a real mystery why it also didn't drag the unconscious Julie into its figurative belly) is eerie despite the cheap effects, with the monster wisely kept hidden in the darkness.

Killers from Space (1954) is generally classified as a lower-case sci-fi film of the '50s, but at its heart it's a giant monster movie; the low budget probably kept the film from fulfilling its potential as such. The plot has to do with a bunch of extraterrestrials who plan to wipe out all of humanity by unleashing hordes of horribly enlarged bugs and reptiles on the planet's three billion-plus population. Nuclear fission expert Dr. Doug Martin (Peter Graves) is presumably killed when his plane nosedives after hitting some kind of fireball, but his body is not recovered at the scene. Martin is dead, but he's brought back to life by the invaders from Astron Delta who want him to spy for them and supply them with information. When he refuses, he's hypnotized into doing their bidding, but after an accident he remembers what happened in the cavern where he was kept captive. As these invaders with their advanced science not only use the power of Martin's atomic testing (to aid in their enlargement of earth fauna), but also siphon off power from the nearest city's power plant, Martin somehow manages to blow their underground complex to smithereens by shutting down said plant after holding a gun on the manager. Earth people are now safe from being devoured.

Killers from Space is not an especially exciting film, but it is competently directed by W. Lee Wilder (brother of the much more famous and talented Billy Wilder), and the cast is professional. The screenplay by Bill Raynor proceeds with the illogic of a child's nightmare or old-time movie serial, and is entertaining on that level. The shrill, melodramatic, mostly string background music by Manuel Compinsky also helps to create a weird, old-fashioned effect. With their big "bug eyes" and jump suits, the aliens are rather comical, but our introduction to them from the point of view of a startled, captive Martin is kind of creepy, probably because they are hovering in eerie fashion over the helpless man whose life they have just saved on their operating table.

For our purposes, the most interesting scenes have to do with the caverns full of what the alien leader Deneb-Tala (John Merrick) refers to as the "menagerie." These, of course, are the genetically manipulated insects and beasts that will make up the invaders' "army." (This is a gruesome concept later borrowed by the makers of the "Mars Attacks" bubble gum cards.) Martin tries to escape from the aliens but winds up in the caverns where they keep these creatures, running from tunnel to tunnel and discovering no escape but only fresh horrors. First he sees giant tarantulas, then a huge salamander that almost seems to snap at him. There are giant cockroaches, more snapping lizards, and two isolated shots of tremendous locusts munching on something or other with great sound effects to match.

Finally, there's a funny-looking, curious lizard that cocks its head at Martin like a dog as it seems to size him up and decide whether or not he'll be a worthwhile morsel. All this is done with effective back projection of blown-up bugs and lizards beyond the actor. Despite the cheap effects, the whole lengthy sequence is rather unnerving. Those critters never get out of the cavern to do any damage; they are all destroyed in the final conflagration along with the aliens. Boo. Hiss. The basic idea of using giant carnivorous critters to wipe out an entire planet's population is utterly horrific and grotesque.

Peter Graves is the only "name" actor in the film. James Seay as Colonel Banks is a familiar face, as are Shep Menkin (who played a French waiter on *I Love Lucy*) as the base surgeon Major Clift and Frank Gerstle as Dr. Krugar. Barbara Bestar, more or less an unknown, is fine as Martin's wife.

One of the most frightening of the humongous movie monsters was the stupendous octopus of *It Came from Beneath the Sea* (1955), which FX wizard Ray Harryhausen worked on with producer Charles Schneer as his follow-up to the very successful dinosaur-on-the-loose movie *The Beast from 20,000 Fathoms* (1953). This was the first of many Schneer-Harryhausen collaborations. Schneer approached Harryhausen through an intermediary, and the FX man was initially leery of the assignment and the problems that animating an eight-tentacled monster via his technique of stop motion would present. Eventually he saw it as a challenge and agreed to do the film. Budget and time considerations necessitated that two of the eight tentacles be dropped from the octopus model, but since most of the gargantuan creature is underwater in its big scenes, audiences would never notice. The city of San Francisco refused to allow the camera crew official access to the Golden Gate Bridge because it gets destroyed in the movie, so Harryhausen and the photographer had to resort to a little subterfuge to get the footage.

When an atomic submarine helmed by Commander Pete Matthews (Kenneth Tobey) is sideswiped by an enormous unknown life form, brilliant marine biologists John Carter (Donald Curtis) and Leslie Joyce (Faith Domergue) are called in by the Navy to examine some flesh torn off from the beast. Matthews is amazed that the big hunk of meat, which we never see, comes from an even bigger animal. The scene when Curtis and Domergue pretend to be looking at this meat inside a dark tank is unintentionally comical, as they're unable to give us the sense that they're actually looking at *anything*. Eventually they determine that it came from a gigantic octopus that was disturbed from the Mindanao Deep by H bombs. Now that the creature is radioactive, its normal prey of fish, equipped with natural Geiger counters, can easily elude it, so it has to take off after higher life forms, including man. The beast attacks a Navy ship, causes more off-screen havoc, smashes a sheriff on a beach (after snatching away an entire family in another off-screen sequence), then finally emerges from San Francisco Bay to destroy the Golden Gate Bridge and send its massive tentacles sweeping through the city to crush and snatch away fleeing pedestrians for food. The octopus also manages to *roar*.

The essential idea of the film is terrifying. This is a monster of such grotesque and impossible size — a veritable Godzilla of octopi — that it can literally kill you without leaving the water. Its tentacles are so long and large than they can reach out of the sea and snake into a city street. No one in the movie ever expresses much of the numb terror and disbe-

The gargantuan octopus of *It Came from Beneath the Sea* (1955) unleashes its huge, people-seeking tentacles on San Francisco.

lief they might feel over the existence of such a monster even after they're finally convinced that it's for real. The octopus is simply another adversary that the U.S. Navy and its draftees — the two scientists — must outwit and defeat. Still, the film manages to exploit this terror in its final scenes, with well-done process shots of the creature's tentacles thrusting up out of the bay. One long shot shows the massive animal leaning against the docks — it's trying to pull itself out of the water although it hardly needs to — as its tentacles hover over a roadway with cars as small as dots passing by below. One shot of a tentacle slapping down and crushing fleeing people, then withdrawing with the people presumably stuck to the huge suckers on the tentacle's underside — a horrible way to die — is chilling (one can only hope they were killed immediately), as is the scene when soldiers use flame throwers to force the tentacles — which might sickeningly crash down on them at any second if their timing is off — back into the water. After fifty years these scenes are still impressive because of the smooth animation, the well-composited shots (one has people running both in front of and behind the tentacle) and the stark contrast in size between the humans and the massive tentacles. (A scene in the remake of *The Blob* has the stop-motion creature growing tentacles at the climax, but it lacks that certain finesse that marks the best of Harryhausen's work.)

Other scenes in the picture are hampered by the low budget. The attack on the ship is fairly exciting, if imperfect, and features a great shot of the wriggling monstrosity kind of wrestling with the ship before it drags it down to the bottom. The Golden Gate Bridge sequence also has some effective shots but it doesn't cover the action from enough angles. A big-budget modern-day movie would show the bridge collapsing behind Curtis just as he's rescued by Tobey. The death of the sheriff on the beach is rather abrupt — a shot of a tentacle flailing about somewhere, followed by a shot of the sheriff backing up and screaming, presumably squashed — although it certainly made audiences of the time jump in their seats. The sequence when Curtis in his wetsuit swims past the octopus — whose eye slowly opens to stare at the tiny man — is marred by poor process work; Curtis is, unfortunately, transparent.

One strange sequence takes place in a hospital where the few survivors of the ship disaster have been taken for examination and questioning. A relatively lucid sailor tries to explain what attacked the ship but can only point to the curved handles of the doctor's stethoscope and say "it was like those," as if he just doesn't know the right word for it. But later on he immediately tells Faith Domergue that the attack was made by "a giant octopus." If he didn't know the word "tentacle," why didn't he just tell the *first* doctor it was an octopus? It also doesn't make sense that the Navy would immediately believe the man's story when they doubted everyone else, including the two biologists who insisted the creature was real.

The movie has a terrific credit sequence which shows the title words rising from a stormy, splashing sea with ominous background music (the score for the film was used for other subsequent Columbia monster and sci-fi movies, including *Earth vs. the Flying Saucers* and *The Giant Claw*). The nominal director, Robert Gordon, was unable to do much to make the talky non-monster sequences come to life, although the three lead actors are all quite competent. Kenneth Tobey (*The Thing from Another World*) was a pleasant, moderately handsome "B" movie actor who could be relied upon to perform adequately in the heroic mold, while Curtis was a likable and acceptable second lead. Faith Domergue, originally a Howard Hughes discovery, gave a creditable performance as an emotionally unstable woman in *Where Danger Lives* (1950) with Robert Mitchum, but soon wound up in increasingly poor — and infrequent — horror and sci-fi films. Domergue was not a bad actress, and used her lips in a way that made her resemble Marilyn Monroe. She also radiated a certain intelligence that doesn't make her seem too ludicrous as a genius-level professor despite her considerable sex appeal.

In addition to some terrific action sequences, the screenplay by George Worthing Yates and Hal Smith tries to create more interesting characters than usual. Domergue's character, Professor Leslie Joyce, was somewhat ahead of her time. While it was common for lady scientists to figure prominently in '50s creature features, Domergue is more warmly human than the lady scientist (Joan Weldon) in *Them!* and is also a decided feminist in a time before the term became common. Her colleague, Dr. Carter, is very pro-female, although he shows absolutely no romantic interest in Leslie and a hackneyed triangle situation therefore never develops. At one point, Commander Pete wants Leslie to run to safety and leave the hard work to the men. Carter tells him that "there's a whole new breed [of women] that feel they're as smart and courageous as men — and they are. They don't like to be over-protected or have their initiative taken away." To which Leslie adds, "I not only don't like being pushed around but you underestimate my ability to help in a crisis." It's interesting, however, that Leslie clearly prefers the more old-fashioned and macho commander — although she's not above telling him off between kisses — to the more with-it and sensitive scientist, even though Carter proves he's just as brave as the military man. Perhaps she senses Carter's indifference to her charms.

The movie has an amusing postscript when the three sit at a table in a bar having a drink after the monster has been defeated. A TV announcer says that there "are three others whose service to San Francisco should not be forgotten." Carter, Joyce and Mathews all smile in readiness for the tribute, but the "three others" turn out to be "civilian defense workers, crossing guards, and street railway employees."

Although the main focus of the movie is a giant man, there are outsized monsters a-plenty in Bert I. Gordon's *The Cyclops* (1957), a nifty little movie that is beloved by some folks and excoriated by others. Gordon — known by his fans as "Mr. B.I.G." — first blew up ordinary animals to giant-size in *King Dinosaur*. He followed this up with the giant grasshopper movie *Beginning of the End* and the credible thriller *The Amazing Colossal Man*. In both the sequel *War of the Colossal Beast* and the unrelated (plot-wise) *Cyclops* Gordon employed actor Duncan Parkin aka Dean Parkin to play horribly disfigured giants. Unlike his other two giant people movies, *The Cyclops* also features some other humongous creatures, including lizards. In *The Cyclops*, however, the big lizards are supposed to be big lizards, not stand-ins for dinosaurs as they are in *King Dinosaur* and countless other movies.

Susan Winters (Gloria Talbott) is convinced that her fiancé Bruce, whose plane crashed in an isolated area in Mexico three years before, is still alive, and flies into the interior with her friend, bacteriologist Russ (James Craig), a down-on-his-luck pilot (Tom Drake), and a financial backer, Marty (Lon Chaney Jr.) who is hoping to stake a claim to some uranium. (He has brought along a "precision scintillator" to detect radium deposits.) Once there they discover that the radioactive quality of the soil, targeting the glands, has enlarged all of the animals — rodents, birds, lizards and so on — to many times their normal size and that there is, as Russ puts it, "no limit to the potential growth of the animal." What's worse, they do find Bruce alive, but he's grown to a height of at least twenty-five feet, can't talk, and has the petulant personality of a deranged child. A huge flap of skin covers his right eye, making him a literal "Cyclops," and his right jaw is similarly mutilated. Russ destroys his good eye with a fiery spear, and the little group — minus Marty, who was killed by the giant — barely evade his out-slung arms as they take to the air and fly back to civilization.

A grotesque and pathetic variation on Beauty and the Beast, Gordon's best movie — a dark fantasy and perverse love story as well as a monster movie — has an underlying romance to it in every sense of the word. The pathos is provided not only by Susan's firm love for Bruce and equally firm conviction that he's alive, but the horrible, undeserved fate that envelops them. *The Cyclops* is hardly profound, but it does present a genuinely tragic situation. Here is a woman who goes almost literally through a kind of Hell for the sake of the man she loves and has never forgotten, and she discovers that it would have been better for both of them if he were dead. While it may seem ridiculous for her not to realize right away that Bruce and the giant are one and the same, this is a woman in serious denial. We learn little about Bruce except that Susan loves him deeply, and since she seems like a very warm, caring person, we have to assume that her love is warranted. Bruce's fate, therefore, seems especially cruel.

The Cyclops boasts an essentially good story bolstered by a snappy script full of seriously screwed-up characters. Susan seems almost morbidly obsessive in her determination (although it turns out that she's right). The pilot, Lee, whose family oil wells have run dry, keeps up a happy-go-lucky front to cover his desperation. Marty is so fixated on finding uranium that he hasn't a shred of sensitivity. Russ is the most grounded of the bunch but, as he puts it, "I'm sick and tired of competing with a dead man."

Most of the actors were in similarly desperate circumstances as far as their careers were going — low-budget monster movies were considered below television level when it came to prestige. Gloria Talbott had some nice small roles in mainstream movies before finding a niche of sorts in such sci-fi–horror films as *I Married a Monster from Outer Space* and *Daughter of Dr. Jekyll*. Talbott was a competent actress who, despite some perfunctory moments, plays with sensitivity in *The Cyclops* and makes the most of her role. Tom Drake had appeared in many A-movies in his younger days and also makes the most of his role of the pilot. He gives all of his line readings an unusual delivery that makes you wonder if Lee is putting the other characters on or if Drake is putting on the other actors. When Susan and Russ are preparing to trek through the canyon (L.A.'s Bronson Canyon), he tells them, "I wouldn't think of letting you two go alone," and you're not certain if he means it or is secretly contemptuous of them. Lon Chaney Jr.'s performance is almost too good for the movie. Whether grousing about staying in the valley "looking for a skeleton" or cringing in the back of a cave in which the Cyclops has imprisoned them, he's thoroughly convincing as the cowardly and expedient Marty Melville. James Craig had been groomed as another Clark Gable and appeared in a few high-profile movies of the '40s as a romantic lead, but despite his handsome features, he never quite caught on with the public. His modest abilities are all too apparent in *The Cyclops*.

Vincent Padua, who plays the governor who refuses Susan permission to fly into the area where Bruce's plane crashed, appeared in a couple of *I Love Lucy* episodes; he was particularly amusing in the episode when Lucy is locked up for passing counterfeit money in Paris. Duncan "Dean" Parkin was a neighbor of Jack Young, who did the makeup for the Cyclops and the Colossal Beast. Although he was not a professional actor — the two "giant man" movies are the only ones he ever appeared in (he also worked on special effects for Gordon's *Beginning of the End*) — he is not bad at all as the child-like, hideous monster, although he had some help from Paul Frees' voice characterization. Parkin told *Filmfax* interviewers Paul Parla and Charles Mitchell that he didn't know he would have to do his own stunts, and was alarmed to learn he'd have to wrestle with a large, aggressive anaconda. Parkin had to wrap the snake around him to make it look as if they were fighting; it was "a harrowing experience ... because the beast did not want to be there, so she became madder with time. I nearly suffocated...." The snake scene is borderline ludicrous.

Gordon not only directed and produced the film, but also wrote the screenplay, which has moments both illogical and amusing. When our heroes' plane encounters the "dangerous down-drafts" the Mexican officials warned them about, Lee tells the others, "Relax — when your number is called, it's called." To which Marty replies: "Yeah, but if your number is called, what about me?" When Marty insists that Lee land the plane and the pilot refuses, Marty actually punches him and knocks him out! The plane goes into a dive as Marty and Russ wrestle with one another; the editing makes it seem as if Susan takes forever to try to revive the unconscious Lee by shaking him awake.

Although one would imagine that Bruce could not make it back to civilization because he crashed in an impassable jungle, the territory we see looks more like the woodland in somebody's suburban backyard. When Susan and Russ start off on their search for Bruce, leaving Marty and Lee to watch the plane, they stop for a rest when they've barely been gone a few minutes. Able to hear the sound of the plane starting, they rush back so quickly that it's clear they were only around the bend.

The effects work in the movie is generally crude, although it could be argued that this adds to its charm. As Russ looks at the first monster, a big lizard crawling over a rock, we see the same shot of the actor turning slightly sideways over and over again, as if Gordon forgot to shoot enough footage of Craig. The scene in which Russ and Susan espy a giant rodent and a huge hawk that swoops down upon it and chews on it is okay. The best scene occurs when Susan, Russ and Lee search for the origin of some roars in the distance. The first creature they come upon is a tarantula that emits a high-pitched squeal. As they absorb this terror, up behind them creeps a big wattled-neck lizard. Susan does what most people would do: She reacts with realistic hysteria, running away with the lizard — and Russ — in hot pursuit. Then another lizard comes in, searching for an easy meal, and the first lizard literally jumps on top of the interloper. (The second lizard was undoubtedly simply thrown on top of its buddy.) Then ensues a fight to the death between the creatures as the others do their best to get out of the way. The fact that you can see through most of the critters doesn't do anything to strip the amusing sequence of its entertainment value.

The Cyclops' makeup isn't terrible — it couldn't have been especially comfortable for Parkin to wear for long periods — even though the snaggled teeth on the right side seem to be part of a mask. An effective touch has us seeing Susan and the others from the point of view of the Cyclops, with a distorted lens standing in for the gargantuan eye as it looks downward. This works especially well as Susan straddles part of Bruce's plane, then looks up to see the Cyclops staring at her and presumably reaching downward to snatch her up in his outsized mitt. There are a couple of forced perspective shots when the party is trapped by the Cyclops in the cave. When the giant reaches in and grabs Susan, Gordon simply makes the whole frame rise up (against a black background) to make it look as if she's being lifted.

There are some decent process shots in the movie. There is a striking shot of the Cyclops stalking the group in the background as they hurriedly sneak through their camp in the foreground. The scene when the little band has to sneak past the Cyclops as he sleeps in a glen is effective, even if it may appear that the giant isn't actually lying firmly on the ground. When the Cyclops raises his arm in his sleep, the others back up from him in a well-timed shot. This is one of two sequences wherein the live characters appear behind the monsters instead of in front of them (as occurs with the use of back projection). The other is when Russ cuts off a slice of skin of the lizard who lost the aforementioned battle to the death. In these cases the creatures are matted into or superimposed over the live action footage.

Although the Cyclops collapses at the very end of the film, it is by no means certain that he is dead (that seems to be the implication, however). Gordon has Russ, who obviously loves Susan, embrace her as they fly away, but it isn't likely that she's going to forget Bruce — alive or dead — all that easily. Russ' blinding of Bruce seems almost sadistic, as if Russ hated his rival and wanted him out of his way once and for all. Blinded, Bruce's fate in a valley of monsters will even more terrible than before.

Albert Glasser, who did many films with Gordon, contributed an effective score for *The Cyclops*, including some violin strains for added pathos when the Cyclops contemplates a sleeping Susan and vice versa. Despite its many preposterous aspects, *The Cyclops* — taken on its own terms — is not a bad movie at all.

Another 1957 release, *The Monster That Challenged the World*, featured gigantic mollusks supposedly of prehistoric origin. The story takes place in and around the Salton Sea in Southern California, "four hundred square miles of salt water in the middle of the desert," specifically at a naval research base where scientists are conducting "top secret atomic experiments." For once these experiments do not create the monsters, which already existed (if only as eggs), but they do create radioactivity in the water. This irradiated water pours into a fissure in the sea floor after an earthquake and helps resuscitate the ancient eggs of a prehistoric mollusk. The monsters make their presence known when people in the area begin to disappear and some of their bodies turn up shriveled and devoid of blood and fluid. Commander "Ironheart" Twillinger (Tim Holt) is the petulant if essentially kind-hearted officer who investigates these deaths; Dr. Rogers (Hans Conried) is the scientist who uncovers the creatures who are responsible and tells Twillinger how to destroy them. The love interest and lady-in-peril is the pretty widow Gail (Audrey Dalton), who has an adorable little girl who loves to go in and sneak a peek at the test rabbits in the lab where mommy works. The picture has a highly effective opening, as over a darkly glistening sea, the words of the title come rushing at us from a distance, first seen as a ball of white light and then forming individual letters.

There is some question as to exactly what the monsters are supposed to be. The term "mollusks," which is what they're called, covers everything from oysters to octopi. Full-scale mechanical models (although only the front end seems to have been built), the creatures actually resemble twenty-foot long caterpillars with big round eyes that dominate the face and moving mouth parts (including two hooks). They are very well designed and quite realistic, but they seem incapable of too much movement aside from wiggling and turning of the head and neck, which in some scenes is more than enough. When one of the creatures emerges from the water to threaten Twillinger, Rogers and others in a boat, its "performance" isn't at all bad, and it's even better at the climax when a larger-scale and longer model emerges from a tank in the lab to terrorize Gail and her daughter.

As for exactly what kind of mollusk it is, Dr. Rogers is no help. He says that it belongs to the same species as the prehistoric Kraken, "a direct ancestor of our modern water mollusk." He shows a 16mm documentary and remarks upon the resemblance of the creatures on screen — common snails — to the monsters in the Salton Sea. However, the monsters don't look anything like snails and even less like squids, which are supposed to be the actual model for the mythical Kraken. There's a gruesome underwater shot of a skin diver caught by the head in the hooks of a creature, screaming and trying unsuccessfully to wriggle out of his predicament, and the corpses are certainly grotesque — remember the creatures suck out all body fluids. (What's really gross are the close-up shots of real snails using razor-like teeth to shred flesh in the film shown by Dr. Rogers.) The monsters rest inside large shells from which they emerge when they're hungry, and their saliva, or mucus, is radioactive.

One scene that makes the audience jump is when an elderly watchman goes out to investigate a noise near the canal. He thinks it may be some swimming youngsters he chased off some time before, but they don't seem to be around any more. He walks around checking this and that, not too concerned — when suddenly one of the creatures, somehow "standing" upright, comes up behind him and envelops him as he screams. The scene is startling even though it's hard to imagine that the old man wouldn't have seen, heard or smelled the creature when it was so close to him all the time.

Pat Fielder's script attempts to add some interesting characters and humanistic touches to the basic monster formula. One touching scene occurs after a woman's daughter and boyfriend go missing, and a little boy shows Twillinger where he found the man's cap on the beach. Finding her daughter's clothing, the woman realizes the girl is dead and breaks down as the little boy, in the background, reaches out to comfort her. After her friend's husband is killed by one of the monsters, Gail is given a good speech when she tells Twillinger about her own reaction to being widowed, but it's nearly ruined by Audrey Dalton's somewhat perfunctory delivery. (Before this speech, Twillinger stupidly asks her "What's the matter?" as if he cannot comprehend why she'd be upset after her best friend's husband is horribly slaughtered.) No-nonsense Twillinger is an interesting, not always likable character, but several scenes show us the warm inner core of the man: when he buys a pen he doesn't really need from an excited boy in a restaurant; tells Gail that he hasn't had supper when she belatedly responds to his earlier dinner invitation (when she calls he's having a sandwich at his desk); and when he gets down on the floor (and looks rather ridiculous doing so) to look for Gail's daughter's missing ladybug. After some good supporting roles in such films as *Back Street* with Charles Boyer and Margaret Sullavan, Tim Holt was excellent as the lead in Orson Welles' production *The Magnificent Ambersons* (1942), but good parts in major films eluded him. He had a good career as a western star, and even had his own comic book at one point. Chunkier and fuller in the face by the time of *Monster*, Holt gives a performance that is adequate but unmemorable, except that he is certainly convincingly frightened and desperate in the climactic scene when he comes to the rescue of Dalton and her daughter. Dalton was a sweet and pretty actress who was not always up to the demands of more serious scenes in the movies in which she appeared.

Other interesting characters include the telephone operator in Twillinger's office who is always on the phone to her mother, and the bizarre Lewis Clark Dobbs, played by Milton Parsons, who looks like everyone's stereotypical conception of an undertaker. Dobbs is

A publicity still for *The Monster That Challenged the World* (1957).

the record keeper who uncovers a map of underground channels and therefore helps Twillinger and Rogers locate the new breeding ground of the mollusks.

Arnold Laven's direction is more than adequate if not especially dynamic. Heinz Roemheld's music covers the action if little else. Whatever its flaws, *The Monster That Challenged the World* is a perfectly creditable little monster flick with some interesting creatures.

There were some extremely interesting creatures in Roger Corman's *Attack of the Crab Monsters*, which was released by Allied Artists in 1957. By this time many bugs and animals had been transformed into giant monsters for the delight of fans, but Corman and his screenwriter Charles Griffith (who was also the associate producer and had a small role in the film) came up with something decidedly different from the usual mammoth-beast-goes-on-rampage-and-attacks-city scenario. *Attack of the Crab Monsters* takes place on an island in the Pacific where there has been atomic testing. An atomic research team headed by Dr. McClain has vanished from the island, and a second team of various kinds of scientists has been sent to continue the work of the first group and possibly find out what happened to McClain and his party. Mysterious deaths, quakes, and explosions clue the group in to the fact that they are in the midst of some truly extraordinary events.

Radiation has created a pair of land crabs the size of automobiles (if there are more than two, they are never seen or mentioned). One of the crabs has devoured all of the members of the first research team, and absorbed their memories and intelligence from their brain tissue. Now its mate, a female, is busy eating the second expedition (why the mate never snacked on some of the first party is never explained). The crabs are tough to kill not only because of their human intelligence, but due to their other unnatural abilities. They can emit "arcs of heat" to cause explosions and send out telepathic voices by projecting their thoughts through metal objects. Via this method they lure unsuspecting victims to their deaths, using the voices of those they trust. There is "no cohesion between the atoms" of their matter which gives them an almost liquid-like consistency, although they are solid enough to grab and dismember their victims. Hoping to devour everyone in the expedition, the crabs reduce the island's size by blowing up strategic portions of it and reducing the area in which their victims can elude them. When only three people are left alone with one crab (the other having been killed) on what is now just a small dot in the sea, a man sacrifices his own life to destroy the female crab and save his two colleagues, the lovers of the group.

To say that the story is outlandish is a major understatement, but it is also clever, imaginative, horrifying, and gripping. The pace never flags, and Corman's direction is not only competent but often very effective. After the French botanist Jules Devereaux (Mel Welles) calls out to the "ghosts" of the McClain party, Corman first cuts to a shot of sea gulls taking flight, and then to a shot of a somewhat freaked Jules from overhead. Corman knows how to create and exploit tension. Charles Gross' editing and Floyd Crosby's photography are similarly adroit, cleverly creating the illusion of a shrinking island with well-chosen angles and shots. One editorial slip occurs during the death of the talky physicist Dr. Karl Weigand (Leslie Bradley), however. First we see the man lying on the ground in front of the crab, with the crab's claw about his neck. The reactions of the other cast members in the very next shot seem to indicate that Weigand has just been beheaded. They run out of the cavern, but then there follows another shot showing the physicist still alive, struggling in the claw. This makes it seem as if his colleagues have simply abandoned him without even making an attempt to save him.

Corman successfully builds up a lot of creepiness and atmosphere during the early sections of the film. There's an interesting bit when two of the scientists leave the complex to

Poor Mel Welles has already lost a hand in *Attack of the Crab Monsters*—now brain-eating crabs are after his head!

investigate a strange crackling noise. They notice a wire scratching at the outside wall, and relax. But after they go back inside, the wire gets stuck in a groove on the wall and the noise continues. Unfortunately, the scariness eventually evaporates due to the matter-of-fact approach during the second half of the film, as well as the prosaic nature of the acting. The cast members are all quite professional and play with some conviction — and we must remember that they hadn't exactly signed up to do Shakespeare — and while some of them seem fairly rattled on occasion, they are generally much too calm considering the grotesque nature of the situation. The island is falling into the sea, the crabs are out to get them, their friends are being eaten one by one and then speaking to them with hatred after they have become crabs, due to, as one character puts it, "the preservation of the species," but the actors never seem more alarmed than if, say, a hurricane were on the way. A hurricane can be pretty devastating, true, but being torn apart and devoured by giant crabs, indeed *becoming* a giant crab? That's a different story.

    Attack of the Crab Monsters is perhaps more frightening in what it doesn't show and say than in what it does. If this improbable situation were to occur in reality, the people involved would not only suffer anxiety at becoming victims of the tearing claws of the crabs, but undoubtedly also wonder what it would be like to have their consciousness inside the body of one of these mutants, sharing it with several other minds, losing their very identity (in more ways than one) in the process. They would also wonder what human flesh would taste like and how it would feel to tear apart one of their colleagues. It would literally be a fate worse than death.

Understandably, there are moments in the movie that give one pause. When one of the crabs smashes through the wall of the complex to destroy the radio, one character remarks that every tube has been snapped neatly in half, a feat that would surely be much too delicate work for the crab's gargantuan pincers. When Jules is killed, the giant claw that grabs his neck doesn't come from behind him but from right in front of him — where exactly was the big thing hiding and why couldn't the scientist see it? (Possibly Jules thought it was a boulder.) When the sailor Tate (Charles Griffith) falls out of a motorboat in an early scene, we see him screaming as if something is biting his leg, but when he's pulled out of the water it's his head that's missing, not one of his lower extremities. His pals don't seem particularly upset over his death, and when one of the scientists pitches a stone at a normal-sized crab, another remarks on how crabs can "finish off a wounded Marine in five minutes." (Well, maybe if they're giant-sized.). Karl insists on following a trail of oil that he's found even though there's no earthly reason for them to bother finding its source. While it may seem ludicrous when Karl (now part of the crab after being eaten by it) talks about planning "our assault upon the world of man" — one crab against the entire Earth? — we must remember that the female is pregnant.

The giant crab (one prop was used for both) was put together by two cast members, Ed Nelson, who plays an ensign (and operates the crab) and Beech Dickerson, who plays another sailor. Decidedly low-tech by today's standards, the mechanical crab is quite a nifty creation nevertheless, an ugly brute that has certain "cute" aspects to it. These certainly include the thing's eyes, which are not on stalks (instead there are two somewhat limp antennae) but smack on its "face." They have a vinyl-like covering that can be pulled up to make it seem as if the sinister orbs are opening. The crab can move fairly quickly, although its motions are jerky. The claws have some limited movement, rising in the air menacingly when required. If the crab were placed in an amusement park, it would probably inspire some admiration today. It looks rather impressive as it comes up out of the sea at the climax and lurches toward the survivors with a certain cheap-jack nobility if not noble intentions.

Despite its many zany aspects, *Attack of the Crab Monsters* is not a parody, but is played straight for the most part, although there is something nearly sublime in the moment when the big crab comes out of the water and reacts to a grenade thrown by one of the scientists: "Foolish, very foolish," it says (telepathically) — in a French accent no less. The makers of creature features of the '50s knew that their movies had amusing aspects which didn't need to be underlined to any great degree. A modern-day remake of *Crab Monsters* would undoubtedly be a campy mess, although some of the actors might react with more realistic dread and terror. Or not.

Of the actors, Mel Welles comes to the edge of campiness at times, but is rather good as Jules. Pamela Duncan, who plays Martha Hunter, is an appealing actress with a vulnerable, quivering quality that works well for the part. She had some of the biggest lips in

Hollywood in those pre-collagen days. Russell Johnson is appropriately stalwart as the radio operator Hank Chapman; Johnson was best-known as the Professor on TV's *Gilligan's Island*. It is clear that Chapman is attracted to Martha — "you can even be lonely in a crowd," she tells him — but she's already planning a "lifetime partnership" with her colleague, Dale (Richard Garland). Chapman's sacrificing himself to save these two at the end adds a small note of pathos. Leslie Bradley is fine as Karl, although the mysterious know-it-all nature of the physicist is irritating, as is Beech Dickerson's small "comedy relief" role of a sailor. Ed Nelson became a regular on TV's *Peyton Place* a few years later. The other actors are all competent if not as well known. Composer Ronald Stein contributed a highly effective musical score. Stein's work, including his music for *Attack of the 50 Foot Woman* (1958), has a strangely tortured and dramatic quality to it although it is certainly not for all tastes.

One would have thought that a gigantic eagle or enormous condor or hawk might have been a good bet to star in a monster movie, but when creature filmmakers finally got around to a monstrous bird in Columbia Pictures *The Giant Claw* (1957), it was like no bird ever found on Earth — literally. Although the ads for the movie claimed that the tremendous bird, which looked quite sleek and powerful in the poster illustration, was from the prehistoric era, it is actually of extra-terrestrial origin. And it looks more like a marionette from the Kukla, Fran and Ollie puppet show than any bird that ever flew through the air or outer space.

Electronics engineer-radar expert Mitchell MacAfee (Jeff Morrow) and mathematician-systems analyst Sally Caldwell (Mara Corday) are engaged in tests on an Air Force base, when MacAfee sees a UFO "as big as a battleship" flying near him, even though nothing whatsoever shows up on the radar screen. Flying home, the couple encounter the UFO again when it hits their plane, killing the pilot and forcing them into a crash landing. It is eventually determined that the UFO is actually a gargantuan bird from an anti-matter galaxy "millions of miles away." Although the bird itself is not composed of anti-matter, it has an anti-matter shield which prevents bullets, rockets and everything else from destroying it. This shield also keeps the bird from showing up on radar. As the bird terrorizes the world, snatching up trains, cars and people and toppling buildings, MacAfee rushes to create a weapon that will destroy it. He comes up with a device that will fire something called "masic" atoms that will destroy the bird's shield and make it susceptible to ordinary firepower. The bird is destroyed and the world is saved once more.

The screenplay by Samuel Newman and Paul Gangelin is workable and has some interesting aspects. The basic idea of a world held captive by a monstrous airborne creature that can fly at extreme speeds, showing up unexpectedly anywhere it wants to — without even a warning by radar — is frightening. Not only is all but military air traffic suspended but the entire world is put on blackout, and even cars, trucks and trains, aside from those on official duty, are banned from the highways and rails. The enormous bird can show up anywhere at any time, swooping down from the heights on victims. There are a couple of scenes that exploit this terror, including one in which the bird snatches a car full of teens, foolishly ignoring the blackout, off a roadway, and another in which it swoops down on a terrified man as he runs down a lonely country byway.

This last scene ties into another interesting feature of the script. After their plane crash, Mitch and Sally hole up with a middle-aged French-Canadian named Pierre Broussard (Louis D. Merrill). Stepping outside his cabin, Pierre sees what he imagines is a legendary witch known as "Kakana," who has the "face of a wolf and the body of a woman" with wings. According to superstition, anyone who sees the witch is doomed to die in the very near future. The Kakana is actually the extraterrestrial terror bird coming to Earth, and it indeed kills Pierre days later as he runs away from its nest in panic.

With an effective monster, *The Giant Claw* might have amounted to more than a amusing time-passer, although it is quite entertaining in its way. If the bird did indeed have "the face of a wolf and the body of a woman" it would have been far more interesting than the silly puppet which the producers somehow found acceptable. There have been lots of funny-looking creatures in low-budget horror films, of course, but they always had some gruesome or ugly element to save them from complete stupidity, such as the crab in *Attack of the Crab Monsters*. The monster bird of *The Giant Claw*, however, has a face that inspires much more laughter than dread (although one still wouldn't want to meet up with a thing that big — it really is "as big as a battleship" — even in broad daylight).

The bird has a very long turkey neck, a ridiculous tuft of hair sticking up on the top of its head, a long thin snout that resembles a crow's (think Heckle and Jeckle), big, bulging eyes that can roll, and large nostrils that can flare and twitch when agitated, such as when its egg is being shot at and destroyed by Mitch and Sally. The bird not only cackles but makes all manner of noises. It actually doesn't look too bad in flight, when that silly face isn't in close-up, and its sinister looking claws are certainly well designed. Hoping to catch sight of the strange UFO that has caused several air disasters, Sally remembers a project she was on in which photos were taken from fixed cameras on balloons for a study of earth curvature calibration. The funniest scene in the movie occurs when these photos are projected in the office of General Considine (Morris Ankrum). We see a shot of the bird's idiotic face with the dumb tuft of hair, then a quick cut to Sally as she covers her mouth and gasps in horror. Undoubtedly the actress didn't actually see what was on the screen or she probably would have burst into laughter instead.

The monster is brought to life by either combining it with miniature props of planes and buildings, including the U.N., which it takes a chunk out of, or by back projecting it behind actors. These process shots are generally effective, such as when the big beak rushes down at the car full of teenagers. Another scene that sticks in the mind is the death of several members of the Civil Aeronautics Board investigating team after they parachute out of a plane that's been attacked, bitten actually, by the bird. The actors are hung from chutes in front of a back projection screen as the bird's head looms larger and larger "below" them, making it appear as if they are falling into the monster's yawning maw. This is followed by a quick cut of the puppet's mouth clamping shut on a toy parachute. This is cheap but effective — and even a bit unsettling. Jumping out of a crashing plane is scary enough, but landing in a monster's mouth on top of it ... ! The scene is an odd juxtaposition of the grotesque and the comical, combining the gruesome deaths with the bird's hare-brained appearance. The sequence when Sally and Mitch find the bird's nest and destroy its sole egg suffers from the fact that we never see exactly where they are in relation to the monster. It is also never explained why there is "no other reason" for the bird to be on Earth "except to make a nest," as Sally theorizes. As the bird goes on a planetary rampage, we see stock shots of fleeing people from previous Columbia films, including *It Came from Beneath the Sea*; it also borrows its musical score from that picture, as previously noted.

The movie is basically played straight, although there are times when the actors strain to make it believable, such as during the "it's just a big bird" scene in the general's office after planes, guns, and rockets have failed to destroy the monster and many pilots have died. A more serious, sleeker, dangerous looking monster would have helped enormously. The screenwriters couldn't resist a few funny lines, however (after spotting the big bird, one pilot says, "I'll never call my mother-in-law an old crow again"; a determined Mitch makes the comment "I don't care if that bird comes from outer space or Upper Saddle River, New Jersey!"). The playfully romantic, mildly antagonistic banter between Mitch and Sally is generally well played by Morrow and Corday, but in the scene in Pierre's cabin after the death of the young pilot, whose body is on the couch only a few feet away from the couple, it seems grossly out of place, with Sally even giggling about Mitch's description of a "flying battleship"; the couple never seem especially affected by the man's death. (It's worth repeating that most actors, unfortunately, seem unable to play more than one emotion at a time. If the script calls for light banter, they will simply deliver the banter without registering any of the underlying tension or depression their characters might be feeling at the time.) To be fair, the screenplay doesn't really give them a chance to react in any concrete way to the pilot's death, at least via the dialogue. Later on, Sally and Mitch engage in similar banter at a more appropriate time when they are on a late night commercial flight to New York. The only trouble with this is that the dialogue is too "cutesy" by far.

Jeff Morrow was a good actor who had starring roles in genre films and smaller roles in "A" movies. After their plane crashes, he seems quite realistically shaken as it explodes and bits of fiery metal rain down upon them, almost as if the pieces unexpectedly came a little too close for comfort, which may well have been the case. Mara Corday was a decorative, engaging beauty of narrow range who appeared in a number of monster movies, including *Tarantula* and *The Black Scorpion*. After a long Hollywood career, Morris Ankrum, a creditable actor, found himself in a great many monster–sci-fi features during this period. In the Andrew Johnson biopic *Tennessee Johnson* (1942) he drew the admiration of critics such as James Agee with his portrayal of a Confederate senator who addresses Congress, with Agee opining that he was the only actor who seemed authentically of the 1861 period. As the scientist who uncovers the true nature of the monster bird, a pained-looking Edgar Barrier is earnest if a little odd. He appeared with Claude Rains in the 1943 version of *Phantom of the Opera*. Robert Shayne, best-known as Inspector Henderson of TV's *Adventures of Superman*, plays a military man who sits in the cockpit with Ankrum in the plane that finally brings down "the big bird." When he laughs following the destruction of the monster, it's hard to tell if he's overjoyed at their victory or just delighted that the damn fool film is finally finished. Reportedly the lead actors had no idea of what the creature would look like until they saw the film in the theaters and were horrified — in the wrong way. It's too bad, because the picture deserved a more convincing monster.

Oh yes, even *The Giant Claw* attempts a moment of limited pathos. As the foolhardy teens fly by Mitch and Sally (who drive at a slower speed with their lights out so as not to attract the attention of the bird), one of the girls says that they're not scared of the bird because "we have salt to shake on its tail"—and holds up a salt shaker. After the teens are carried off by the monster (a couple fall to the ground and are taken to a hospital), Sally finds the unbroken salt shaker and picks it up with an ironic motion.

Director Ray Kellogg came out with two low-budget but nevertheless memorable out-sized monster movies which played on a double-bill in 1959: *The Killer Shrews* and *The Giant Gila Monster*. *Killer Shrews* takes place on an island where scientists are conducting genetic experiments which backfire, unleashing a horde of shrews that are as big and ravenous as wolves. (While these animals are not gigantic per se, at 50 to 100 pounds apiece they are certainly giant variations of the tiny species.) Because of a storm, the scientists are trapped on the island along with the captain of a supply boat. After several people fall victim to the shrews, the survivors manage to make their way to the boat and safety. The shrews will presumably turn upon one another and the last one will starve to death.

Before the credits, an off-screen voice tells us of the eating habits of the shrew, then intones with childish glee: "First in Alaska, and then invading steadily southward, there were reports of a new creature—the *giant killer* shrew." However nowhere in the film that follows is there any mention of giant shrews coming down from Alaska; they seem to have been created on and limited to this small island. Dr. Craigis (Baruch Lumet) is an amiable if somewhat daffy doctor who is concerned with the increasing threat of overpopulation. To this end he has decided to do experiments in order "to decrease size [of animals] and increase their lifespan." As he puts it, "If we were half the size we are now, we'd live twice as long." Not only is there no reason to assume this theory has any validity, it hardly makes sense to deal with overpopulation by shrinking everyone—a subway car crammed full of midgets instead of normal-sized people would still be uncomfortable for the people inside regardless of their height. Jay Simms' screenplay doesn't delve into any of this; the experiments are just an excuse for coming up with a respectable menace. There is also no explanation for why the test animals, the cute little shrews, grow into giants instead of getting smaller. Craigis' assistant Jerry (Ken Curtis, who also produced the picture) accidentally let the mutated beasts out of their cage while he was drunk. Now they have multiplied and are freely roaming the island, munching on the wildlife. Only the wildlife is running out.... Guess who's next on the dinner plate menu. However, the shrews don't have to eat you to kill you. One bite and you're a goner. The poison with which the scientists tried to kill them has only become absorbed into their salivary glands.

Kellogg manages to work up an atmosphere of nervous dread in the early scenes of the movie. Pretty Ingrid Goude, who plays Craigis' daughter Anna, may not be a great actress, but she's quite good at getting across her jitters over everyone's uncertain future. She knows that there are 200–300 carnivorous, starving monsters outside their cabin refuge, but certainly takes her time letting Captain Thorne Sherman (James Best), the supply man, know what's up. Her father doesn't do much to soothe the poor woman's nerves. A sequence while he goes on and on about the shrews' eating habits as Anna freaks out behind him borders on black comedy. The tension is also increased by frequent cuts to the shrews as they try to bite and claw their way into the cabin. (The walls are adobe, which easily crumble under the monsters' teeth, increasing the peril and tension.) Anna is perplexed at Sherman's lack of curiosity over everything, wondering why he didn't ask about such things as the boarded-up windows and "my accent." While it may be strange that Sherman didn't ask many more questions, he certainly wouldn't have needed to ask about Anna's accent as only seconds before she had mentioned that she was Swedish.

Killer Shrews features some atmospheric photography, including a nice pastoral shot early in the film of Sherman and his sidekick Rook rowing to the island's dock in a smaller boat, the larger supply boat in the background. The island looks consistently stark and forbidding, bristling with unseen menace. The film is very well-edited, particularly a sequence with effective cross-cutting when Sherman tries desperately to get inside the doors of the compound — which cowardly Jerry has locked — before the shrews can reach him and tear him to shreds. The climax is quite good, as the doctor, Anna, and Sherman tie several upside-down metal drums together and crouch underneath them so that they can make their way to the beach and have some protection from the shrews. The giant shrews are dogs tricked up with extra large teeth and shaggy hair; luckily the camera never lingers on them for very long. In close-ups when the shrews bite somebody's leg or ankle, puppet heads with fake fangs are employed.

The hero of the film, James Best, was a dependable second lead and character actor who had an interesting career, appearing with Jerry Lewis in *Three on a Couch* in 1966 and ten years later playing the older man with whom a despondent Billy Joe McAllister (Robby Benson) has sex before throwing himself off the Tallahatchie Bridge in the dated *Ode to Billy Joe*. In *Killer Shrews* he makes the best of an under-written part as a nice, un-curious fellow who just wants to get on with his life. As noted, Ingrid Goude was mostly decorative but effective enough as the nervous romantic interest. Baruch Lumet is acceptable as the talkative, amiable, clueless doctor who chatters unceasingly about shrews and "liveschtock." As Sherman's obese black assistant Rook, who makes a super-sized meal for the shrews early in the picture, J. H. Dupree is likable if stereotypical; he does not really appear to be an actor. The same is certainly true of Gordon McLendon, who plays Craigis' colleague, Dr. Redford Baines; McLendon tries to act but has absolutely no aptitude for it. McLendon, who was one of the film's financial backers (as well as of *The Giant Gila Monster*), was the millionaire owner of several Texas movie theaters. Pointing with his ever-present pipe, he scrunches up his face behind his glasses in an attempt to come off as what he imagines is an earnest intellectual; instead he seems like an idiot. When Baines is bitten by one of the shrews, and sits down at his typewriter to "record every symptom and reaction right up to the moment of [my] death," McLendon's ineptitude strips the scene of any intended pathos. The best performance in the movie comes from *Gunsmoke* regular Ken Curtis, who is excellent as the intense, frightened, often drunken Jerry, who was briefly engaged to Anna before his stupid blunder in letting the animals go free. His drunk scenes, such as when he banters with the doomed servant Mario in his bedroom (Mario is also bitten by a shrew), are very convincing. Curtis alone is successful in creating a portrait of a flawed but realistic human being, while the others never go beyond being types.

A cut below *Killer Shrews*, *The Giant Gila Monster*, also written by Jay Simms, is not without its amusing moments. In a small town in Texas, livestock and people begin disappearing amid reports of a large lizard roaming the desolate wooded areas on its outskirts. Embroiled in the mystery are the sheriff (Fred Graham) and a young man, Chase Winstead (Don Sullivan), who works in a garage and helps the sheriff look for some of Chase's missing friends. The giant gila monster crashes through a trestle and causes a train wreck, and enough survivors see the beast to make it clear that the rumors of its existence are true. When the monster bursts into the gymnasium where local teens are holding a dance, Chase uses his prized hot rod and two containers of nitroglycerin to blow it to smithereens.

The film is full of sympathetic characters, including the sheriff, who is friendly instead of at odds with the teenagers in town, and Chase, who is a few years older than his friends. Chase's ambition is to be a rock 'n' roll singer, and he sings some of his own songs (written by Don Sullivan, who plays Chase) throughout the movie. Some critics have seen Chase as being too good to be true, but the world then and now is full of perfectly decent people who hope for a break and are not disillusioned and bitter. Chase gets along with everyone, is kind (if testy at times) with his pretty French girlfriend, Lisa (Lisa Simone) — another sympathetic character — and adores his crippled young sister who is just learning how to walk with her new braces. The child is cute if perhaps just a bit cloying. Also taking up

The giant lizard prepares to go on a rampage, or what passes for same in *The Giant Gila Monster* (1959).

much screen time is the town's friendly drunkard, a colorful codger named Harris (Shug Fisher). The disc jockey, Steamroller Smith (Ken Knox), whose car is towed by Chase is also a friendly sort who does his bit to help Chase's recording ambitions. As Chase, Sullivan is a very likable and competent leading man, but Graham and Fisher give the most professional performances. Chase's mother and sister have Southern accents, but Sullivan doesn't. As Mr. Wheeler, the excitable father of one of the missing teenagers, Bob Thompson, an obvious amateur, mostly lacks the resources to get across his character's fear and anguish, but he's nowhere near as bad as Gordon McLendon in *Killer Shrews*. As with *Killer Shrews*, Ray Kellogg's direction is fairly adroit, and Aaron Stell's editing (he also worked on *Shrews*) makes the most of the situations.

For a low-budget movie, there is quite a bit of the giant gila monster on screen, although it is never seen in the same shot with live actors (there are *no* process shots in the movie). The monster is brought to life by filming a real gila monster, a big, beaded beauty, on miniature sets and combining them cleverly — and sometimes not so cleverly — with other footage. The road walked on by the gila monster does not quite match the (same) road which Steamroller Smith is driving on when he nearly runs into the beast. However, the miniature ravine set is a good match for the real ravine, and the set with the miniature trestle is also effective. (The crashing train is an obvious phony.) Still, the shot of the gila monster creeping slowly back to the wrecked train to presumably munch on victims is creepy, as are all the shots of the beast wandering the back woods and spying on potential suppers, such as a salesman who's menaced as he waits on the side of the road (why he was dropped off in the middle of nowhere is a question). Sometimes the gila monster seems to be crawling around a sandbox or dry aquarium, in its own private universe, but clever inter-cutting makes it seem to be licking its chops as it watches Chase and Lisa searching the ravine for their missing chums. You could swear it's about to pounce on them at any second in the suspenseful — and rather funny — sequence. For the scene when it crashes through the wall of the gymnasium, a miniature was built of the building, as well as of the inner wall through which it thrusts its wet, black snout. In two sequences when the beast creeps up and kills victims, a shot of its giant foot (an effective prop) coming down toward the camera is employed and works very nicely.

Described by the sheriff as being "as big as a bus," the monster appears to be about fifty feet long. The sheriff theorizes that the creature's pituitary gland is out of whack, and briefly talks of alleged instances of gigantism and its causes in other areas of the world. As with *Killer Shrews,* the pre-credits sequence's narrator tries to increase the terror quotient of the creature by claiming that the story takes place in an area "where the gila monster still lives" as if to suggest that it's extinct like a dinosaur. "No one knows how large the dreaded gila monster grows," he intones, which might be news to biologists. One particularly stupid aspect of the movie is the way the train wreck sequence is followed by an utterly prosaic scene of comedy relief with the sheriff and Harris. The sheriff explains that he's not out at the train wreck because "it's not my department." One can't really imagine any small town sheriff staying away from the scene of what would have to be the worst disaster in his county no matter who might be officially in charge.

Don Sullivan's songs include the mediocre "My Baby, She Rocks and Rolls" and the derivative "Laugh, Children, Laugh." He was a much better singer than he was a composer. Sullivan was probably like many good-looking young guys who have dreams of stardom as either actors or singers, but whose careers never quite take off for any number of reasons, including bad breaks or no breaks. Although undoubtedly more sophisticated than his character, he could have been a perfectly nice guy like Chase Winstead.

In the late fifties and early sixties British actor Michael Gough nearly had the title of "Vincent Price of England" along with Christopher Lee and Peter Cushing, all because of *Horrors of the Black Museum* and *Konga* (1961). The latter features a giant monster which, like the she-giant in *Attack of the 50 Foot Woman*, grows to outsized proportions and terrorizes everyone in the film's final minutes.

Gough is Dr. Charles Decker, who has been presumed dead after a plane crash in Africa. Actually he survived the crash, continued his experiments in secret on the dark continent, and as the film begins has returned after a year to resume his teaching at the university. In Africa he discovered some bizarre plants which had, as he puts it, "human characteristics" and some seeds that can make anyone subservient. He uses a formula derived from the plants in order to get his pet chimp, Konga, whom he also brought with him from Africa, to murder his enemies, but only after injecting the animal with another formula that makes him grow to the size of a full-grown gorilla. At the end of the film, Decker's jealous "housekeeper, secretary and assistant" Margaret (Margo Johns) injects Konga with more formula which makes the ape as big as a house. Although Margaret has ordered the gigantic chimp to kill Gough, it first kills her and then marches through London with the not-so-good doctor in his hairy paw. Soldiers shoot at Konga as he stands before Big Ben; the Big Ape dashes Gough to the ground, killing him. Finally the bullets put an end to Konga.

Konga is a strange, rather ludicrous, entertaining movie. Although much of the dialogue by screenwriters Aben Kandel and Herman Cohen (who also produced) is literate, the basic plot is an oddball cornucopia of various horror subgenres, never neatly settling into any one of them. Gough is a typical mad scientist, who thinks of no one but himself, his dreams, and his experiments, making *Konga* first and foremost a "mad doctor" movie. The killings-by-ape then turn the film into a gorilla-on-the-loose flick. When Konga suddenly grows fifty feet tall, it becomes a giant monster movie. Director John Lemont keeps things moving at a fast enough pace to keep you from getting bored or from analyzing the picture too intensely, which is a good thing.

The oddest thing about the movie is how Decker's scientific goals seem to change at the drop of a hat just to suit the convolutions of the plot. He talks with much animation of the fascinating new plant life he's discovered (as if Venus fly traps were something new) and all the things he can do with it — including mind control. Then he starts jabbering about creating things of "huge proportions" — out of nowhere. In other monster movies (such as *Tarantula* and *Beginning of the End*), scientists experiment with the growth of normal animals and vegetables as a way of relieving the world's hunger, but Decker seems to have no real objective. Herman Cohen probably thought a Kong-sized ape would be good for box office, so Konga grows — and grows.

A subplot concerns Decker's relationship with pretty student Sandra (Claire Gordon) and her jealous, rather smothering boyfriend (Jess Conrad). While the audience can well understand why Decker has a lech for the shapely Sandra, it's much less believable that she would rather spend time with Decker than with her handsome young boyfriend. Sandra is supposed to be very "into" science — hence her interest in her teacher — but she does not exactly look or behave like an intellectual. A hilarious exchange has Decker telling Sandra "I can't believe how you've grown." She replies "Well, you have been away a year." A small child may "grow" a lot during a year, but a grown woman? Decker talks about Sandra as if he hasn't seen her since she was a little girl! On the other hand, the script is often intentionally amusing, such as when Decker and Margaret have an argument at breakfast. "If there's anything I can't abide it's hysterics," Decker sneers, "especially in the morning."

Michael Gough gives a terrific performance in the film, and is far better than the picture deserves. He turns the dialogue into poetry, snaps each line with authority and conviction, and offers as smooth, professional, and chilling a portrait of a self-absorbed, calculating, ruthless sociopath as has ever been seen. Watching him take control of virtually every frame of the movie is primarily what holds your attention. One marvelous shot has him exhibiting a look of supreme disgust behind Margo Johns' back after he agrees to marry her to keep her from going to the police about his activities. Johns isn't bad as the woman who loves him unconditionally — she only turns against him when she learns he plans to replace her — but compared to Gough she's merely competent. Claire Gordon as Sandra is little more than decorative. Jess Conrad as Bob shows genuine potential in his scenes when he confronts the older man who has designs on his girlfriend.

The color film was touted as being shot in "Spectamation," a meaningless term that could have stood for "cheap effects due to meager budget." The transformation of Konga from chimp to gorilla is achieved via a "wavy" visual effect on the screen and simply substituting a man in a gorilla suit for the chimp. The wavy visual is again employed when Konga changes from gorilla to poor man's King Kong, and this time the actor in the gorilla suit also moves toward the camera to make it seem that he's growing. Miniature sets of a laboratory and the doctor's house (this particular miniature is well-crafted) are used once Konga has grown to giant size. To blend Konga in with screaming people, a split screen is used, as well as back projection. One effective shot shows Konga reaching over a building from behind to try and grab up some of the people in the street in front of the building. The first floor is a live action shot, while the second floor is a miniature with the actor standing behind it; then the two images were combined. Another effective shot is taken from below as dozens of screaming people rush toward the camera as Konga, in the background, looms above them. A forced perspective shot with the actor in the suit standing on a rooftop and shot from behind makes it seem as if a giant beast is standing tall above the crowd. In the long shots, a puppet is substituted for Michael Gough. Medium shots show Gough held in a large prop ape hand combined with the blown-up Konga behind him. The Venus fly trap and other carnivorous plants in Gough's hothouse are well-designed and credible.

The climax has a hilarious aspect to it in that the soldiers shoot thousands of bullets and rockets at Konga but most of them, incredibly, seem to fly past the beast and up into space. If these guys can't hit a target the size of Konga then they *literally* can't hit the side of a barn. It takes forever for the fusillades to finally bring the animal down. Gerard Schurmann's indifferent score takes on an "epic" tone as Konga dies. A bit of pathos has the huge creature turning back to the small, harmless chimp lying in the street next to the dead body of its master after its death.

Konga is by no means an especially memorable monster movie, but it does have its pleasures for devotees.

By the time of the next film version of *Mysterious Island* in 1961, Jules Verne was again "big" in Hollywood, with successful adaptations of *20000 Leagues* from Walt Disney, *Journey to the Center of the Earth* from 20th Century–Fox, and now *Mysterious Island* from Columbia. The picture was another collaboration between special effects wizard Ray Harryhausen and producer Charles Schneer, with highly felicitous results. Although the movie follows the basic plot of Verne's novel, it does add two ingredients that are nowhere to be found in the original: giant monsters and women. The latter are two shipwreck survivors who wash ashore on the island, and the former are Captain Nemo's experiments to end war by increasing the world's food supply. As he puts it: "Imagine wheat growing forty feet high and sheep as big as cattle." Needless to say, it isn't sheep nor wheat that show up to menace the protagonists.

Captain Harding (Michael Craig), infantryman Herbert (Michael Callan) and freed slave Neb (Dan Jackson) escape via balloon from a Confederate prison during the 1865 Siege of Richmond. Along for the ride are Union war correspondent Gideon Spilett (Gary Merill) and a Confederate sergeant named Pancroft (Percy Herbert). The ragtag group eventually lands on a strange island inhabited by giant animals, and are later joined by two female shipwreck survivors. During moments of crisis, a guardian angel of sorts seems to look out for them, providing them with the very goods and implements that they require, as well as blowing up a ship full of sinister pirates with bad intentions. This angel turns out to be Captain Nemo, who has docked his crippled *Nautilus* in a cavern beneath the island. Nemo helps the group get off the island before the volcano explodes, but dies before he himself can join them.

Laid over Verne's basic premise, which was influenced by *Robinson Crusoe*, is Ray Harryhausen's superlative stop-motion monsters. These include a giant crab (for this Harryhausen simply animated an actual crab instead of a model), a big bird or chicken, humongous bees, and a bad-tempered squid-like creature which waits for our heroes at the bottom of the sea. Under Harryhausen's magical touch, the crab is a scuttling, busy horror, a juggernaut of clacking limbs and sucking, whooshing mouth parts. The bird, a semi-comical creation, is a squawking, foul-tempered fowl that pecks and scratches with its beak and feet and is altogether more dangerous than its appearance might suggest. (The original plan was for the island to be a time-lost oasis full of prehistoric monsters, and the big chicken was to be a creature called a phorohacos.) The bees are handsome things that studiously buzz about as if concerned with matters of great importance. Although one of them seals up the young lovers Herbert and Elena (Beth Rogan) in a honeycomb, the bees never seem especially dangerous. The squid is one of Harryhausen's most masterful creations. We are introduced to it as the camera slowly moves in through darkness to the giant opening eye of the sea monster (in a scene much more effective than a similar one in *It Came from Beneath the*

Sea). The squid, which only battles the men underwater, has a baleful eye and sinister gaze to go with its busy, grasping tentacles. The only problem with the sequence is that it is much too brief.

There are other interesting effects besides the monsters. While the matte paintings are generally pretty but unconvincing, sometimes they have a certain magic. On their way underwater to repair a sunken pirate ship so they can use it to leave the island, the adventurers come across an "ancient city of a forgotten civilization" consisting of ruined buildings and toppled statues; these shots, with the men tramping past the remains of the city with their "electric guns" and "leaded shoes," are very effective. Originally this city was supposed to be Atlantis, but in the finished film it is never named, perhaps because Atlantis had already been (over) used in *20000 Leagues* and *Journey to the Center of the Earth*. Another impressive sequence, which also combines live action, studio sets, and matte paintings, is when Herbert and Elena discover the secret underground grotto where Nemo has hidden his *Nautilus*. The Nautilus itself is a fairly impressive 19th century–type creation with an especially beautiful interior design. This sub is quite different from the one in the Disney version.

Herbert Lom is effective as Captain Nemo, even if the script does not develop him very much. A man of many facets in Verne's novels, here he is simply a benign if grumpy fellow who wants to bring peace to the world. There are some arguments over his methods in the screenplay by John Prebble, Daniel Ullman, and Crane Wilbur, but these are set aside rather quickly to get back to the action. Michael Craig seems to be exerting most of his energy in disguising his British accent so that he can sound one hundred percent American, a feat which he manages to achieve for the most part. His performance is perfectly professional, but he plays Harding so rigid and by-the-book that the character is absolutely devoid of charm. Gary Merrill invests his rather unlikable, totally unsentimental Spilett with plenty of charm, however. Michael Callan is quite believable as the shy, frightened young Herbert trying so hard to be a man. Beth Rogan hasn't much to do but be pretty as Elena, and to sport a shockingly short skirt that was very 1960s and definitely not 19th century. (Wanting to marry Herbert, she suggests that Captain Harding can do the honors. "But he's a land captain, not a sea captain," Herbert protests. "Well, we're on land, aren't we?" Elena retorts.) Joan Greenwood is good as the girl's fluttery, affected, smoky-voiced aunt, Lady Mary. Dan Jackson plays the noble, affable, warm-hearted Ned with dignity and veracity.

Wilkie Cooper's photography is what you would expect from this talented veteran, but Cy Endfield's direction shows no special flair for the material whatsoever. It is up to Harryhausen and the actors to keep *Mysterious Island* humming, not to mention Bernard Herrmann's rich and exceptional musical score. Herrmann brings up the excitement level right away with his dynamic and beautiful opening-credits music, and, as usual, enriches every subsequent scene, adding that certain "wondrous" undertone to the sequence with the ancient underwater city and so on. *Mysterious Island* remains a very entertaining adventure movie even today.

Hammer–7 Arts released *The Lost Continent*, based on Dennis Wheatley's 1938 novel *Uncharted Seas*, in 1968. In this a group of sailors and passengers on the tramp steamer *Corita*, traveling to Caracas, have to abandon ship when a hurricane threatens to blow up the illegal cargo of explosives on board. Aboard the lifeboat are the loathsome Captain Lansen (Eric Porter), who only wants to retire after making a killing with the illegal cargo; Eva Peters (Hildegard Knef), who is hoping to be reunited with her little boy after being forced to flee South America years before; Unity Webster (Suzanna Leigh) and her unpleasant father Dr. Webster (Nigel Stock); a drunken ne'er-do-well named Tyler (Tony Beckley); and others. Traveling in circles, they come upon and re-board the abandoned *Corita*, only to discover that they're trapped in a bizarre land in the middle of the Sargasso Sea along with dozens of ships down through the centuries. The descendants of the shipwrecked survivors have divided into two groups, friendly farmers and sinister Spanish "conquistador"-types who prey upon them. Attacked by a variety of weird and dangerous monsters, the group from the *Corita* manage to rescue those of their number who are kidnapped by the Spanish, and begin to make their way back to civilization.

Wheatley's novel is an entertaining and occasionally imaginative read, but it is also hopelessly racist, with the industrious farmers on one island constantly set upon by the other island's vicious, primitive blacks, who kidnap their women for sex slaves and murder all of the men. Each newly arrived ship gets the same treatment. The seaweed- encrusted water which traps the ships is also home to countless giant octopi whose tentacles can reach up at any moment to ensnare a victim. To avoid these monsters, the islands' inhabitants use huge balloons to kind of hop over the seaweed and perhaps avoid the tentacles. In the film version, the balloons they wear are so small that they don't, and couldn't possibly, provide any elevation, so there seems little point for the islanders to wear them. On the other hand, the sea of lost ships, bathed in a dingy yellow glow, looks eerie and marvelous, a triumph for art director Arthur Lawson.

The film employs all of Wheatley's monsters and then some. In the novel the seaweed is just seaweed that creates a stranglehold on the ships. In the movie, the seaweed or kelp is alive — it constantly makes a noise like amplified crickets — and its tentacles, once wrapped around an arm, squeeze until either the limb or the tentacle is severed. We only see one octopus, a large monstrosity with a big yellow head, long, thick tentacles, and an eye like a glass porthole that glows bright green. This whole sequence is positively smothered in thick fog, probably because the octopus is not remotely convincing, even though it was worked on by Robert A. Mattey of *Jaws* and *20000 Leagues Under the Sea* fame. On a small island between the *Corita* and the main island where the Spaniards live, some of the group encounter a giant crab and scorpion. The crab has an ugly wizened face with deep-set green porcelain doll's eyes, a slithering wet maw that is constantly *gooshing* in and out, two black claws with limited movement, and a brown body inside a very large shell. It looks much worse than the crab in *Attack of the Crab Monsters* but is about the same size. It kills the likable steward Pat (Jimmy Hanley) by grabbing his neck with its pincer. Then it has a ludicrous battle with a giant rubber prop scorpion whose movements seem limited to the ability to rush in a forward direction with rapidity (it's probably actually on wheels). Both of these monsters, despite some cute and disgusting aspects, are rather pathetic, especially in comparison to the excellent art direction. *The Lost Continent* could certainly have used some of Ray Harryhausen's magical touch with humongous monsters.

Another monster created specifically for the film is simply a terrible writhing orifice under a trap door, a pore or mouth in the seaweed that has several layers, as well as short, red, tongue-like tentacles and stubby round teeth with darkened centers. This monster is well-designed but unconvincing. The nasty little boy El Supremo (Darryl Read), puppet ruler of the Spaniards, feeds subjects who disappoint him to this wriggling, hungry orifice and watches with cackling glee as they are being devoured. It is somewhat disappointing that this midget monster is simply taken off with the "good guys" at the end of the film as if he were just some adorable, misunderstood child. Similarly, it is irritating that Captain Lansen survives intact, considering all the people who died due to his criminal actions and utterly self-centered nature. Lansen was not a character in the novel, and the whole business with the illegal explosives was cooked up by the screenwriter, Michael Nash.

Eric Porter turns in a solid if unexciting turn as the nasty Captain, while Hildegard Knef is excellent, far above the level of her material, as Eva Peters. The other cast members are all quite professional, doing their best to bring the mostly stock characters to life. Michael Carreras' direction can best be described as unobtrusive, although some scenes, such as a lifeboat fight that leads to Dr. Webster being eaten by a shark, are well-handled. Gerard Schurmann's musical score is forgettable, as are the songs by Ray Phillips, especially the awful title tune, jazzy junk with background organ that does nothing to suggest the events to follow.

A major publicity campaign was mounted for *The Lost Continent*. It was, perhaps, one of the last films to employ that now old-fashioned approach in the newspaper ads, with sidebar boxes depicting scenes from the movie with the words SEE: MAN CONSUMED BY CRAB CREATURE! SEE: ATTACK BY CRAZED KELP MONSTERS! and so on. Even more publicity was generated by the amply endowed actress Dana Gillespie, who played one of the islanders understandably pursued by the Spaniards. Clad in an outfit with plunging décolletage, Gillespie certainly ignited the fantasies of many a schoolboy.

The last word on *The Lost Continent* belongs to critic William Wolf, who wrote of the film in *Cue* Magazine, "Continents may come, and continents may go, but bosoms can always be found."

One of the most bizarre monster movies of all time was released in 1972: *Night of the Lepus*, directed by William F. Claxton. The screenplay by Don Holliday and Gene R. Kearney was based on a satirical novel by Australian writer Russell Braddon entitled *The Year of the Angry Rabbit*, not a good bet for filming to begin with. The book, although it had something to do with the population explosion of rabbits on the continent, had absolutely *nothing* to do with giant monster rabbits. But when MGM decided to make a film "based" on the novel, that is exactly what they came up with.

In Southeast Arizona, rancher Cole Hillman (Rory Calhoun) is having a problem with rabbits over-running his property. He contacts a university friend, Elgin Clark (DeForest Kelley), who puts him in touch with a husband-and-wife team of scientists, Roy Bennett (Stuart Whitman) and Gerry (Janet Leigh). The two come up with a formula that, as Gerry explains to their daughter Amanda (Melanie Fullerton), will "make Jill more like Jack and Jack more like Jill ... so they won't have such large families." Amanda surreptitiously switches one of the test rabbits she likes with a control animal, and the rabbit is accidentally released into the wild. Before long there is a huge herd of hundreds of rabbits "as big and as ferocious as wolves" (they are actually much bigger), savaging the livestock and inhabitants of the nearby communities. With the aid of Sheriff Cody (Paul Fix), Hillman and Bennett manage to kill some of the rabbits in a mine cave-in, and destroy the others via use of an electrified train track.

Night of the Lepus might have made a perfectly reasonable monster movie if the special effects crew had been on their toes. If a formula can make giants out of rabbits, it might be expected that it could also mutate them into rather fearsome-looking creatures with huge fangs, shortened ears, and a wholly formidable and horrific appearance; rabbits are rodents, just like rats, after all. Instead, the movie simply uses actual cute, cuddly, adorable — and normal-looking — bunny rabbits as the monsters! The sight of these frisky critters running down miniature roads and attacking toy cars approaches the cosmic level of the *Giant Claw* puppet as it makes beautiful Mara Corday gasp in shock and terror. To be fair, this writer would not especially care to run into a giant rabbit, even if it were still cuddly, and close-up shots of their teeth combined with the roars cooked up by the sound department make these rabbits a little unnerving to behold at times. Still ... one has to ask, "What were they thinking?"

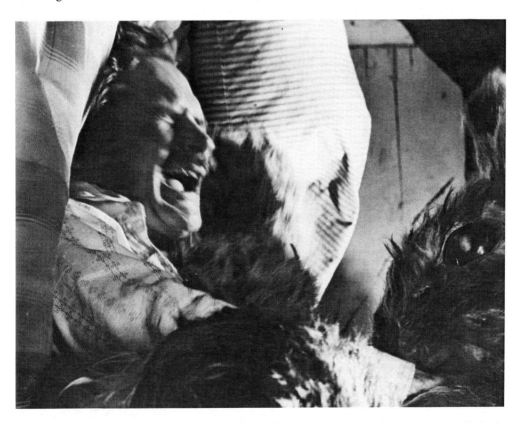

One of the giant bunny rabbits of *The Night of the Lepus* (1972) attacks a screaming victim it wants to make a meal of.

The FX people were also a little out of sync with the screenwriters when it came to the size of the rabbits. More than once they are described as being "as big as wolves" but they are more along the lines of baby elephants. This is true from the very first process shot showing Calhoun and Whitman discovering the bunnies' lair in an abandoned mine and remains consistent throughout the movie. Another clue to how big they actually are is the sound they make when they run — like stampeding horses, a much heavier animal than a wolf. After attacking people, they leave behind lots of body parts, which may seem illogical given how numerous they are and how hungry they must be, but perhaps they do not actually eat people, only attack them (this may not be true of the horses and cattle they hurl themselves upon). But in a fantastic film like this, it's not a stretch to imagine that the formula that made them grow also made them carnivorous. Herbivorous monsters aren't very scary, after all. The rabbits make squealing, grunting, growling noises like feral pigs which helps a bit to make them seem fearsome.

The rabbits are brought to life via process shots, forced perspective shots, and the use of miniatures, which are excellent, whether they are of landscapes, bridges, country roads, highways, the outside of buildings, or the inside of farmhouses. The irony is that the sight of the rabbits running down roads and across fields is not as ludicrous as one might imagine once you get used to their appearance. The prop bunnies that are used for close-up attacks (and which we never see for too long, luckily) are as cuddly as Teddy bears and about as scary. (After one such attack, Janet Leigh says to an injured man, Jed, "Calm down, the rabbit's gone, calm down," as if she were speaking to a child.) Trying to circumvent the impossible problem of the rabbits' non-frightening appearance, the FX crew at times shoots them in slow motion to get across their bulk, as well as from below, making them appear quite huge. This is particularly effective for the scene when the rabbits study a group of horses from the top of a hill and actually lick their chops in anticipation of dinner. A clever use of close-up photography helps a lot but can only go so far.

Oddly, *Night of the Lepus* still manages to be creepy and suspenseful at times, such as when the rabbits sneak up on a trailer, infest the tunnels of a mine, and approach isolated farmhouses en masse. One of the better scenes has Gerry and Amanda caught in the dark when their trailer breaks down. As Gerry struggles to make repairs, we see two giant bunnies in the left foreground (a forced perspective shot achieved simply by putting two rabbits quite close to the camera) ominously biding their time until they and the others can attack. Bennett saves his wife and daughter just in time by making a rescue in a helicopter.

One of the more absurd scenes has the sheriff announce to the customers at a drive-in movie: "There's a herd of killer rabbits heading this way and we desperately need your help!" The idea is to use the car lights to attract the rabbits, who will then be fried by the high electric charge on the railroad tracks. But this has to wait until a slow freight finally gets off the track, adding some minor suspense. Everyone dutifully lines up their cars on the other side of the track as the sheriff directs, when in reality most people — hearing talk of "a herd of killer rabbits" — would either think the man was drunk or head in the opposite direction as fast as they could go, especially those with children in the back seats! The rabbits that aren't killed by electricity are picked off with shoguns. (The film does not go into what might happen when predators, pests and parasites get wind of all those giant rabbit carcasses.)

Night of the Lepus is not the first nor last movie in which the experiments of well-meaning scientists lead to the creation of horrible monsters that take scores of innocent lives. What's amazing is that in most of these movies the scientists don't even look embarrassed. This is certainly true of *Night of the Lepus*. The Bennetts cannot argue that the outbreak only occurred because their little girl switched rabbits on them, because the test animals would have grown to giant size in any case and broken out of their lab (in fact, it's never explained why this hasn't happened). In real life there have been many cases of people responsible for the deaths of innocents who are so guilt-wracked that they attempt suicide, but Roy and Gerry don't even have the decency to look mortified when dozens of people are being torn apart and trampled because of their stupidity. They were supposed to fix a problem and only created a much worse one.

Part of the problem is that the acting is largely perfunctory. Janet Leigh was essentially a limited actress of light romances who found herself inappropriately cast in horror items because of the success of *Psycho*. Rory Calhoun is not at all bad in the movie, but he was also a romantic lead of B movies, not a serious dramatic actor. DeForest Kelley was in the post–*Star Trek* slump of his career and is at least professional. Stuart Whitman was a fine actor who starred in the British production of *The Mark* (1961) wherein he gave an excellent performance as a tormented and guilt-wracked convicted child molester trying to start his life over. His performance in *Lepus* is, again, professional but by-the-numbers. Many good actors, confronted with scripts along the lines of *Night of the Lepus*, figure there's little point in pulling out all the acting stops, but this attitude doesn't do much for them or the picture.

Night of the Lepus is played totally straight, without a tongue-in-cheek line or a single pun. As a director, William Claxton keeps things moving but little else. Composer Jimmie Haskell provided the fairly ominous theme music. The well-done sound effects, however, build up more chills than any music. Despite its zany "monsters," *Night of the Lepus* has its charms for the rabid monster fan. All of its enduring clichés — a formula gone awry, sheriffs scratching their heads, isolated attacks followed by the beasts going on the rampage etc. — make it somewhat endearing in spite of its zaniness.

Bert I. Gordon resurfaced in 1975 with his second adaptation of H. G. Wells' novel *The Food of the Gods*, which was only fitting as the book was the first work of popular fiction to deal with the theme of gigantism, Gordon's specialty. In 1965 Gordon came out with a film entitled *Village of the Giants* that was loosely based on the later chapters of the book. Wells' novel deals with a mysterious substance or "food" that can make animals, insects, and people grow to tremendous size. Wells meant the giant people to be metaphors for man's need to escape pettiness, expand his consciousness, and explore his own nature and the nature of the universe. But their huge size also makes them extremely dangerous — monsters — in the literal sense. The novel, although entertaining and thought-provoking, never quite reconciles these two opposing aspects. In the rather dreadful *Village of the Giants*, teenagers in a small town drink a formula, grow into giants, and create campy mayhem. In the better *Food of the Gods*, also loosely based on a "portion" of the novel, modern-day humans in a small island community are beset by outsized chickens, wasps, and rats. Both films attracted droves of teenage fans and others and both received massive publicity campaigns. The poster for the first film showed a teenage boy hanging on for dear life to the bra straps of a huge bosom. The poster for the second showed a huge rat on a tree branch hovering over a supine, screaming woman.

Football player Morgan (Marjoe Gortner), the team's P.R. man Brian (Jon Cypher) and another teammate, Davis (Chuck Courtney), travel to the island where Gortner grew up (actually Bowen Island in British Columbia). While hunting, Davis is stung and killed by dozens of wasps that are as big as large dogs. The other two men come across an old woman, Mrs. Skinner (Ida Lupino), who has some extremely large chickens out in her barn. Seems she and her husband have a white substance bubbling up from the ground and have been feeding it to their hens, mixing it with their regular meal. Mrs. Skinner explains that it only made the baby chicks grow big, and as soon as they did the full-grown ones "got et by the real big ones." Unfortunately, some wasps and rats have also gotten into the food and are now killing people on the island, including Mr. Skinner (John McLiam). Others who are menaced by the voracious creatures include businessmen Bensington (Ralph Meeker), who wants to buy the rights to the "food"; his assistant Lorna (Pamela Franklin), a bacteriologist; a pregnant woman, Rita (Belinda Belaski); and her husband Thomas (Tom Stovall). As Rita gives birth, the rats attack the Skinner cabin where everyone is holed up. Morgan manages to unleash a flood that drowns the beasties and, temporarily at least, ends their threat to civilization. Some of the food trickles into a stream that provides water for cows, whose milk is given to schoolchildren, and so on...

The Food of the Gods got some good reviews and might be considered Gordon's best film for those who are immune to the charms of *The Cyclops*, *The Amazing Colossal Man*, and *The Magic Sword*. The film is generally entertaining and the rat-attack scenes in the cabin genuinely harrowing. There are even a couple of decidedly scary scenes, such as when the huge rats approach in the distance as Meeker and Gortner have an argument outside the cabin. But the production is still rather cheesy in a strictly negative sense, and the low budget, plus Gordon's distinct limitations as a director, reduce its potential.

As with *The Cyclops*, Gordon's screenplay is full of both illogical and amusing moments. When Gortner and Cypher are attacked on the road by the rats, Cypher is dragged off

Ida Lupino has her hands full with giant worms in *The Food of the Gods* (1976), another Bert I. Gordon production.

by about half a dozen of the things while only one descends upon Gortner. Gortner never kills the rat, it just seems to disappear so that he can continue to appear in the movie. Cypher had previously told Gortner, "In this open Jeep we don't stand a chance" but Gortner takes the Jeep out *again* after the other man's death despite the fact that on both occasions he could have taken Meeker's sedan. When the young husband Thomas steps out of his trailer, turns around, and sees a huge rat on top of the trailer, he stupidly asks his wife to step outside when it would have made much more sense for him to hop into the trailer at lightning speed and slam the door behind him. But the couple has to run away from the trailer so they can be present at the big climax in the cabin, where Rita gives birth at a most inopportune moment.

On the other hand, it's very funny to hear Gortner scream at Lupino "Where did you get those goddamn chickens?" after one tries to peck him to death. Later, after Franklin has had a narrow escape in a tunnel filled with rats, all Meeker can say to her is "Thanks to you we missed the last ferry!" Meeker thinks he'll get rich solving the world's hunger problem by creating giant animals. "Wouldn't bigger animals have bigger appetites?' Franklin wisely asks (it's hard to believe she wouldn't have brought this up long before). Meeker counters that he'll also make bigger plants. Lupino says that the food was a "gift from God"—presumably the Christian God—but the jars of the stuff in her kitchen are all labeled "F.O.T.G." for "Food of the Gods."

The effects in *Food of the Gods* are typically — for Gordon — uneven. He turns the camera this way and that but it doesn't disguise the phoniness of the big chicken prop that pecks at Gortner in the barn. Consisting of a big rubber chicken head with claws, the prop is not capable of much movement and looks ridiculous. This is followed by a process shot blending the actor with some blown-up fowl, about six feet tall, who seem more confused than dangerous (the attack-fowl was presumably a rooster). In long shot the wasps are see-through buzzing things of little distinction; Gordon also turns the camera at dizzying angles during these sequences to little avail. The rubber prop wasp used for close-ups also seems incapable of much movement. The worms or maggots that bite at Lupino as they come up out of the drain in her sink are credibly slimy and disgusting; they seem to writhe in the actress' hands but they are also immobile props. The giant rats, which are nearly man-sized, are created via the use of process shots blending them with live action, or by stuffed mock-ups used for close-ups. These stuffed rats are well-designed but immobile. They do their best acting piled up as water-logged corpses at the end of the film. There are occasional shots employing real rats and miniature cars and the like. The two elements of the process shots aren't always properly aligned; Gortner will point to the rats on the other side of a fence, but he's pointing slightly to the left or right of where the rats actually are. However, the climactic shots of the surviving cast members standing on a roof terrace after the flood, with rats drowning in the water all around them, is nicely done and effective, and it even impressed a number of critics.

As in *The Cyclops*— as indeed most of Gordon's films — the actors were mostly in a state of career decline (Orson Welles had even appeared in a Gordon film, 1972's *Necromancy*). The star of the film, Marjoe Gortner, had been the subject of the Howard Smith documentary *Marjoe* three years earlier; it detailed his life as an amiable phony evangelist. His undeniable charisma netted him a short-lived Hollywood career, but after appearances in such high-profile movies as *Earthquake* (1974), and then *Food of the Gods*, little was heard of him. His performance is perfectly competent but he was definitely a case of personality triumphing over limited talent. Child star Pamela Franklin appeared in quite a few films as an adult, including the aforementioned *Necromancy*, but *Gods* was not one of her distinctive credits. Ralph Meeker, who had had a notable Broadway career before doing such films as *Kiss Me Deadly*, is fine as the crusty, reprehensible Bensington. Ida Lupino was a major Hollywood star of the 1940s and '50s, and had also directed some films herself. She essays Mrs. Skinner with her customary professionalism although her big false eyelashes are a bit out of place. The film's musical score is completely unmemorable.

Fourteen years after the Gordon film was released a follow-up was made by a completely different creative team: *After the Food of the Gods*. This was eventually released under the title *Food of the Gods II* and is also known as *Gnaws*. Although the film manages to hold the attention, it is even more cheapjack than Gordon's movie, and often borders on parody. The story, unrelated to Wells' novel, has animal rights activists accidentally letting loose a horde of man-eating giant rodents. This all begins when a lady doctor beseeches a scientist working in a college lab to look for a cure for a little boy whose growth has spurted alarmingly after a growth hormone reacted to something in his blood. Giant rats are created when the scientist, looking for answers, creates a growth formula and injects it into a rat. (Other rats eat giant tomatoes and ingest the formula that way.) Before long the rats are running wild, chewing on everyone in sight.

Director Damian Lee is too inexperienced to do much to save the movie. He isn't helped by the inexperienced and downright inept cast. The script is often groaningly derivative: the dean of the college stupidly and irrationally downplays the serious menace of the rats because the new gym building is about to open and he's afraid he'll lose students (figuratively speaking) and their parents' dollars. (Read: the "summer dollars" of *Jaws*.) Characters always act with little reason or logic. The editing is crude and the musical score jumps from style to style without ever helping to build scares or move the picture along.

Although the rat attack scenes are sometimes exciting, they are filmed with little elan. The big scene when the critters attack at the opening of the gymnasium is busy and frenetic without really being well done. The effects consist of a very few process shots employing real rats, along with unconvincing, immobile rat props — mostly heads and teeth — applied to the cast members along with lots of stage blood for especially gory sequences. The best bits in the movie actually have to do with giant people: the first sight of the outsized little boy, ten to twelve feet tall, generates a quiet shock; and there's a great dream sequence, complete with an overgrown penis prop, in which the hero imagines he's grown to giant size while having sex with a campus Lolita. The lensing is crisp and professional, but this is a cheap and generally unmemorable production.

A gigantic bear was the star of *Grizzly*, a *Jaws* knock-off that was released in 1976. A grizzly bear from the Pleistocene era (as one character theorizes) somehow survives into modern times and attacks numerous campers and others in a national park. There is no explanation for how the grizzly (or its genus) survived or where it came from, and no one seems remotely concerned about it, either. The bear is fifteen feet tall and weighs 200–300 pounds.

It is also smarter than most bears, toppling a ranger station tower to get at a victim in one fairly exciting sequence. Taking its cue from *Jaws*, the film has an irritating political type who is at odds with the sheriff (Christopher George), and even a scene when another ranger (Andrew Prine) tells a "true" horror story about man-eating grizzlies during a quiet "just us guys" campfire sequence in much the same way Quint tells about the U.S.S. *Indianapolis* and sharks in Spielberg's film. The movie has a deceptively tranquil opening with trivial "TV movie"–type music (the whole score is pretty awful), but soon turns quite ugly with a girl camper getting her arm torn off by the bear, and another woman losing her face as her helpless lover screams in horror. The bear attacks four women, including a nudie under a waterfall, in quick succession.

Under William Girdler's mediocre direction, the pacing is too leisurely, and the movie is rarely scary nor especially atmospheric. A somewhat chilling sequence has the bear covering up one still-living victim with dirt so that he can come back later to have him for a meal. The ranger wakes up and shakes the dirt off, happy to be spared, but it's too late — the bear has returned and is hovering just above him — pow! The best scene deals with the grizzly's attack on a little boy and the brave mother who tries to save him. One has to wonder why after all the deaths, many more than in *Jaws*, the National Guard isn't called in to put paid to the bear. While many sea and land animals were called into duty as menaces after the success of *Jaws*, *Grizzly* is one of the few that made their animal into a literal monster — not just prehistoric, but of tremendous, unnatural size, which is why it is included in this chapter.

Q (AKA *The Flying Serpent*) could be seen as a remake of either *The Flying Serpent* or *The Giant Claw* if only it were half as entertaining as either of those earlier films. Written and directed by Hollywood schlockmeister Larry Cohen, it deals with a giant serpent that attacks and consumes New Yorkers. Somehow the creature has been brought to life (it is never really explained how this is done) in some supernatural fashion by a series of human sacrifices wherein willing victims of a latter-day Aztec witch doctor are either skinned alive or have their hearts torn out; the monster is "prayed back into existence," as one character puts it. It is also "getting bigger every day." Officers Shepard (David Carradine) and Powell (Richard Roundtree) are assigned to both cases — the bird, as it's called, and the human sacrifices — and figure out that they're connected. In the meantime, an out-of-work piano player, petty crook, and full-time loser named Jimmy Quinn (Michael Moriarty) discovers where the serpent-bird has built its nest, but barters this information for money. The creature is eventually destroyed but at the cost of many lives.

"Q" stands for Quetzlcoatl, the Aztec god or feathered serpent. There was also a huge flying reptile of the prehistoric era — an especially large pternandon — that scientists christened Quetzlcoatlus, but it is never suggested that the monster of *Q* is a Jurassic leftover. It also does not resemble a pterodactyl.

Q received some surprisingly respectful and even admiring reviews from the critics, but they were not from real fans of monster movies, who want to have plenty of monster for their dollars and to hell with all the boring extraneous stuff. The one main problem of *Q* is that there is far too much of Michael Moriarty and not nearly enough of The Monster. Far too much of the running time is given over to Moriarty's involvement with some hoodlums and a robbery that goes awry, as well as his relationship with his wife, Joan (Candy Clark). To make matters worse, Moriarty's performance is showy without being particularly good. Moriarty started out as a New York theater personality — he got plaudits for his performance as a male hustler involved with a married bisexual man in *Find Your Way Home*— and played the head prosecutor on *Law and Order* in pre–Sam Waterston days. He did another horror film with Cohen, *The Stuff,* in 1985, and was similarly over-the-top. David Carradine and Richard Roundtree give generally good, if standard, performances; it's too bad that Cohen's apparent fascination with Moriarty deprived the other actors of some good scenes. But nothing can make up for the sheer lack of monster that does *Q* in worse than Moriarty's hamminess. Some critics, who do not really care for the genre, think a monster movie is good if it's full of other things that somehow make it less of a monster movie.

The monster of *Q* is sleek, brown, with large wings, a long neck and a small head with a turtle-like beak. At its largest it appears to be the size of a small plane. Stop motion animators Randy Cook, David Allen and others brought the beast to life; the animation is fairly smooth and the process work not badly done. Stop motion animation was time-consuming and expensive, which is why Cook and Allen turned out a number of low-budget features with well-done animation but an insufficient number of FX shots. In that respect, *Q* is no different. When the monster shows up it looks quite good, but its appearances are too infrequent until the climax. The serpent's battle with the police who are waiting for it in its skyscraper nest is exciting and horrifying, but also a case of too little, too late. One of the most effective shots in the movie doesn't feature the bird at all, but rather its ominous and enormous shadow on skyscrapers as it flies by.

Considering the lightness of its tone, *Q* is full of a lot of ugliness. The first victim of the serpent is a window washer whose head is snapped off. Later the beast makes off with a sunbathing beauty whose blood drips down onto several appalled pedestrians. The severed foot of a construction worker is found in the street, and many passersby see the monster flying above. Yet the continuity of the film is so poor that it seems to take quite some time after these incidents for the authorities to acknowledge the existence of the bird. One chilling, if illogical scene, has the serpent overlooking the women standing around a rooftop pool and dipping into the pool itself to drag out the screaming man who just dove in.

Cohen's screenplay is full of interesting and macabre touches, but he should have trusted his tale to the monster and reduced the Moriarty character to a bit. The viewer does not really need to know all about the pathetic Jimmy Quinn's life and times. The authorities give in to Quinn's demands for money in exchange for information (although the way things play out he doesn't get the cash) when in reality they could have charged him with at the very least depraved indifference to life and a dozen other things, including leading two hoodlums to slaughter at the beak of the bird (he told them the jewels they were after were in the nest but didn't warn them about the serpent). To be fair to Cohen he does introduce a note of personal responsibility with the Quinn character. Even Quinn's wife is appalled that he did not immediately go to the police with what he knew and perhaps prevented further deaths. But this aspect isn't well-developed enough to justify all the footage of Quinn.

The flippant tone of the movie is often at odds with its events. The climactic battle features the terrifying deaths of several police officers, including an obviously scared young man who's pulled out of the tower by the monster's beak and thrown many stories to his death. Carradine merely says "It's big" for a quick laugh, but the script allows him no reaction at all to the deaths of his colleagues. Robert O. Ragland's musical score is mediocre.

In short, *The Giant Claw* is a classic compared to *Q*.

FOUR

Nature Turned Nasty Part One — Birds, Bugs, and Bats

Every day we intermingle without conscious thought with Earth's other creatures, most of whom seem to have little interest in intermingling with us. A popular theme in films has been the idea of animals we never give a second thought to, animals that only on rare occasions are dangerous to humans (or dangerous animals that most humans rarely encounter), becoming certified menaces to mankind on a massive scale. While Alfred Hitchcock's *The Birds* has remained the most famous of these nature-gone-berserk movies, it was not the first. This chapter generally focuses on killer insects, birds, and bats — things that fly, crawl, and hop — with an occasional detour when warranted.

One of the earliest nature-gone-amok films — although the "monsters" don't behave in any particularly unusual manner — was *The Naked Jungle* (1954), which was based on Carl Stephenson's short story *Leiningen vs. the Ants* and produced by George Pal. To pad out the running time, the screenwriters concocted a half-baked domestic drama that defies credulity. In 1901, Joanna (Eleanor Parker) comes from New Orleans to a cocoa plantation in South America after marrying the owner, Christopher Leiningen (Charlton Heston), by proxy — sight unseen. Although Leiningen's brother disagreed that she would be the best candidate, Joanna convinced him that she would make the perfect wife. However, Christopher is deeply disturbed to discover that Joanna is a widow, and virtually shuns her. We later learn the trouble is that Christopher is a virgin (Heston was thirty-one years old at the time of the picture's release)! Apparently Chris left for South America while a teen and never wanted to use any of the local Indian women for sexual purposes. Joanna is a bit too "experienced" for the nervous fellow.

While Chris and Joanna try to deal in their own way with their horniness, the audience has to wait an interminable length of time for the real menace: billions and billions of soldier ants ("marabunta") that devour everything in their path. If it weren't enough that the viewer has to suffer through all the dull domestic sequences, the picture doesn't become that much more exciting even when the ants finally do appear. The "attack" on the plantation — which Christopher aborts by smashing a dam and washing away the ants along with the furniture — happens only in the final moments and by that time most viewers probably felt like they had ants-in-their-pants. In spite of this, *The Naked Jungle* got some respectful reviews, possibly because the subject matter seemed unusual and some of the close-ups of the ants were creepy. There is a quick shot of what appear to be stop-motion ants crawling on a branch, but otherwise the special effects are limited to some good miniatures that are destroyed in the okay but unspectacular climax when the dam bursts.

Director Byron Haskin's direction can most charitably be described as stodgy, the pace being slack even in the final quarter. It doesn't help that the screenwriter has Joanna sitting down and playing piano when the audience is much more interested in ant action (what little of it there is). His libido stimulated by approaching death, Chris finally makes love with Joanna before the final onslaught of the marabunta. Charlton Heston is appropriately rigid as Christopher, but Eleanor Parker is all breathless, "actressy," and unreal as Joanna. Parker was a very good actress but she could be very affected if a director didn't rein her in, and Haskin was not the man to do it. One can't even call Parker's performance entertaining because she makes Joanna completely humorless. The best performance is given by William Conrad as the commissioner, who stood in for Parker during Christopher's proxy marriage to Joanna in a sequence that was fortunately never filmed.

The same year of *The Naked Jungle* came William Dieterle's *Elephant Walk*, another over-baked melodrama with dangerous "normal" animals waiting impatiently in the background until they take center stage at the climax. (Obviously neither birds, bats nor bugs form the menace in *Elephant Walk*, but it's included in this chapter as a companion piece to *Naked Jungle*, which it resembles.) In this, John Wiley (Peter Finch) — improbably, as *he* is apparently not a virgin — can't seem to find time for his absolutely luscious wife Ruth (Elizabeth Taylor at her sexiest), whom he has brought home to his tea plantation in Ceylon; therefore friend and associate Dick Carver (Dana Andrews) makes advances. Wiley's late father, a stubborn, imposing man, built his huge, equally imposing estate right in the middle of an ancient pathway that the elephants have always used to make their way to the water. Decades later, they still try to use the path and have to be beaten back by people bearing torches (this happens a couple of times as the story progresses, whetting our appetites for the inevitable rampage).

At the finale, a malaria outbreak fells most of the native people, who aren't on hand when the elephants decide to literally crash through the estate en masse and use the traditional pathway. Unlike the lackluster climax in *Naked Jungle*, *Elephant Walk* delivers the goods as dozens of pachyderms storm through the living room and nastily try to smash the staircase upon which La Liz seeks to effect an escape. The ants in *Naked Jungle* may just be doing what comes naturally, but even if one buys the idea of elephants-who-never-forget being unable to adapt to another pathway after many years, their stopping to try to kill Ruth and others instead of simply marching to their objective, the river, puts them squarely in the nature-run-amok category. The rampage scene is extremely well done, employing what presumably were trained elephants and rarely using stunt doubles for the heroic Finch and Taylor.

The Birds (1963) was suggested by a short story by Daphne Du Maurier which was published in 1952. Wealthy playgirl Melanie Daniels (Tippi Hedren) is intrigued by a San Francisco lawyer named Mitch Brenner (Rod Taylor) and follows him out to Bodega Bay, where he lives, on a pretext. As Melanie gets to know Mitch's widowed mother Lydia (Jessica Tandy), young sister Cathy (Veronica Cartwright), and old girlfriend Annie Hayworth (Suzanne Pleshette), who is the local schoolteacher, birds in the area begin acting strangely.

Melanie is attacked by a gull, and a flock of gulls soar down at the children at Cathy's birthday party. Lydia then discovers that a neighbor has been pecked to death by birds. An attack by crows on the schoolchildren is followed by an attack on the town itself by gulls and other birds. Mitch boards up his house to protect them from a frightening bird onslaught that comes at night. Investigating a noise in the attic, Melanie is assaulted by dozens of birds and requires medical attention. The film ends as the Brenners and Melanie drive off, millions of birds watching them ominously as they go.

The Birds is full of classic set-pieces and some of Hitchcock's most audacious cinematic tricks. Somehow it doesn't matter that it takes a while for the birds to do their thing, because the first half of the film is so smooth and entertaining. The attack on the children at the birthday party is comparatively mild, but provides just the right touch of menace. The business with the sparrows coming down the chimney is not an "attack" at all but it's an unnerving, well-done scene in spite of it. The sequence when Lydia drives to a neighbor's house to talk about the behavior of his chickens and discovers the man's corpse with his eyes pecked out is the first time we're aware of how serious a threat the town may be facing. The three successive shots bringing us closer and closer to the dead man's disfigured face offered quite a shock in its day and still has impact.

The monkey bars sequence — Melanie smokes a cigarette outside the school, unaware that a mass of crows are gathering on the monkey bars behind her — leads into the still-disturbing attack on the children as they race down the road toward town and safety. Some may question the wisdom of letting the kids leave the building in the first place, although Annie may have felt they would be better off getting far away from those crows. This frightening sequence shows the crows clawing and pecking at the children, badly scratching one little boy's face and drawing blood, knocking a girl to the ground, all with a background cacophony of screaming birds and crying youngsters. Children had been in danger, even killed, in earlier movies, but this was perhaps the first scene of its kind, with *many* children in mortal danger and terror at the same time — and with a particular *emphasis* on their terror. Was this Hitchcock being in a gleefully perverse, anti-child mood, or was he simply breaking more taboos as he had with the shower murder in *Psycho*? Probably both. In any case, the scene has an undeniable poignancy for anyone who loathes the idea of children being hurt or terrified.

The next big sequence is the attack on the town itself. This begins when a gull knocks a gas station attendant unconscious and the gasoline from the pump spreads across the ground toward another car. As the driver of the second vehicle lights a cigarette, Melanie and others in the diner yell at him a warning not to drop the match. After he does, there are quick shots showing the fire following the trail of gasoline inter-cut with frozen, *still* shots of Melanie, her head facing in four different directions as her eyes follow the fire moving from right to left. (Some people find this very effective, while others think it just looks silly.)

There is a striking shot of the gulls descending from high in the air down toward the town below, the conflagration at the gas station seeming to attract them. Hitchcock filmed the attack that follows from the viewpoint of Melanie as she seeks shelter inside a phone booth. While this approach could be considered somewhat constricted, it makes sense as

There was a tremendous publicity campaign for Alfred Hitchcock's *The Birds* (1963), one of the master's most fascinating pictures.

Tippi Hedren tries to fight off an attack of *The Birds* (1963).

Melanie is the film's constant focal point (as well as the focus of Hitch's attention). Although very few birds appear in the scene, the attack on the Brenner house that night is also unnerving, an aural assault as the birds squawk, cry, and chip away frenetically at the doors of the house and the boards covering the windows. The assault on Melanie as she opens the attic door and gets trapped inside is almost a replaying of the shower murder, as if Hitch were punishing this beautiful woman for being so abjectly out of his league (the scene took a week to film as well as both an emotional and physical toll on Hedren). The birds come at Hedren almost one by one — or at least only a few at a time — as the rest sort of flop around in the background instead of smothering Hedren, but — as Du Maurier's story suggests — the birds were slowly learning how to work together. (Annie is attacked en masse and killed by the birds but the attacks may not have been too vicious *at first*.) Throughout the film the birds, although very well-trained by Ray Berwick, don't seem particularly intelligent. Certainly not intelligent enough to act in concert and dispatch Melanie in a matter of moments.

In fact, one might ask, why does one gull throw itself suicidally at Annie's front door, stupid bird? For Hitchcock it was a way of telling the audience not to be impatient, that the birds were indeed coming after all the exposition, but it begs the question of what the gull hoped to achieve by thumping into a doorway and offing itself. At the same time it has to be remembered that the birds' behavior is strangely affected in different ways — some chickens won't eat, for instance — so a kamikaze gull may not be as strange as it sounds. In the short story, the birds are perfectly willing to kill themselves for the cause — the cause of inexplicably killing off humankind.

The Birds has been analyzed — and over-analyzed — almost as much as *Psycho*, with much debate centering on the meaning of the film. One prominent critic has theorized that the film deals with the loss of complacency, which is certainly true of Du Maurier's story, which also deals with denial and how it leaves people open to a terrible fate. Some have seen the birds as old-fashioned furies or harpies called down by the emotional state of the characters, although this interpretation doesn't seem to hold water. Hitchcock himself suggested it was an "end of the world" story and this scenario makes the most sense. There is no explanation for the bird attacks, just as there is none in Du Maurier's story (a masterpiece which, if anything, is much grimmer and more relentless than the film, with no comedy relief whatsoever). It is the coming of despair and hopelessness, mankind obliterated by the simplest and least offensive of creatures. Hitchcock and company were less interested in being profound than they were in providing a good, money-making thrill for the audience, but if there is any meaning — or at least subtext — to the *film*, the clues may be found in the main character of Melanie Daniels (neither she nor any of the other characters in the film appear in the short story). Melanie is by no means a moronic, déclassé Paris Hilton type, but she is still very much the spoiled and immature heiress. When she knocks on Annie's door, the teacher asks "Who is it?" from around the corner. "Me," says Melanie. Annie can't possibly know who "me" is but in a light-hearted way this illustrates Melanie's self-absorbed sense of self and entitlement. Later, when Cathy tells her the story of Mitch's client who shot his wife in the head six times, Melanie reacts with the same callous glee of the much younger child, who can't quite grasp the tragedy of the situation or feel empathy for the dead woman. As the film proceeds, Melanie does begin to feel empathy, to care about someone other than herself. Not the romantic figure of Mitch, but Cathy, and especially Lydia.

In the scene between Mitch and Melanie during the birthday party, Melanie reveals her bitterness over being abandoned by her mother. This, of course, means she both needs Lydia's approval — especially as she's after her son — and resents her as well, just as Lydia resents the intrusion of Melanie into her life. Both women are defensive with each other, but by the end of the film both have learned to care about one another. The loveliest shot in the film is when they both sit in the back seat of the car, about to leave the house, Lydia cradling the injured Melanie in her arms. Melanie looks up at her, vulnerable, needing her affection and concern, as Lydia looks down at her warmly, as if Melanie's another one of her children. Both women have learned to accept each other and pull together during the crisis, which, the film suggests, may only just be beginning.

Although 33 at the time, Tippi Hedren had only had a tiny bit in one film when a smitten Hitchcock signed her to a contract after seeing her in a commercial for Diet Pepsi. Hitchcock must have been extremely infatuated with the gorgeous model to cast someone so completely inexperienced in as major and difficult a film as *The Birds*. Hedren is not only the leading lady and appears in virtually every scene, but is the focus of the entire movie. That was an awful lot to put on one person's shoulders, especially someone who had yet to have a major or even minor role in a motion picture.

Hedren is actually quite good in the light romantic scenes that form much of the first half of the picture. The bedroom sequence where Hedren converses with Jessica Tandy as Lydia voices her apprehension, regrets and loneliness—clearly Tandy's scene, and she is brilliant—illustrates the difference between consummate acting ability and what could be called attractive posing. In this scene Hitchcock intelligently directs Hedren as to how to react to Tandy, down to her expressions and exactly when she looks away and where. It is a manufactured performance at this point, but it works well enough. During the scene when Melanie and Mitch talk on the dunes overlooking the birthday party, Hitchcock has Hedren turn away from Mitch and the audience when she gets emotional remembering her mother because she probably wasn't up to a sudden outburst of tears. She certainly appears to be crying when her back is turned, but when she turns around her expression is too gay and her eyes dry, which usually solicits laughter from the audience. However, Hedren is not bad in the film by any means; in fact, it's a wonder she's as good as she is. The following year she would give a genuinely creditable performance in the title role of Hitchcock's *Marnie*. Mother of actress Melanie Griffith, Hedren has acted sporadically in the 30 years following *The Birds*.

Jessica Tandy was always a superb actress and she gives another strong and intelligent performance in *The Birds*. Although Suzanne Pleshette had started out as a sexpot in steamy soap opera-like movies, she emerged a confident and strong player and is excellent as Annie Hayworth, albeit a bit too glamorous. It's hard to imagine a woman as attractive as Pleshette burying herself in Bodega Bay as she pines for a man. Pleshette's facial expressions make it clear that despite what she says to Melanie, she's still very much in love with Mitch. She's told herself that she can accept him just as a friend, but there's no doubt that she still harbors hopes of something more happening between them. Rod Taylor could be a fine actor with the right material—his performance as an astronaut whose comrades begin to drop out of existence on a classic *Twilight Zone* episode was haunting and passionate—but in *The Birds*, while competent, he merely seems stalwart and stereotypically "heroic," possibly because his role isn't as well-written as the ladies.' Once she was grown up, Veronica Cartwright appeared in a number of genre films, including *Alien* and two remakes of *Invasion of the Body Snatchers*, and here she certainly shows her acting chops in the scene when she tearfully tells Mitch and Melanie how Annie saved her life, virtually dying in her stead.

The Birds is also full of flavorful performances by some fine and familiar character actors, including Elizabeth Wilson as a peppery waitress in the diner, Ethel Griffies as the elderly bird-fancier Mrs. Bundy, and Ruth McDevitt as the slightly vague San Francisco bird shop owner. Charles McGraw, who starred in many *films noir* in the fifties, is the charter boat owner Sebastian Sholes, while Richard Deacon ("Mel Cooley" of *The Dick Van Dyke Show*) plays a neighbor of Mitch's in such a way that you're not certain if he's going to hit on Melanie, as she tries to deliver some love birds, any second or not. Doreen Lang makes an impression as the woman who complains that the diners are frightening her children with all their talk of killer birds, but clearly is much more petrified than they are. We never learn what events in her life have made this woman so excitable and neurotic even *before* the birds have attacked the town.

The Birds may not seem to hold together as well as it used to, but after forty-five years it's still a fascinating picture. The trained birds, combined with superimposed birds, or birds even drawn directly onto the celluloid, are wonderful actors. Hitchcock's use of the subjective camera, such as when Melanie sneaks away from the Brenner house after leaving the love birds for Cathy, is as adroit and compelling as ever. The considerable amount of humor in the film never quite dissipates the tension or suspense, although some of it is certainly questionable. Evan Hunter's screenplay is full of incisive characterizations that lift the movie above the level of the usual creature features (among other factors). However, Annie's speech about how Lydia is not really a "jealous, possessive woman," that she isn't afraid of losing Mitch but rather fears being abandoned, doesn't make much sense — isn't that the same thing? (Pleshette's delivery of these lines is so good that it disguises their gobbledygook nature.) Hunter is not to blame for an improbable aspect of the monkey bars sequence: when the schoolchildren sing the nonsense song as Melanie waits outside, they never laugh or giggle at the dopey lyrics, sounding instead like a well-rehearsed chorus of professional singers.

The photography by Robert Burks is outstanding. The final shot as the car drives away, comprised of 32 separate elements, is so stunning that it alone is almost worth the price of admission. Robert Boyle's production design is also first-rate. George Tomasini's editing is as skillful as ever. Although Bernard Herrmann was "sound consultant" on the film, there is no music, but rather "electronic sound production and composition" — the noises of birds — expertly provided by Oskar Sala and Remi Gassmann. Ub Iwerks from the Disney Studios helped immeasurably with the composite shots of birds and Albert Whitlock provided some excellent matte paintings.

It was hoped that *The Deadly Bees* (1967) would be an insect version of Hitchcock's *The Birds*, but this cheapie from England's Amicus, although not without merit, was never in the running. Vicki Robbins (Suzanna Leigh), a pretty pop singer, collapses during the taping of a show due to exhaustion. Her doctor sends her for a rest cure to an inn located on quiet Seagull Island. The owners of the inn, Mr. and Mrs. Hargrove (Guy Doleman, Catherine Finn), have a strained relationship, and the husband raises bees, as does a friendly old neighbor named Manfred (Frank Finlay). Mrs. Hargrove is killed by a swarm of killer bees, and other people — including Vicki — are attacked as well. Convinced that the dour Hargrove is the culprit, Vicki takes refuge at the home of Manfred — only to learn that he has bred a strain of bee that is twice as large and many times as lethal as the regular kind. Hargrove and the constable save Vicki, and Manfred dies at the stingers of his own creations.

The Deadly Bees was based on the novel *A Taste for Honey* by H. F. Heard, in which one of the characters — omitted from the film version — was a retired if unnamed Sherlock Holmes. Originally the leads for the film were to have been horror stars Christopher Lee and Boris Karloff, which certainly would have increased the box office. While Doleman and Finlay are perfectly adequate, one can only imagine the tension and fireworks that might have resulted had Lee and Karloff been retained for the film.

122

The attack bees in *The Deadly Bees* (1967) go after Catherine Finn.

The highlight of *The Deadly Bees* is the unnerving attack on Mrs. Hargrove, despite the fact that the process work showing bees swarming all around her head is poor. The sequence works because of the actress's performance, the extreme, gross close-ups of bees leaving their stingers (like tiny hypodermic needles) in human flesh, and the angry clusters of bees covering and mutilating her face. The other attack scenes are not as intense nor detailed. The film is suspenseful and fast-paced but the conclusion is too drawn-out. And we never learn the mad bee killer's motives. Jealousy over who has the better bees? The dreary island setting, with a sky that seems permanently gray, is also a plus.

Another plus is Wilfred Joseph's intelligent, unusually orchestrated musical score. Jangling and exciting, it mirrors and responds to the frenetic, agitated activity of the killer bees. Vicki is also given a song at the opening entitled "Stop the Music!" The song is amusing because it tells the highly dramatic tale of a girl who goes out for a smoke and comes back to find her boyfriend dancing with somebody else — only she reacts as if she found him in bed having sex with another woman. Vicki seems very well-adjusted for a pop star, not the neurotic, head-shaving Britney Spears type at all.

Suzanna Leigh, who also appeared in *The Lost Continent*, makes an attractive, competent heroine as Vicki. Michael Ripper is effective as the local constable and pub owner. Catherine Finn, however, walks off with the acting honors as the bitter, doomed Mrs. Hargrove. Robert Bloch and Anthony Marriot turned in a good script, and Freddie Francis' direction, although devoid of real cinematic flair, is at least well-paced and professional. There was a spate of killer bee films made for TV and cable a few years after the release of *Deadly Bees*; most of these were inspired by news of the African killer bee.

Despite the major success of *The Birds* and the comparatively minor success of *The Deadly Bees*, it wasn't until the advent of *Jaws* that filmmakers became serious about making movies with killer birds, bugs, and bats.

The last film produced by William Castle was *Bug* (1975), which Castle co-wrote with Thomas Page, the author of its source material, *The Hephaestus Plague*. An earthquake in a small town unleashes a flood of "firebugs," incendiary cockroaches, an unknown species that can burn anyone who touches them, and can set things aflame. Biology teacher James Pamiter (Bradford Dillman) studies the bugs and mates them with a common household roach. The results are winged cockroaches that have properties of the two parents, but are also different from both of them. Inexplicably, these roaches seem to have a hive mentality as well as abnormal intelligence, and they are also responsible for several deaths. Before long they're writing out Pamiter's name on the wall with their bodies, as well as the words "We Live." Horrified, Pamiter tries to destroy them, but they fly en masse into the house to attack him, setting him on fire. Pamiter falls into the crevice from which the original roaches came (and where the hybrids have set up house) and, presumably, he and the bugs are burnt up together.

The bugs are played by large South American cockroaches (as well as beetles) tricked up with outer carapaces that resemble sea shells. Ken Middleham's extreme close-up photography of the insects is good, and the scene where the bugs spell out words on the wall is clever. Model roaches were substituted for the real thing, and placed on a flat horizontal surface that was photographed to make it seem vertical.

There are several "shock" scenes in the movie, most of which involve women. A firebug clings to a telephone receiver and jumps onto a girl's ear when she answers the phone. Drawing blood, it grinds into and burns the flesh on the side of her head. Pamiter's wife (Joanna Miles) is killed when another bug climbs up her back, crawls across her neck, and sets her hair, and then her clothing (and eventually nearly the whole house) on fire. The problem with this scene is that it's hard to believe the woman wouldn't feel a roach that is nearly two inches long climbing all over her even through the material of her blouse. Near the end of the film, the wife of Pamiter's colleague drives out to the farmhouse where he's staying and runs afoul of nasty hybrid bugs, one of whom drops down from above right onto her eye. As the bug and her eye begin to sizzle, she runs about in futile panic until succumbing. The shot of the woman with the huge bug covering half of her face made for a very effective poster image for the movie.

One might think the roaches (or the filmmakers) had it in for women were it not for the movie's creepiest scene, when the hybrid roaches crawl out of their confinement and cover Pamiter in his bed as he's sleeping. Having developed a fondness for fresh meat, they proceed to chew into Pamiter's skin. The blood they draw doesn't look real, but the roaches are real enough and Bradford Dillman probably deserves a special award for having the guts to interact with moviedom's most disgusting co-stars. Dillman's performance in the film is excellent, but one suspects his revulsion as he jumps up and hurriedly pulls off the roaches is not just good acting. Patty McCormack, who played *The Bad Seed* in 1956, also has a role.

Bug has an absorbing if illogical storyline, but the film is not well-served by the usual insufficient direction of master hack Jeannot Szwarc, who betrays no style or panache with this kind of material (or anything else, in fact). The picture would have also been improved with a more traditional score instead of the irritating electronic soundtrack it has. Still, it's one of the better "killer bug" films of the seventies.

Squirm elicited some interest and praise from horror fans when it was first released in 1976. During a severe storm, the electrical tower in Fly Creek, a small town in Georgia, crashes over and sends 300,000 volts running through the ground, the wet mud acting as conductor. This has the result of driving thousands of worms from the earth, and also somehow turns them into aggressive man-eaters. Mick (Don Scardino), an antiques dealer from New York who has come to visit Geri (Patricia Pearcy), finds himself embroiled in the horror when the two discover skeletons of local residents eaten alive by the worms. When night comes the worms burst from the earth in full force and nearly devour everyone until the attack ends at daylight and everything is seemingly back to normal.

Squirm isn't bad at detailing a gross worm infestation, even if most of the worms are played by wiggling strands of rubber. There are many inserts of close-ups of actual worms with hook-like mouthparts emerging from their slimy "faces." For some reason the worms squeal like pigs. Other sound effects help add to their general creepiness. Worms pour out of a shower nozzle just above Geri at one point, and fill not only her bathtub but her entire house to a level of several feet. In a scene set in a rowboat on a lake, the worms burrow into the face of Geri's amorous friend Roger, this set to throbbing electronic "music." (The film in general would have benefited from a more traditional and exciting score.) One of the best scenes has a huge tree (upended by thousands of worms digging through the roots) smashing into Geri's living room as she, Mick and her mother and sister have dinner. Both the outdoor shot of the tree smashing down, as well as the indoor shot of it splitting the ceiling and walls over the actors' heads, are very convincing.

Despite a few okay scenes, *Squirm* is schlocky and forgettable. There's a great deal of talk and wandering around and the pace drags even at the climax. Whatever initial impression the film made, it just doesn't hold up today. Joseph Mangine's photography is professional, but director Jeff Lieberman is unable to sustain tension and interest for the film's length. Patricia Pearcy makes a very effective heroine, and Jean Sullivan (a former ballet dancer, soap star, and a theater-trained actress) makes a distinct impression as her mother, Norma. Fran Higgins is appealing as the younger sister, Alma, although she seems to be mere local talent. R.A. Dow scores as the simple-minded if sexy worm farmer who has his eyes on Geri but winds up on the worms' menu. Don Scardino isn't bad as the somewhat geeky city boy, Mick, a fellow who doesn't seem too bright. Exiting a bus on a lonely country road surrounded by miles of forest, he asks the driver where he can find a men's room. When Geri tells him about the worm farm, he assumes the worms are eaten by the locals! A peculiar aspect of the film is that everyone refers to Mick as being "from the city," which makes you assume he's from Atlanta — after all the film takes place, and was shot, in Georgia. But, no, he's from *New York* City, which makes you wonder why nobody mentions this when they speak of him.

Kingdom of the Spiders (1977) also got some respectable reviews when it was released but seems pretty mediocre today and is a cheapjack production to boot. In the small Arizona town of Valley Verde, animals disappear and livestock inexplicably become ill. Diane Ashley (Tiffany Bolling), an entomologist, reports that the cows have been pumped full of spider venom. Teaming with the local vet, "Rack" Hansen (William Shatner), she discovers huge spider hills which contain millions of aggressive (normal-sized) tarantulas. Her theory is that DDT has killed off most of the spiders' normal food supply so they are going after larger animals. Hard to kill, the spiders are responsible for several deaths before they invade a lodge where the main characters hole up, and then cause mayhem in the town itself. At the conclusion the spiders seem to have won the battle, spinning a huge silken cocoon around every building in town.

Kingdom of the Spiders proceeds at a pace charitably described as stately. Director John "Bud" Carlos betrays no particular feel for this kind of picture and there are no real moments of inventiveness or inspiration. A big problem is that the tarantulas, as ugly as they may seem to some viewers, don't really exude much menace — they're just big, fat, slow and dumb, hardly anything to work up a sweat over. It is up to the actors to try to dredge up as much excitement and sense of peril as they can. There are some harrowing moments — a pilot who sprays the spiders freaks out when they crawl all over him in the cockpit, causing him to crash; the spiders gather en masse outside the lodge and try to sort of pour their way into the building — but the big attack scene on the town is completely unconvincing.

Cardos tries to create a sequence along the lines of the big bird attack scene in *The Birds* (the one with the diner, gas pumps, phone booth, etc.) but hasn't the resources to pull it off, nor the sense to realize it wouldn't work in any case. It's one thing for diving, swooping birds to rush down and attack people, causing panic; quite another for slow, crawling, earth-bound spiders to create the same reaction, their lethal bites notwithstanding. Hence the scenes of people running about screaming, banging on the police car door to be let in, going berserk with terror, seem not only borderline comical but inexplicable. Spotting an army of tarantulas heading down the road, most people would have simply driven away. It's not that millions of tarantulas couldn't cause plenty of death and destruction, but not necessarily in the way it is presented here — Cardos just doesn't pull it off. There are never any close-ups of the spiders biting into people, so the only excitement comes when the sheriff's car crashes into the water tower and sends it toppling down on him. The tarantulas never seem to actually "attack" anyone in any case; they're just placed here and there on the set or all over the wriggling, uncomfortable extras.

There are times when the film almost works up a sense of quiet creepiness, but this doesn't reach fruition until the film is over and we see the long shot of the entire town covered in spider webs. Apparently the tarantulas have left and will come back to eat everyone at their leisure. There is no real resolution. The one memorable scene in the picture has nothing to do with spider attacks but occurs when the sheriff (David McLean) goes to tell Birch, the rancher's wife, that her husband is dead. It's an affecting moment when he pulls the woman to him and both break down in tears.

William Shatner gets by on the boyish charm and charisma that's worked for him from *Star Trek* to *Boston Legal*. Tiffany Bolling is fine as the haughty but likable entomologist, although she's not always up to her more emotional scenes. Sammy Davis Jr.'s wife, Altovise Davis, was introduced in this film as Birch Colby, and while she has her moments, she's not in the league of intense, believable Woody Strode as her husband. Lieux Dressler scores as Emma, the lodge owner, who's been carrying a torch for the sheriff for several decades, although she underplays a bit too much when she realizes the man is probably dead. The movie opens and closes with a pleasant country song, "Peaceful Valley Verde," that does little to summon up *frissons* of fear or horror. The screenplay by Richard Robinson and Alan Caillou is perhaps above average for this type of picture, but is done in by inferior direction and editing.

As for the tarantulas, they look real because they are real, but as both monsters and actors they're a complete wash-out, placing a distant second fiddle to their great big sister of *Tarantula*.

Bad-tempered cockroaches figure in the most memorable scene in *Damnation Alley* (1977), which was allegedly based on a science fiction novel by Roger Zelazny. None of the actors seem all *that* upset that nuclear war has wiped out most of the human race, but a bunch of Air Force veterans decide to drive cross country along a path they call "Damnation Alley" until they reach Albany, where they hope some tatters of civilization might remain. The fallout has not only tilted the Earth on its axis and caused crazy weather conditions — along with striking color schemes in the sky — but it's also (wouldn't you know it?) caused scorpions to grow bigger than the motorcycle ridden by Jan-Michael Vincent. Crudely superimposed onto the desert scenery, the scorpions never seem to actually occupy the same space as the actor. Ken Middleham provided some nice creepy close-ups of the scorpions' faces, however.

The crew encounter the cockroaches after first picking up Dominque Sanda (an actress who made a memorable impression in *The Garden of the Finzi-Continis*, but whose Hollywood career was badly mismanaged) in Las Vegas. The next town they arrive at is infested with a plague of large (but not giant) man-eating roaches who leave absolutely no meat on the bones once they are done snacking on any unfortunate who gets in their way. Since roaches are notoriously unreliable when it comes to taking direction, prop roaches were laid end to end on thin sheets which were then pulled along the ground to make it look as if all the roaches were heading in the same direction with single-minded purpose. Unfortunately, all this looks like is a bunch of prop roaches being pulled along on sheets.

Most of the footage in *Damnation Alley* is not taken up with malevolent bugs but with encounters with horny rednecks, storms, flash foods, and arguments between George Peppard and supposed anti-hero Jan-Michael Vincent. Under Jack Smight's utterly uninspired direction, the film never really takes off, but it has an inevitably moving conclusion (as most apocalyptic movies do) as our heroes discover that some fragment of civilization has indeed survived in Albany. Jerry Goldsmith's score does its best to add to the minimal excitement.

Based on a popular novel by Arthur Herzog, Irwin Allen's production of *The Swarm* (1978) was hotly anticipated by creature-insect fanatics who had enjoyed the book. Unfortunately, Allen modeled it on his other big budget "disaster" movies and employed the exact same formula: an all-name cast of second-tier and once-big thespians playing a variety of characters whose stories took up much of the running time even as the actors used up most of the budget. Viewers who were hoping for a kick-ass horror thriller were sorely disappointed.

Everyone on a midwestern ICBM site is found either dead or dying, and the cause is a swarm of mutated African-Brazilian killer bees whose sting is incredibly virulent. Dr. Bradford Crane (Michael Caine), an entomologist who has been tracking the bees, shows up at the base and alienates the brass — even more so when the White House puts him in charge. He assembles a team of top experts to combat the menace even as the bees gather in the nearby town of Marysvillle. Neither the military nor the scientific establishment is able to stop an attack that nearly wipes out the town nor a devastating assault on a train evacuating the survivors. The bees make their way to Houston and take over the city, until Crane comes up with the idea of using sonics to draw them together over the water where they can be safely bombed out of existence.

The attack scenes consist of slow-motion shots of victims flailing around in a mist of puffed rice. There are no close-ups of stings entering flesh as in *Deadly Bees*. Occasionally a bees-eye view will be presented by shooting through a prism. The long shots of the swarm of bees are effective, however. As presented, the bees aren't dramatic enough on their own so we get scenes of a train wreck, an explosion of a power plant, and a bit where a man wielding a flame thrower against the bees catches on fire, crashes through a window, and falls to his death like something out of Allen's *The Towering Inferno*. The sequence when the bees bring down two helicopters employs some excellent miniature work. Veteran effects man L. B. Abbott worked on the picture.

The Swarm doesn't work up enough fear or suspense but it briefly comes alive during the well-handled, chilling train wreck, and during the climax in Houston. The talky film has a good story but works better as a minor drama than as a thriller, and the more memorable scenes are quieter moments: Dr. Krim (Henry Fonda) trying a vaccine on himself in his lab and having a very convincing heart attack; Slim Pickens cradling his dead son, a soldier, in his arms; Crane confronting a general (Richard Widmark) who wants to use chemicals to kill off the bees; a teacher (Olivia de Havilland) reacting to the sight of corpses outside of the school after a massive bee invasion. Some of the subplots in Stirling Silliphant's

Killer bees and an all-star cast couldn't keep *The Swarm* (1978) from the scrap heap.

script, such as a cutesy love triangle among senior citizens which is cloyingly performed by some veteran actors, should have been scrapped.

There are the inevitable dopey moments in the picture. Crane and Dr. Anderson (Katharine Ross) are shown still standing outside during the bee attack on Marysville even after we are shown numerous shots of dead and dying victims; it makes no sense that the two wouldn't run for shelter as there's nothing they can realistically do to help anyone. When one young survivor keeps seeing an hallucination of a giant bee, Crane tries to calm him and says "there" as the bee vision disappears — but how could he know that the bee was gone when he couldn't possibly see what was only in the kid's imagination? The kids covering themselves with garbage cans as they run from the bees reminds one of *Killer Shrews*, and using sonics to draw the bees together is reminiscent of the climax of *Beginning of the End*.

The large cast does its best with the material, with Katharine Ross doing an especially nice job, and Silliphant's dialogue is often trenchant and amusing. But *The Swarm* deserved its fate of fading away into oblivion, like the bees that cause its characters so much trouble.

Like *The Swarm*, *Nightwing* (1979) was much anticipated by creature feature fans who had admired the Martin Cruz Smith source novel. The mysterious deaths of animals and people on a Native American reservation in Arizona confound Deputy Duran (Nick Mancuso) and his girlfriend, a health professional named Anne Dillon (Kathryn Harrold), among others. Crusading biologist Phillip Payne (David Warner) shows up and tells them that the problem is a swarm of 30,000–40,000 killer vampire bats who are not only vicious and voracious blood-drinkers but who carry bubonic plague. After more people are killed in a horrible mass attack, Duran, Anne and Payne enter the caves where the bats reside and try to destroy them, which the deputy does by setting fire to an oil reserve as a last resort.

During the 1970s and afterward, writers and filmmakers began to explore the world of Native Americans and their supernatural legends. Sometimes this was done with intelligence and a sense of social justice, sincerely examining the plight of a neglected minority, but other times it was merely exploitative, using "Indian" ways and life on reservations as the backdrop for the story or creating monsters supposedly drawn from native superstitions. *Nightwing* seems to be somewhere in the middle, exploring the poverty of, and condescension toward, Native Americans while also adding elements of the supernatural. The high priest (George Clutesi) of the Maskai Indians keeps showing up as a ghost after his death and is determined to let the killer bats wipe out civilization even as his nephew, Duran, tries to stop them. The supernatural aspects of the film are foolish and unconvincing, Duran's visions of his uncle much too literal, and frankly the Native American material ultimately becomes little more than a distraction from those wonderful bats.

Nightwing is one of the few creature features that seems to have improved with age. The puppet-mechanical bats by Carlo Rambaldi look very realistic and emote convincingly in some startling attack sequences. Occasionally flying black bats are simply drawn onto the film the way birds were layered onto the film in Hitchcock's classic. The bat attacks, well-edited by John C. Howard, are the highlights of the film.

The first of these occurs during a picnic, a scene that starts out as black comedy (due to the somewhat geeky quality of the victims) then turns horrifying as panic sets in and the helplessness of the people caught in the onslaught becomes obvious. Two other women are caught in the open as Anne and the men in the group manage to find safety inside their van. Both women try to get into the van but the man at the door is too petrified to open it and let them in. One woman quickly succumbs to the bats, while the other crawls beneath the vehicle for safety only to have her spine crushed when the van takes off without her. The callousness and cowardice of the men (who temporarily survive) makes the sequence that much more disturbing. The only problem with this protracted sequence is that it doesn't make sense that the bats wouldn't completely cover the bodies of their victims. They do drink blood, after all.

The second attack scene occurs when Duran, Anne and Payne are outside the cave in a mesh cage for protection. The cage has been electrified and as the bats arrive Payne gives the signal to turn on the juice. Unfortunately the switch won't work and there is a lot of harrowing business as the highly realistic bats begin to claw their way in to the cage as the trio try desperately to turn on the current. One shot of a bat flying directly into the cage has an almost 3D effect to it. The current is finally turned on just as things look hopeless for the threesome. Another suspenseful scene has Payne dangling from a rope over an underground lake with the bats on the walls all around him and trying to swing himself to safety without falling onto the rocks at the edges of the lake — all without arousing the horde of vampire bats.

If *Nightwing* works, it is because of editor John Howard and Carlo Rambaldi, not Arthur Hiller, who directed the film. Hiller moves from genre to genre, picture to picture, and leaves no directorial mark or particular stamp on any of them. If the pace meanders a bit and the film isn't quite taut enough, it is more likely Hiller's fault than Howard's. Cinematographer Charles Rosher provides sweeping vistas of the deserted plains of Nevada and New Mexico where *Nightwing* was filmed. Henry Mancini's musical score does no real damage.

The cast helps put the movie over as well. Eternally smirking Nick Mancuso makes an effective Duran, and Kathryn Harrold and David Warner are excellent support. Stephen Macht also scores as a businessman who clashes with Sheriff Duran. Warner is given the standard scene wherein he describes the formidable nature of the vampire bat which, as he says, consumes one and one half times its weight in blood. George Clutesi played a similar role of a wise old — and much more benign — Native American in *Prophecy*.

George Romero, the director of *Night of the Living Dead*, and Stephen King teamed up for the black comedy *Creepshow* (1982), a quintet of tales in the style of the old E.C. horror comic books. In the first four stories a hated old man comes back from the dead; a simple-minded farmer turns into a fungus; a husband gets diabolical revenge on his cheating spouse and her paramour; and a hen-pecked professor kills his wife via a carnivorous critter that hangs out in a crate. For our purposes the final story is the most interesting. In *They're Creeping Up On You*, E. G. Marshall stars as cruel, wealthy financier Upson Pratt, who has a thing about germs — and especially bugs. In his sterile, white, ultra-clean penthouse apartment with assorted computer consoles and an old-fashioned jukebox that plays big band tunes, some cockroaches come a-callin'. These are big South American roaches from one to three inches long. Finding the insects in his cereal, crawling up his leg, on his desk, filling up his sink, and so on, he complains to everyone he can while fielding calls from a woman whose husband he drove to suicide. Pratt eventually retreats behind the glass door of his bedroom to escape the infestation, but discovers that his mattress is virtually alive with the bugs, giving him a heart attack. The next day there isn't a single roach to be found in the penthouse. They have all holed up *inside Pratt's body* and come bursting out at the conclusion, giving the audience a gross-out moment to reckon with. An obviously fake body of Marshall was substituted for the actor for this shot, pretty much telegraphing what is to happen. Except for this last bit, the roaches pretty much behave as roaches do, if a bit more aggressively than most. With his hair sticking up on either side of his bald head like an aged Bozo, Marshall is both a comic and horrible figure, and his performance is dead-on. He and the bugs provide the viewer with *Creepshow*'s most memorable minutes. Tom Savini, responsible for the film's special makeup effects, was no fan of roaches and recalled finding himself suddenly on the other side of the sound stage after one of the little darlings got too close to him.

Fear of spiders was exploited in *Arachnophobia* (1990), which has a decent prologue and goes downhill from there. In an isolated area of the jungle, a bored, testy photographer is accompanying entomologists who hope to gather unusual, perhaps unknown, species of insect (and of course arachnids). There's a genuinely macabre scene when they spray the trees and loads of dead bugs clatter down into several pans set up on the ground to receive them. *Clunk.* One of the pans has captured something rather large. *Clunk.* There's another. And these fist-sized spiders (the size of Arnold Schwarzenegger's fist, that is) are still alive. One of them bites and kills the photographer and hides out in the wooden coffin taking his body to the victim's home town in America.

After a series of misadventures (such as being carried off by a crow which it kills), the spider winds up in the local doctor's barn, where it mates with a more common spider and unleashes from its gigantic webbing a whole slew of deadly offspring. These spiders don't seem intent on taking over the world like the ones in *Kingdom of the Spiders*. They generally only bite people when they touch them accidentally as they, say, put their foot into a slipper, or their hand on a lamp, where a spider is resting. There's the obligatory scene with a naked girl and a spider in the shower. These scenes are moderately suspenseful and vaguely amusing. Later, whole masses of arachnids invade the doctor's house, but even then they seem not to have a master plan or evil intent — they're just *there* (which for most people is bad enough). The finale has the doctor in the cellar where the mother spider has taken up residence, doing his best to stop the next generation from hatching. There's a creepy moment when the she-spider *rushes* at the doctor from across the room, but she gets impaled, and fire takes care of her babies.

In spite of a few jolts, *Arachnophobia* isn't directed with any particular finesse by Frank Marshall; it's just a light entertainment with no real shocks, horror, or intensity, a horror film that the proverbial "schoolmarm" could sit through (unless she suffers from you-know-what). The ads tried to make *Arachnophobia* out to be some wild, campy parody ("eight legs, two fangs, and an attitude") but the film is straight-faced if not very serious.

Critics approved of the movie, mostly because of its sense of humor and Jeff Daniels' amiable impersonation of the small town doctor, a likable hero who is better developed than usual. The trouble with Daniels' performance is that he's supposed to have a deadly terror of spiders himself, but when he confronts the eight-legged horrors he seems no more nervous than the rest of the cast, who don't suffer from arachnophobia. In reality, a true arachnophobe would probably be completely unable to interact in any manner with these big nasty spiders — but then the doctor couldn't get to save the day. Daniels just doesn't get across that this is a man triumphing over an affliction out of sheer desperation. John Goodman is fun as an exterminator who finds himself unable to cope with the "invasion" and Julian Sands has a nice bit as a grim if funky entomologist who comes to town to see the spiders and winds up getting killed by them.

The effects are first-rate. Spider puppets and animatronic arachnids were employed along with actual spiders, and as it's hard to tell the difference for the most part, one can assume that the spider-fakes deliver the goods in stellar fashion.

Monster movie fans were excited by the news of an upcoming creature feature entitled *Bats* (1999), but only because they thought it might be the feature film version of Jeff Rovin's wonderful novel *Vespers*, which featured two helicopter-sized bats on the loose in Manhattan. Unfortunately, *Bats* was unrelated to Rovin's book. Dr. McCabe (Bob Gunton), a very mad scientist, has inexplicably created a mutated species of bat which is extra large in size, infected with a deadly virus, more aggressive than usual, omnivorous, and able to work together to launch organized attacks on people. The bats escape from a lab and wind up in Gallup, Texas, where Sheriff Kinsey (Lou Diamond Phillips), biologist Sheila Cooper (Dina Meyer), and her assistant Jimmy (Leon) team up to put a stop to them. Finding the nest of the bats in a large cavern, the trio manages at the last moment to freeze them into submission. A single bat escapes but is squashed by a truck.

One thing the film has going for it is some interesting monsters, even if they never quite seem to be alive. The bats have a demonic, almost humanoid appearance that gives them an added creepiness; their eyes seem to blaze with wicked intelligence and they almost appear to have human chests on their large bodies with big square heads like bulldogs and a wingspan of a couple of feet. Unfortunately—unlike the bats in *Nightwing*—the puppets and animatronic bats never seem more than "good-looking" but phony props. However, the computer-generated images showing them in flight, soaring across the moon, are impressive.

Brisk editing is usually a plus in a horror film, but Glenn Garland's work is often *too* frenetic. Perhaps in an attempt to disguise the phoniness of the bats, Garland's rapid cutting often prevents the viewer from clearly seeing what's going on. A case in point is the opening scene depicting a bat attack on a young couple in a car. Everything happens so quickly that it's nearly impossible to follow the action. A subsequent attack on a laboratory is just busy and messy instead of exciting. The attack on the town itself is somewhat better, but Garland really comes through in the climax. In this excellent sequence, Cooper and Kinsey race out of the bat caverns with the bats chasing after them through tunnels and up ladders, following them as they ascend in the cage up the elevator shaft, with the desperate couple not only trying to stay alive but rushing to get out before the military can blow the whole place to smithereens. If the whole movie had been on the level of this one sequence, it might have been a contender. It's also fun to watch the bats turning on their creator and feasting on wacky scientist McCabe, who is the nuttiest doctor since Bela Lugosi in *The Devil Bat*. At least Lugosi was given a motive for creating and using his bats as assassins, but McCabe, as several critics noted, merely seems gleefully demented, creating these monstrosities simply because he *can*.

The whole film, in fact, approaches black comedy at times. Cooper and Kinsey fall through a hole in the bat cave and into a pool of bat guano. "I'm up to my waist in bat shit!" screams the sheriff. Preparing to take on the bats, the sheriff plays a recording of Montserrat Caballe singing an aria from *Lucia di Lammermoor*. While there's nothing wrong in exposing monster fans to a little culture, it makes little sense that Kinsey would choose *that* moment to play some opera. (Opera fans tend to listen to their favorite recordings when they can *concentrate* on the music, not when they're busy figuring out how to wipe out a horde of man-eating killer bats!) Dr. Cooper's assistant, Jimmy, is supposedly an educated scientist but his constant jive-talking and flamboyant jittery nature sometimes makes him seem like a kind of latter-day Stepin Fetchit—or at least Mantan Moreland.

Dina Meyer and Lou Diamond Phillips are not bad at all in the leads, although they show little reaction when they see the bodies of very young soldiers who have been killed by the bats outside their cave. Even given the emergency situation they find themselves in, it makes them seem a little inhuman. (Far too many actors feel that if a certain reaction isn't *specifically* called for in the script, they aren't required to deliver it; the more intelligent thespians deliver it anyway.) Bob Gunton plays the impossible part of zany Dr. McCabe with a certain gusto. John Logan's script is fairly predictable although it does provide some good situations, and director Louis Morneau seems to have let editor Garland do most of the work.

FIVE

Nature Turned Nasty
Part Two — Fish Stories

Publishers often make a mighty effort to turn a book they think has strong potential into a bestseller, and this was certainly the case with Peter Benchley's manuscript for *Jaws*. Even after being worked on by a battery of editors, the novel remained hopelessly mediocre, but the story intrigued and attracted filmmakers. Although it was not director Steven Spielberg's first directorial assignment, the success of *Jaws* (1975) put him on the map — and begat a whole series of films about "ordinary" sea creatures (and even land animals) relentlessly hunting humans. While *The Birds* engendered a very few copies over the years, *Jaws* practically provoked a cottage industry of "fish stories" in addition to its several sequels.

Amity Island is plagued by a series of attacks on bathers by a rogue Great White. Chief Martin Brody (Roy Scheider) wants to close the beaches but the mayor (Murray Hamilton) reminds him that tourist season is in full swing and they will lose all the "summer dollars" if they do. After Brody's own son witnesses an attack and nearly becomes a victim himself, Brody insists that they hire an expert, Quint (Robert Shaw), to hunt and destroy the Great White. Accompanied by a shark expert named Hooper (Richard Dreyfuss), the men set out in a creaky boat to tackle the 25-foot, three-ton fish, ultimately resulting in the deaths of both Quint and the mighty Great White.

The "old-fashioned" pre-computer imagery effects of *Jaws* may make it seem a bit dated to some viewers, but the mechanical shark built by Robert A. Mattey is a marvelous, superbly designed creation that is often very convincing. It is, however, pretty easy to see when a real shark has been substituted for the mechanical one, even taking into account the fact that human actors are never in the water with an actual Great White. Mattey also built the giant squid for *20000 Leagues Under the Sea*, but his shark is more memorable.

There are some wonderful scenes in *Jaws*, such was when Brody, failing to close the beaches, sits nervously trying to keep his eye on the swimmers as dozens of people, unaware of the danger, splash around in the water. There is a scary and amusing scene when two men use a holiday roast to attract the shark, and one of them nearly winds up in the Great White's stomach after it pulls apart the dock that they're standing on. Quint, who is a survivor of the U.S.S. *Indianapolis* disaster, tells a chilling story about how 1100 men on the torpedoed ship went into the water and only 316 came out, the rest eaten by sharks who picked them off one by one. (This is a true story, and is more nightmarish than anything that happens in *Jaws*. It was also made into a film years later.) And the sequence when the

The shark of *Jaws* (1975) goes on the prowl by night.

huge shark smashes at the underwater cage to get at Cooper is intense and exciting. (No one gives the obligatory lecture about how formidable the shark can be; this is demonstrated and commented upon throughout the movie. At one point Brody looks through a coffee table book with photos of victims of shark attacks and the like.)

But there are flaws in *Jaws* as well. It very much begins as a horror film, a monster movie — with the cause of isolated attacks being argued over as in many creature features — but then becomes more of an adventure movie, returning to its horror roots only in the final moments. This is when the shark behaves in an unnatural manner, going so far as to haul itself out of the water and attacking Quint and Brody in the boat. The middle section of the film is slack, with the tension undercut by the antics of Quint and Hooper comparing bite marks on their legs and the like. Even when the film finally picks up speed again, there are way too many lulls. John Williams' score doesn't help, as it often sounds like the sort of stuff you'd hear in a nature film about sea life and does nothing to create suspense during the dull bits. The ominous two-note theme became famous but the score really isn't that good.

Although the film has many similarities to previous, less acclaimed creature features, it does have better developed characters than most. The three men who go after the shark are a study in contrasts, and each is made very real to the viewer, in large part because of the convincing playing of the actors. Even the minor characters who pop up, the islanders themselves, are a flavorful and well-cast bunch. It isn't explained why Quint, a survivor of one of the worst mass shark attacks in history, would even want to go out on the water again let alone tackle a huge Great White, but in the end it seems as if the sharks have finally caught up with him. Brody is meant to be a stand-in for the audience, an everyman who is not-so-secretly petrified of the shark as most sensible people would be, and who keeps telling the others that they should get a bigger boat — again as most sensible people would suggest. This doesn't make him a weak man. What makes him a weak man is that he doesn't stand up to the mayor and put up the "No Swimming" signs; his inaction results in the horrible death of an innocent child. He is, in fact, one of the most despicable "heroes" in the movies, worse than the mayor because the mayor is an ignoramus.

The death of the boy Alex Kintner is a pivotal moment, but Spielberg doesn't give it or its repercussions enough impact. There are no scenes showing the townspeople reacting to the boy's death or sympathizing with the heartbroken mother. The scene when the mother confronts and slaps Brody isn't nearly powerful enough, with Brody's internal reaction underplayed to the point of virtual non-existence. If Brody thinks about the dead boy or wonders how he'd feel if something happened to his own son, it isn't really shown; we're just given a dinner table sequence where Brody sits and broods and his youngest son mimics his facial expressions and actions. It hints at the sheriff's moral quandary but it just isn't enough. Brody never even apologizes to Mrs. Kintner.

The townspeople, especially the mayor, seem somewhat demented. Human nature can be odious and even stupid, but their refusal to accept that they, their families, and all of the tourists with their "summer dollars" are in terrible danger is patently unrealistic. There has been at least one death per day at the teeth of the Great White, but these people *just don't get it*. The merchants of the town not only seem stupid and callous but positively inhuman. The mayor is so oily, rigid, and staggeringly moronic that he almost seems comically unreal — partly because of the unsubtle (to put it mildly) performance of Murray Hamilton. Mayor Vaughn became the prototype of many similar characters that popped up in all the *Jaws* imitations that followed.

Roy Scheider is convincing as a man who is out of his depth, but he is much too controlled in the film's final moments, acting all heroic simply because the plot calls for him to be. Robert Shaw could not have been improved upon as the crusty Quint. Richard Dreyfuss has the least defined character but is charming and capable. The film has an especially classy look because of Bill Butler's superb cinematography which takes full advantage of scenic vistas and the sweeping ocean, giving the film a handsome look in every sequence. During key sequences, Verna Fields' adroit editing is probably more responsible for these moments' effectiveness than Spielberg's otherwise smooth direction.

A strange moment in *Jaws* has one of the big fishermen who captured a shark (wrongly believed responsible for the attacks) turning to Hooper after the latter tells him it's not a Great White but a tiger shark. The fisherman says "[It's] a *what?*' in a rather effeminate manner. Moments later, however, when this same man is arguing with Hooper, he seems very gruff and "macho." It may not have been that Spielberg wanted to get a cheap laugh

The shark attacks by day in *Jaws* (1975).

(which the scene usually gets) by implying the man was stereotypically gay but simply could have thought it would be a bit of "comic relief" to have a "girly"-sounding voice inexplicably coming from such a hefty fellow, even if only momentarily.

Jaws was not the first movie to show shark attacks — Howard Hawks' adventure-drama *Tiger Shark* (1932) had some pretty raw, gruesome (if less graphic) sequences, for instance — but it was the first to exploit the public's fear of and fascination with killer sharks and their infrequent attacks upon humans. Following the lead of previous creature features in many regards, *Jaws* created its own conventions and clichés, and engendered three mostly unnecessary sequels.

In addition to three sequels, *Jaws* spawned a score of imitations, only one of which was sued out of existence by Universal — *Great White* (1982) — possibly because its ad art too closely resembled the ad campaign for *Jaws*. (The film starred James Franciscus and Vic Morrow and had a largely Italian crew.) Most producers steered clear of the fury of *Jaws* and lawyers by using other types of animals and sea creatures (even if the general tone was clearly inspired by Spielberg's movie), but there were a couple that couldn't resist using sharks as villains, changing the storyline and using a breed other than a Great White.

For instance, William Grefe's *Mako: The Jaws of Death* (1976) stars Richard Jaekel as a shark admirer who uses the title creatures to kill off anyone who dares to mistreat them.

In spite of a low budget and a pedestrian approach to the material, the film makes its mark through a clever plot, grotesque situations, and some superb underwater photography. Jennifer Bishop is quite good as a young lady who has an unusual nightclub act: she jiggles in a glass-enclosed aquarium and even uses a shark as a dancing partner. Unfortunately, said shark gets its teeth in her and sharply diminishes her odds for attaining stardom. The movie is fun in its way. *Tintorera* (1977) also avoided the pitfall of using a Great White, but the film is neither original nor compelling, the photography murky and unimaginative. Most of the film deals with a *menage à trois* between two male shark hunters and the woman they share (Susan George). They enjoy an idyllic three-way relationship until poor "Miguel" is chewed alive by a huge tiger shark. The infrequent shark attacks are gruesome, showing stuffed dummies spewing gallons of blood and lots of stringy offal. There are some amazing shots with live actors and presumably drugged sharks in the water together, but virtually every scene is handled ineptly by director Rene Cardona Jr.

Other minor productions employed a variety of sea creatures. In Harry Kerwin's *Barracuda* (aka *The Lucifer Project*, 1978), the inhabitants of a small California coastal town are the unwilling subjects of a secret government experiment in which human beings are imbued with extra aggression in order to turn them into better "combat units." A young biologist is alerted to the danger when barracudas are accidentally contaminated along with humans and begin to eat innocent swimmers. The movie has few thrills and is full of typically jerky fish-versus-people camera movements. The best bit has to do with a girl and her dog who discover that a scuba helmet lying on the beach has somebody's head in it.

The monster in Oliver Hellman's *Tentacles* (1977) appears to be an actual octopus (a normal-sized one, as opposed to the monster of *It Came from Beneath the Sea*) playing with undersized props, as well a phony mock-up or two. The problem is that the creature is given little to do in the script, which is about a large cephalopod that chomps on divers, snatches babies from the shore, and smashes boats, little of which is shown in any great or interesting detail. There's one decent night-time attack scene—which is gross and startling—in which the octopus gets its slimy tentacles around a screaming young woman who seems to be performing a ballet or achieving orgasm, or both, within its grasp, but otherwise it's a long, dull time between the sea beast's infrequent appearances. The baffling script and lethargic music defeat a perfectly workable premise. Such seasoned professionals as Shelley Winters, John Huston, Henry Fonda, and Bo Hopkins (doing his perpetual smirking James Dean impersonation) wander about as if they're in different movies.

Italian producer Dino De Laurentiis was determined to make a film that out-grossed *Jaws*, and his first attempt was the abysmal *King Kong* (1976). When that didn't do as well as he hoped, his next attempt was an actual fish—or rather mammal—story entitled *Orca* (1977), the first of the bigger budgeted *Jaws* knock-offs. Oceanologist Rachel Bedford (Charlotte Rampling) tries to dissuade fisherman Nolan (Richard Harris) from attempting to capture a killer whale. As she feared, Nolan only succeeds in accidentally killing a female orca and her baby, enraging the surviving mate. The male killer shark tracks down Nolan and his crew, killing two of them and causing havoc at the coastal town where Nolan makes his home. Nolan, who lost his wife and child to a drunk driver, feels compassion for the whale but is angered by its attacks on the innocent. He sets sail to have it out with the whale once and for all. One by one the orca picks off the rest of his crew, confronting and killing Nolan on an ice floe.

As killer whales are more intelligent than sharks and can be trained, they make more versatile performers, and the whales in *Orca* do a marvelous job. There are beautiful shots of them jumping out of the water by moonlight. If there is any problem with them, it is that despite the unnatural way the male orca behaves in the film, they are not really viewed as "monsters" the way sharks are. Despite the fact that the orca kills several people, he is never especially frightening, even after your initial sympathy for him starts to waver.

Angered by Nolan's actions, Rachel perhaps gives the orca more credit than it deserves. She later confesses that she isn't really sure if it's getting revenge because of what happened to its mate and baby. Nonsense! It's clearly doing just that, its grief — as Rachel suggests — making it almost sociopathic (if never quite as "evil" as the shark in *Jaws*). Early in the film Rachel gives one of those obligatory "this creature is the deadliest" lectures wherein she mentions that orcas can grow to forty-five feet in length (this one seems to be about twenty-five to thirty feet), weigh six tons, and in the embryonic state have hands with five fingers. And pretty big brains to boot.

There are some good sequences in the film. First there is the attack on Nolan's home, which juts out over the water on stilts. The orca attacks the stilts and the whole building begins to tip over, sending Ann (Bo Derek), a colleague of Nolan's, tumbling toward the water. Although the men try to pull her to safety, the orca bites off her leg at the knee. The climax on the ice floe, when the orca pulls itself out of the water and causes the tip where Nolan is standing to rise up in the air, is effectively handled. Orca then flips Nolan to his death. In general the movie is well-produced and fairly easy on the eyes.

Unfortunately *Orca* is also a bit too dull and talky. The premise is interesting, as are some of the characters, but the movie meanders instead of generating tension. Michael Anderson's direction and the editing are not up to par, and the action scenes — not always as well executed as they could have been — seem to exist in a vacuum. Rachel's narration also serves to slow the film's pace. Ennio Morricone's music, languid, majestic, and just a bit sappy, is no help.

Richard Harris is not the perfect choice for Nolan, but he isn't bad in the film. Charlotte Rampling has beautiful eyes and a glacial expression that makes it seem as if all warmth has been sucked right out of her; she's competent if no more. Keenan Wynn is a welcome presence as another colleague of Nolan's who becomes an early victim of the orca's teeth. While attractive, Bo Derek certainly does not in any way look like she would become an international sex symbol two years later when she starred in Blake Edwards' *10*. She has little to do in *Orca* but is more than adequate.

Piranha (1978) got a lot of attention and praise from critics and fans when it was first released but it's another creature feature that hasn't stood the test of time. Often described as a "spoof," in some ways it's really just another rip-off. A skip trace investigator named Maggie McKeown (Heather Menzies) encounters a gruff, antisocial, divorced man named Paul Grogan (Bradford Dillman) while looking for two missing teenagers. The pair come upon an abandoned Army research station where the two teens took a dip. Draining the pool to find their bodies, Maggie unwittingly unleashes a horde of mutated, super-dangerous piranha into the nearby river. She and Grogan try to get authorities to warn everyone about the killer fish, but the piranha attack a summer camp and a tacky resort on grand opening day. Grogan destroys the fish by unleashing poison from a shuttered underwater refinery.

The fish are portrayed by cut-outs streaming along in the water, or by puppet fish seen in close-up biting into victims in a frenzied flurry of blood and movement. The shots are very quick, giving the audience no chance to get a really good look at the piranha. We also see prop fish chewing on rubber limbs upon which are strips of fake flesh and dyed bloody patches. The quick editing and eerie vibrating noises on the soundtrack help to make all of these scenes reasonably effective. A more interesting effect is a tiny kind of lizard-man, stop-motion-animated by Phil Tippett, which is seen briefly in the Army laboratory. The special makeup effects were supervised by Rob Bottin.

In one memorable sequence, the fish nibble at the ropes tying Grogan's raft together as he, Maggie and a young boy desperately try to reach land before the logs come apart and they're all dumped among those hungry piranha. The climax, when Grogan holds his breath and tries to unleash the poison in the underwater control room before the piranha can make short work of him, is also quite suspenseful. Then there's the bit with a water skier who sees a gruesome corpse in the water and signals the boat driver to slow down, only to realize that the last thing he wants to do is come to a stop in the water. He desperately shouts

One of the killer fish in *Piranha* (1978) nibbles on a victim.

out to "go faster!" before the fish can get him. Guilty over having created the piranha, Dr. Hoak (Kevin McCarthy) sacrifices his life in an attempt to save the aforementioned boy whose father was just eaten by the voracious fish.

Despite all of the above, *Piranha* is a bit boring and the killer fish are off-screen for too much of the time. As in *Jaws* and so many other *Jaws* imitations, the owners of the resort refuse to postpone opening day, etc., etc., against all logic, never considering that lawsuits resulting from death and injury to guests will cause much more financial ruin (not to mention bad publicity) than closing down for a few days. The illogic persists in such moments as when a piranha, for no good reason (except for the victim's unlikable charac-ter), jumps out of the water to attach itself to the face of the unpleasant camp owner (Paul Bartel). Grogan's little girl Suzie (Shannon Collins) summons up her courage to go onto the water in a boat when the fish attack the summer camp, but she rescues two grown-up counselors instead of her fellow youngsters.

Then there's the question of why the Army abandoned the base where the fish were mutated and left all of the animals behind in the first place, and the bigger question of why the piranha simply didn't eat each other long ago. Dr. Hoak remains in the lab, yes, but everything seems shuttered and dusty and he seems too batty to be left in charge of any-thing. *Piranha*, like many films of the period, has an anti-military stance which (while not necessarily without some foundation) stretches credulity at times.

Piranha was helmed by Joe Dante, who (along with Mark Goldblatt) makes a better editor than director. Like the summer camp attack, the attack on the resort is busy and fre-netic but hardly entertaining, except perhaps for the moment when the callous Colonel Wax-man (Bruce Gordon) falls into the drink and gets devoured. A clip from *Monster That Challenged the World* only reminds the viewer of a much more entertaining picture. Pino Donaggio, who wrote some memorable scores for Brian De Palma films, doesn't turn in one of his better jobs, although the music is still too good for Dante's movie.

John Sayles' script has some interesting aspects although it never really breaks free from formula. Taking a cue from *Jaws* and expanding upon it, its attack-on-children scenes are disturbing and repellent. Critic Andrew Sarris once theorized that films with evil tots like *The Omen* were mere expressions of child hatred, and one has to wonder about movies like *Piranha*, which present dozens of screaming, injured and dying children for our "pleasure." These scenes in *Piranha* are much uglier and much less artful than anything in *The Birds*.

Sayles does at least offer a twist on the old scene where the heroine tries to seduce a guard, in this case an Army sentry, in order to escape from a jail cell. "What if he's gay?" Maggie asks Grogan. "Then I'll do it," Grogan retorts. Scenes like this rarely deal with the fact that the jailer could be gay, much less that there could be gays in the military. The sen-try is played by John Sayles himself in a cameo.

Bradford Dillman is excellent as Grogan, maintaining a light touch without descend-ing into parody or making fun of the proceedings. Heather Menzies plays it a bit too cutesy at times, but she isn't bad. Dick Miller delights as the unsavory Buck Gardner, who owns the resort, and Barbara Steele classes up the production a bit in her turn as the sinister Dr. Menger, an old colleague and lover of Hoak's. (The aforementioned little animated lizard man, crawling about the lab early in the picture, was to have made a re-entry right after

Barbara Steele intones "There's nothing left to fear"—and he would have been sixty feet tall. Unfortunately, the low-budget precluded what would have been a marvelous closing sequence.) As Hoak, McCarthy offers a good performance, but Paul Bartel proves that he's no real actor in the role of unpleasant Mr. Dumont. Keenan Wynn is fine in his second "killer fish" story after *Orca*.

The original lead of *Piranha* was to have been Eric Braeden, who decided to bow out. He later became the star of the popular soap opera *The Young and the Restless*, on which he's been starring as the ruthless "Victor Newman" ever since. The actress who plays his TV wife Nikki, Melody Thomas-Scott, appears in *Piranha* as a counselor named Laura. Braeden can still be seen in long shots during the *Piranha* climax.

In real life, piranha really don't strip a man down to a skeleton in seconds (as happened in *You Only Live Twice* and other films), and even the fish in *Piranha* are not quite so voracious. Since the fish are mutated they are much more aggressive—and hungry—than real piranha. In any case, piranha, like sharks, continue to maintain a certain fascination over the public. After the inevitable sequel in 1983, *Piranha* was remade for cable in 1996 with William Katt (of *Carrie*) in the lead, and yet another remake (with *prehistoric* piranha) is in production as of this writing and may be released in 2008.

Piranha was followed by *Piranha 2: The Spawning*, a 1983 Italian-American co-production directed by James Cameron, later to win acclaim for his work on *The Terminator*, *Aliens* and *Titanic*. In this sequel, four canisters of fertile piranha eggs accidentally sink into the sea near a shipwreck off the shore of a sprawling Caribbean resort. Only three of these canisters are recovered. The death of one of her students alerts diving instructor Anne (Tricia O'Neil), her estranged cop-husband Steven (Lance Henricksen), and a make-out artist named Tyler Sherman (Steve Marachuk) to the danger. Tyler turns out actually to be a biochemist who worked on the original project that created the fish in *Piranha*. He tells Anne that these new piranha fish have been genetically combined with both flying fish and grunions (fish that can walk on land) in order to make them the ultimate weapon. Now it's almost time for the first full moon after spring equinox, when the grunions (as well as the piranha-grunions in that fourth unrecovered canister) will come ashore at night to find mates and spawn. Tyler wants to avoid the wholesale slaughter that will inevitably result. Naturally the resort owner balks at the idea of curtailing all underwater activities for the guests' safety and fires Anne when she suggests it.

Aside from a couple of brief isolated attack scenes, the first half-hour of *Piranha 2* is tedious, detailing the activities of a rather grotesque collection of guests whose antics are meant to be humorous but are merely silly. Eventually the picture manages to work up some suspense and chills, beginning with the scene when Anne takes an unsuspecting Tyler to the morgue to get a close-up look at the dead diving student. They have not been granted permission to see the corpse, and are chased out of the building by the Jamaican cleaning woman. As the woman starts to push the dead body back into the refrigerator, a flying piranha fish suddenly jumps out of the butchered messy mass of the dead man's raw, half-eaten stomach, bites her on the neck with such force that she crashes into the opposite wall, and then flings itself out of the window and into the darkness. These flying piranhas—clever rubber models with flapping wings that the camera wisely never dwells on for too long—

are about the size of cats, with big mouths and rows of pointed teeth. The sound effects cooked up for the fish — sort of the noises one would imagine a wet, fishy bat would make — make them seem even more ferocious. The same can't be said for the utterly bland musical accompaniment throughout the picture.

Another darkly amusing scene occurs when the hotel guests wait en masse on the beach at night to see the cute little grunions come ashore to spawn. Whoever catches the most of these adorable fish will win a prize. "Let's go get 'em!" shouts an unctuous master of ceremonies, completely unaware that they are about to be visited by a plague of flying, walking piranhas that will do whatever "getting" there is to be done. However, the mass attack scene that follows is rather brief and disappointing, especially after all the lip-smacking build-up. (Perhaps movies such as this, with mass victims so ripe for the slaughter going blindly to their fate, appeal to viewers because of the basic repressed contempt for humanity that virtually everyone shares.) The ending of the film, with Anne and Steven going underwater to plant charges that will kill the fish, is too similar to the ending of the first *Piranha*. But *Piranha 2: The Spawning*, in spite of slow stretches, is entertaining. It contains a lot of cute, fun ideas and macabre sequences that easily make it superior to most of the other evil fish-marine monster films made during the same period.

This includes Anthony Dawson's *Killer Fish* (1979) in which crook James Franciscus stocks a Brazilian body of water with deadly piranha because he's concealed diamonds in the bottom of it and doesn't want any of his associates stealing them before he's ready to get his share. There are plenty of other complications — explosions, typhoons, boat wrecks — and a party of models accompanied by a 300-pound male photographer who was born (in this film's mindset) to become an eventual victim of the nibbling, voracious fish. That and other attack scenes aren't badly handled, but, excluding Karen Black, the second-rate actors (Gary Collins, Lee Majors, Margaux Hemingway) don't lend the production much veracity. Marisa Berenson at least exhibits a nice personality and has natural ease in front of the camera (if not in front of those piranhas).

John Sayles, who wrote the script for *Piranha*, also did the honors for *Alligator* (1980). In a prologue, Marisa, a little girl, has her pet alligator flushed down the toilet by her mean father. Presumably this pet grows into a 30- to 40-foot giant that inhabits the sewers of Chicago and begins munching on people. The size is the result of chemicals dumped into the sewer system by Slade Pharmaceuticals. Marisa is now a grown-up alligator specialist (played by Robin Riker), and she teams up with a rough-hewn cop, David Madison (Robert Forster), to track down and destroy the beast, which they do with explosives after much death and mayhem.

The effects throughout *Alligator* are not very impressive. A real alligator is placed among smaller props such as automobiles to make it look much larger than it is. A full-scale mechanical alligator is used for scenes when it munches on and swallows up assorted actors. Generally this phony gator is seen in long-shot or in very quick cuts. The whole production has a cheapjack quality to it.

In its treatment of children, *Alligator* is even more vile than *Piranha*. One little boy helplessly witnesses a cop being torn apart by the gator. In a later scene an even younger boy is forced to "walk the plank" over his swimming pool by an older boy, both of whom are unaware that the gator has taken up residence at the bottom of the pool. In the next second, the terrified child falls in the water and is bloodily devoured by the monster as his parents, presumably, watch. *Alligator* is typical of many modern horror films in which very ugly sequences are interspersed with light ones or moments of black comedy. The light tone of the film is in direct contrast to such disturbing moments as when a cop is pulled out of the water and is shown to be missing the bottom half of his legs.

The best scene is the tense climax in which Madison leaves a time bomb underground with the gator, then discovers that someone has parked a car over his manhole exit, trapping him with both gator and bomb; Marisa tries desperately to get the woman behind the wheel to finally move her car. It also has to be said that Great Macho Hunter Colonel Brock (a dramatically effective Henry Silva) has a notable exit as he's slowly, munch by munch, pulled down whole into the gullet of the monster as he wriggles and screams in pain and terror. This, of course, reminds one of Robert Shaw's death in *Jaws*, which *Alligator* apes to a great extent.

The "big" scene is when the gator shows up at the wedding of pharmaceutical king Slade's (Dean Jagger) daughter to the man who runs illegal tests on animals for him. A politically incorrect gator, the creature eats the mayor, bashes in the roof of Slade's car with his tail, crushing him, but also swallows up a screaming waitress and other innocents. The whole sequence is entirely forgettable and doesn't even make any kind of satirical statement.

Alligator holds the attention and moves fast under the helm of Lewis Teague, but is ultimately mediocre. John Sayles' highly derivative screenplay makes an attempt to present likable three-dimensional characters and this may be one of the reasons why many critics severely over-praised the film. (Sayles also wrote and directed "serious" films so it was witlessly believed that he, therefore, could write a "better" monster movie. Not so.). Robert Forster is excellent as the smirking, world-weary Madison although the references to his receding hairline seem awkwardly thrown in to give him some suspect vulnerability. (A love scene with Robin Riker reveals that Forster simply isn't hirsute enough to be actually suffering from male pattern baldness, which is caused by an excess of testosterone that makes the body hairy if not the head.) Madison has a nightmare about the gator and wakes up to find himself watching a clip from *The Lost World* (1960), in which a lizard with a bib is roaring at the audience. Like most monsters in these movies, the gator leaves behind many body parts, even though most predators rarely leave anything behind—why should they?

Riker is appealing and competent as Marisa even if she doesn't quite make a strong enough impression. As Police Chief Clark, the grizzled, gravelly voiced Michael Gazzo comes off exactly as he does in every other role he's played, be it good guy or bad—others can call it "acting" if they wish. Comedian Jack Carter, playing the mayor, proves that he is no actor at all. Sidney Lassick is properly repugnant as the slimy pet shop owner who steals people's pets and sells them to Slade's future son-in-law; also properly, he becomes lunch for the gator. Perry Lang is fine as the cocky young cop who volunteers to search for the gator with Madison and is killed, giving the guilt-wracked Madison the impetus to go on fighting the monster even after he's kicked off the force (for making waves with Slade, who is a close friend of the mayor's).

The appearance of Bart Braverman, who is on the money as an insolent reporter who also winds up as a blue plate special, is notable because Braverman—under the name Bart

Bradley — appeared as the little boy who finds the cylinder that contains the Ymir (or Venusian monster) in *20 Million Miles to Earth* (1957). He also played Guiseppe in the "Lucy Gets Homesick in Italy" episode of *I Love Lucy* the previous year.

Other gator "epics" include *The Great Alligator* (1981) and *Crocodile* (1981). Despite its title, the former concerns a great beast in a river teaming with *crocodiles* that harasses the crew and guests at an isolated resort even as they must contend with an annoying local uprising. Sergio Martino's film (shown only on TV in the United States), a dubbed Italian production starring Barbara Bach and a hapless Mel Ferrer, is very busy and reasonably entertaining. The special effects are downright lousy, but there are tense, gruesome moments and some suspense in the final quarter. *Crocodile* is a Thailand import packaged for American shores by schlock producer Herman Cohen. It features a huge plaster-of-Paris-type title monster that snacks on cattle and can carry whole families away in its jaws.

Deep Blue Sea (1999) was one of the best — if not *the* best—of the films inspired by *Jaws*. Dr. Susan McAllister (Saffron Burrows) has determined that shark brains contain a protein that can stimulate human brain cells and possibly provide a cure for Alzheimer's, which affects 200,000 people nationally per year. She arrives at Aquatica, a floating undersea research station where the sharks are kept, with Russell Franklin (Samuel L. Jackson), who is there to investigate the results of her research. It turns out that Susan has illegally used gene therapy to increase the sharks' brain mass so that they can provide more protein. Unfortunately, this has the side effect of making the sharks much smarter. Before long, everyone at the station is fighting for their lives against three 8000 lb., 45-foot-long Mako sharks. The sharks are destroyed one by one but only shark expert Carter (Thomas Jane) and "Preach" the cook (LL Cool J) survive.

The deadly sharks were brought to life (by a huge number of technicians) via computer animation, animatronics, and mechanical sharks that interact credibly with the live-action actors. There are shots of real sharks as well. Although large, the Makos never appear to be 45 feet long, however. The miniatures of Aquatica are expertly constructed, and all of the pyrotechnics, such as when a helicopter crashes into a building on the surface and explodes, are highly convincing. Other effects, such as when a huge underwater window breaks and lets in tons of water, are all first-rate.

The effects crew decided to go a little over the top when depicting the carnage inflicted on the assorted victims of the monsters. The characters are not just carried off but torn apart, savagely dismembered, before being stuffed into the Makos' mouths. It was decided that they would make the deaths gruesome enough to please the average "frat boy." However, the film is good enough that it doesn't have to rely on extreme gore to be entertaining. In any case, these mutilations are usually shown in long shot.

When a researcher loses an arm at the jaws of a supposedly tranquilized Mako, there begins a series of very exciting sequences. First a copter tries to lift the injured man, secured to a cot, from the surface of Aquatica, but a storm has come up and there are terrible winds and choppy waves. The copter crashes and the injured man winds up in the drink, where one of the Makos grabs him in its teeth and pitches him at the aforementioned underwater window. The scene when the glass slowly begins to crack and then the water pours in is impressive, but perhaps isn't as exploited for maximum suspense as much as it could have been.

Hyper-intelligent sharks with enlarged brains are the threat in *Deep Blue Sea* (1995) with Thomas Jane.

The death of Russell Franklin offers a quick moment of shock and surprise. The imposing Franklin has just made a speech telling the panicky researchers that they must pull together and they'll all survive, when a Mako jumps out of the pool behind him and grabs him in its teeth. A second later, Franklin, the natural leader, is *gone*. There is also an excellent sequence in an elevator shaft, with fireballs dropping down on the cast from above, as the water rises in the shaft below them, with the sharks not far behind. One shark grabs up a woman whole in its mouth. The stunts and action in the film are all well-handled, although director Renny Harlin injudiciously uses slow motion on occasion. It must be said, however, that the pace of the film rarely flags.

The script provides few if any memorable or well-realized characters. While they may make more of an impression in other films, the cast members all seem to be trading on personality instead of exhibiting any great acting ability. This seems especially true of Michael Rapaport (as "Scoggs") and rap singer LL Cool J, who does not seem to be an actor at all. LL Cool J provides the number "My Hat Is Like a Shark's Fin" that plays over the closing credits. The song is snappy enough, but you probably won't want to hear it more than once. Trevor Rabin's musical score makes no impression at all.

Thomas Jane, who appeared in several independent productions before getting a big Hollywood break in this film, is suitably heroic, but seems a trifle miscast, his swagger too artificial. At the end when Jane and LL Cool J are the only ones left alive, they both act a bit lackadaisical considering the events that have just transpired, and the deaths of so many friends and colleagues. Jane's (or a stunt double's) two rides on the backs of the Makos are thrilling, however.

Deep Blue Sea is entertaining, and has few lulls (unlike *Jaws*), and its premise is a novel variation on the killer shark formula. It is also a bit depressing, considering the high body count and the utter failure of Dr. McAllister's noble if ill-advised experiment.

If anyone were to wonder if it were possible to make a dull movie about a 60-foot prehistoric shark they need only sit through *Megalodon* (2004). Most of the movie takes place on and beneath an off-shore oil rig called the Colossus, which plans to drill deeper than ever before, concerning environmentalists. But there are other things to worry about besides seismic reactions. First the crew unearths a kind of prehistoric cod that munches on the hand of one of the workers (Steve Scionti). Then a giant prehistoric shark called a Megalodon — supposedly extinct for 65 million years — appears and begins to kill off more of the crew. Ultimately one of the men (Al Sapienza) sacrifices himself in order to blow the monster in half. An epilogue shows the pretty reporter (Leighanne Littrell) who covered these events relaxing in a yacht off the coast of France. Another giant shark unaccountably swims under her boat. *Fade out.* Few in the audience were hoping for a sequel, however.

The shame about *Megalodon* is that its production values are pretty good and the capable, professional and attractive cast is much better than the movie deserves. The special computer effects are very uneven, unfortunately. There's a school of fleeing "cod" that looks quite good, and the shark looks fairly realistic when it chases after Ross at the not-so-thrilling climax. On other occasions the megalodon looks about as real as a cartoon shark in a computer game. And it doesn't appear often enough to satisfy most monster fans. In fact, the megalodon doesn't even show up until 53 minutes into an 80-minute running time. Most of the footage has the cast talking, talking and talking. The professionalism of the assorted actors help hold the attention but after awhile it's pretty clear this is a film that should have gone direct to the Sci Fi Channel. There's hardly a thrill in the movie. The actors deserved better. Hell, the shark deserved better.

Gary J. Turnicliffe (who also co-scripted) and Pat Corbett move things along at a fairly brisk pace, but there's simply not enough shark action on screen. The musical score does very little for the movie although the music that plays over the closing credits is pretty snappy. The environmentalist who briefly appears is called "Robert Armstrong" and there's a reference to an unseen character named "Carl Denham." The aforementioned Sapienza, Scionti and Littrell (she has a nice moment reacting to the death of her photographer) all acquit themselves very nicely, as do Robin Sachs (as the CEO of the company that owns Colossus) and Red Belford (as Jake the photographer), among others.

Some years before the film came out, Doubleday published a novel by Steve Alten entitled *Meg* about a giant prehistoric shark, promoting it heavily because it had been pre-sold to the movies. The film version of the indifferently written *Meg* never materialized (as of this writing, the film is due to be released in 2008), although its storyline was more exciting than the one used for *Megalodon*, which used an original screenplay. The Sci Fi Channel showed a film entitled *Shark Hunter 3: Megalodon* (2002), which was also much more entertaining than this *Megalodon*, its shark carrying away whole boat-loads of people in its humongous maw.

Six

Nature Turned Nasty
Part Three — Day of the Animals

In their relentless pursuit of the almighty dollar by way of *Jaws*-like creature features, producers may have exhausted every sea beast known to man, as well as all the known insects, arachnids, and flying creatures, but there were lots of land animals left to demonize. One of the earliest nature-gone-amok thrillers (that didn't features bugs or sea creatures), made long before the *Jaws* craze, was actually a cheap but curious item entitled *The Beast with a Million Eyes* (1955) which looks as if it were shot in about two or three days on a minuscule budget.

Allan Kelley (Paul Birch) is a rancher who's fallen on hard times. This has put an added strain on his marriage to unhappy, frustrated Carol (Lorna Thayer), who takes out her misery on their teenaged daughter Sandy (Dona Cole) and mute, simple-minded handyman (Leonard Tarver). Their domestic problems become secondary, however, when a spaceship bearing a hostile alien descends on their town and the malevolent unseen presence takes over the minds of various animals. Birds, cows, chickens, and dogs begin attacking people and Carol is forced to take an ax to the family pet. The family and the sheriff (Dick Sargent) track the alien to its spaceship in the desert and defeat it with the power of their love. Transforming his consciousness into a lowly mouse, the alien is snatched up by a hungry eagle in what the others see as an act of divine intervention.

The Beast with a Million Eyes holds the attention and has an intriguing premise. It presents bird attack scenes years before *The Birds*, although *Beast* is in no way in the league of Hitchcock's film and the bird scenes are unmemorable. The birds used in the film are blackbirds "led" by a much larger crow. The birds are simply filmed flying in one direction, generally toward the camera — supposedly heading toward the actors — as the latter run for safety. Also, nature goes "berserk" only because an alien intelligence is directing them to. There isn't much of an "invasion," but the alien tells the humans that it is only one of many advance scouts looking for a planet they can conquer.

Paul Blaisdell's effects are as cheap and inventive as his work in other low-budget movies. The spaceship looks like a big coffee urn with different spouts, a revolving head piece and flashing lights all over it. The alien — or rather the creature that the alien has used to pilot its spaceship (it has no material form of its own) — is a silly "fearsome" puppet with two big fangs and eyes, a human-type nose, and webbed arms. The effect of the

The Beast with a Million Eyes (1955; aka *The Beast with 1,000,000 Eyes*) featured a tiny puppet alien that didn't appear until the very end of the film.

alien preparing to "attack" our world in the prologue consists of a shot of rippling water overlaid over a globe and an eyeball.

Some of the attack scenes work better than others. The sequence when the bull (although referred to as a cow by the cast, it has a pair of horns) goes after Carol is well-shot and edited. The dog attack scene doesn't work well because the German Shepherd, despite close ups of it snarling at the camera, just looks like a big puppy running around hoping to find someone to play with. The "crazy animal revolution," as Carol puts it, also causes the chickens in the coop to go on the warpath although they merely jump and squawk as the actors react in horror. Most of these scenes are presented in quick cuts that help to disguise that there really isn't that much going on.

The script by Tom Filer tries to present real people in an extraordinary situation and almost succeeds, helped by some good actors. Filer provides some decent dialogue, such as when the mother says of her daughter: "Sometimes when I see her so young and pretty, with all the years ahead of her, years I missed — yes, sometimes I think I do hate her." The backdrop of a family in crisis gives the film an added strength, although in no stretch of the imagination could it be called a strong domestic drama. And there's way too much talk at the climax. A strange aspect of the screenplay is the way it treats the handyman, who is called "him" throughout most of the movie because, as the daughter puts it, "nobody knows his name." Yet Allan clearly calls the man "Karl" just before he dies. A moment later he tells his wife and daughter that Karl was in his unit in World War II and suffered brain damage due to a bad decision made by Allen; ever since he's felt responsible for him. Yet he lets his family call the poor guy "him" instead of his name?

Most of the actors give solid performances. Laid-back Paul Birch is contrasted well with the much more intense Lorna Thayer as his wife. Fifteen years later Thayer would play the impatient waitress dealing with Jack Nicholson in the famous "Chicken salad sandwich" scene in *Five Easy Pieces*. Leonard Tarver manages to make an impression without saying a word. Richard Sargent, the second "Darren Stevens" on TV's *Bewitched*, is competent as the local sheriff and Sandy's boyfriend. Dona Cole, who plays Sandy, is an actress best described as bizarre. Although playing a nubile teenager, she reads all of her lines as if she were a cloying eight-year-old, almost coming off like a cartoon character *à la* Rocket J. Squirrel. *Beast* would be the last of two movie appearances for her.

The "music" by John Bickford seems to consist of various classical themes used in an inappropriate manner. One minute you'll hear the "Magic Fire" music by Wagner, then a riff from Tchaikovsky. There are some good locations, such as a grove with rows of eucalyptus trees. Producer-director David Kramarsky keeps the action moving.

Eye of the Cat (1969), although more of a psychosexual suspense thriller than a creature feature, could be looked at as a fascinating variation of the killer cat picture. In this a hairdresser named Kassia (Gayle Hunnicutt) teams up with a young reprobate, Wylie (Michael Sarrazin), to get the latter into his rich Aunt Danielle's (Eleanor Parker) will. Although the woman suffers from serious lung disease and is on her way out, Kassia has no problem in hurrying her along. A bigger problem is that Wylie suffers from a morbid fear of cats ever since one crawled into his crib, and his aunt's San Francisco mansion is now home to about a hundred of the furry critters. When the overly devoted aunt learns of his phobia, she gets rid of the cats but one of them makes it way back and interferes when it comes time to turn off the old dame's air supply, resulting in Kassia's death. It turns out that Kassia was actually scheming with Wylie's younger brother Luke (Tim Henry) to not only murder Danielle but Wylie as well, so the twosome could live happily off of Danielle's money.

Some critics complained, who on earth could be scared of a bunch of pretty pussycats? (Although the one that sneaks into the crib in a flashback is a sinister black cat, the ones in Danielle's home are all adorable light-colored tabbies.) But director David Lowell Rich is able to take us into Wylie's mind and show us the effect these pretty cats have on *him*, which is more to the point. The only cat that acts strangely is the one that figures in the climax. As Kassia tries to shut off the valve on Danielle's oxygen tent, the cat jumps forward and scratches at her arm, hissing at her and waving its outstretched paw in her face as a warning. Later the cat follows Kassia around the house and "corners" her in the hothouse, where the woman climbs a ladder to get away from the snarling creature. The cat follows her up the rungs and Kassia falls to her death. The only problem with this sequence — aside from the cat's inexplicable behavior, a nature-gone-wild (or at least supernatural) occurrence that seems to come out of nowhere — is that one can easily imagine a cold, hard-bitten dame like Kassia simply giving the creature a good kick to send it flying; it was never established that she has any particular fear of cats. It is also true that the screenplay by Joseph Stefano, which is otherwise quite effective, never introduces any kind of psychic bond between Danielle and any of her cats. The cat simply does what it does to add a touch of irony to the proceedings, particularly as it follows that Wylie was apparently faking his phobia all along (in a very confusing and unconvincing denouement that almost puts the kibosh on everything that came before).

One has to ask, if Wylie was faking, then why did he have such trouble rescuing his aunt when her wheelchair shorted out simply because a cat jumped into her lap? (Rich makes the most of these scenes, showing Sarrazin frigid with fear and unable to approach the aunt until sheer nerve pushes him ahead.) This is by far the best sequence in the movie. Wylie tries to save Danielle as her wheelchair plunges down a steep incline towards the roadway below, but every time he does the cat gets in the way and he's forced to retreat. His brother eventually comes to the rescue. The coda shows the wheelchair being smashed by a truck, a chilling reminder of what probably would have happened to Danielle had she not been rescued. Due to sharp acting and superior editing, the tension is sustained for several minutes.

Trained by Ray Berwick of *The Birds* fame, the "killer" cat Tullia is a top performer but she's matched by some of the humans. Eleanor Parker is in the same airy, breathless mode as in *The Naked Jungle*, but in this case it's perfectly appropriate and she etches an interesting portrait as the head of a highly dysfunctional family. Michael Sarrazin is on occasion a little too "cute" and self-conscious, but he's generally very good as he wrestles with his (alleged) ailurophobia and never gives away that he's not *quite* the bad guy he's pretending to be. Gayle Hunnicutt does her best with an under-written "femme fatale" part and Tim Henry plays Luke with an amiable blandness that helps to disguise the twist ending, although Luke's apparent lack of interest in all the loot should have been a giveaway.

Eye of the Cat has some strong dialogue, as well as a great premise and situations, but none of the characters are completely well-developed and none of them are remotely likable. The film moves at a very snappy pace, has a nice score by Lalo Schifrin, and is genuinely entertaining, but when all is said and done it's just so much kitty litter.

Busy character actor Marc Lawrence, who acted practically up to the day of his death at 95, helmed the film *Daddy's Deadly Darling*, starring his daughter Toni Lawrence, in 1972. The film was re-released under the title *Pigs*, probably in an attempt to cash in on the then-current killer animal craze. Lynn (Toni Lawrence) is raped by her father and stabs him to death. She escapes from a mental institution by dressing up as a nurse, and winds up working for Zambrini (Marc Lawrence), who feeds dead people to his pigs. Lynn helps him raise the body count by castrating and slashing a man she beds, as well as another man who comes looking for her. She eventually kills Zambrini and feeds him to his pigs, then plants some of her clothing around so that the sheriff (Jesse Vint) will also think she was eaten by the swine. In truth she has driven off to a new life — or death. Picking up a hitchhiker, she tells him that he reminds her of her father.

Throughout the movie there are lots of shots of those pigs squealing, eating, rolling in the dirt, doing whatever pigs do, but the hoped-for Rampage of the Pigs never materializes. You would think it would have occurred to Lawrence, who also wrote the screenplay under the pseudonym F. A. Foss, that a climactic scene of the flesh-hungry sows tearing up the town and its citizenry would have appealed to the audience. Instead we get a half-baked psychosexual thriller that provides little insight into what makes these people tick. The murder scenes are quickly edited but done with little finesse, and in general Lawrence's direction has little style or inspiration. It all comes off like a vanity project for him and his daughter, both of whom give solid, professional performances (Toni had a brief career after this film), as do others in the cast. A particularly vivid performer is Katharine Ross, not to be confused with the actress of the same name who appeared in *Butch Cassidy and the Sundance Kid* and *The Graduate*. This Ross is perhaps a better actress and makes the most of her scenes as the slightly dotty Miss Macy, who lives next door to Zambrini and has a strong idea of what he's up to.

The film seems to have been shot at different times, possibly months apart. The production values of the opening scenes — the rape and institution — are bottom of the barrel. Things improve a bit once Lynn winds up in the country with the pigs, although many scenes are under-lit to the point of eyestrain. This at least provides some atmosphere-by-default. Lawrence also directed *Nightmare in the Sun* in 1965. Rumor has it that the pigs of *Pigs* all applied for the lead role in *Babe* but were turned down for being too old or too hammy. In any case, they are well cast in Lawrence's forgettable opus.

Although *Frogs* (1972) may have been played more or less straight by the cast, at least AIP's advertising department had a sense of humor. The ad showed a giant frog (the frogs and other creatures in the film are actually normal-sized) with a hand sticking out of its mouth. "Today the pond — tomorrow the world!" read the ad copy. If only the movie itself had been as good.

Pickett Smith (Sam Elliott) is in the Everglades doing a photo piece on pollution for an ecology magazine when he almost literally runs into some members of wealthy paper mill magnate Jason Crockett's (Ray Milland) family, all of whom are being compelled to celebrate the old man's birthday in a week-long fete. Smith comes across the body of one of Jason's missing employees, who has apparently been bushwhacked by snakes. As dozens of noisy bullfrogs creep closer to the estate, all manner of amphibious creatures start acting abnormally, causing the deaths of several of the celebrants. Gators, spiders, lizards, turtles, and birds go on the warpath, leading Smith to take the few survivors and run for safety. Stubborn Jason refuses to leave and faces a contingent of "angry" frogs who give him a fatal heart attack.

Frogs is not exactly an amphibious version of *The Birds*. Although unintentionally comical at times, *Frogs* is not a black comedy and should have been, as it's not well made enough to deliver any serious thrills. Although there are potshots at the dumb and greedy family members, *Frogs* isn't intelligent enough to be taken as some kind of witty satire on the evils of industrialists or an allegory about nature striking back at those who corrupt it. No real explanation is given for the behavior of the critters. The competent enough actors are lost in a travesty completely devoid of style, pace, and cinematic inspiration.

Frequently the animals don't so much as attack but simply take advantage of the helplessness of the blundering humans. When one character accidentally shoots himself in the knee and collapses to the ground, the spiders simply come forward to cover him as he screams. On the other hand, in a scene that takes place in a greenhouse, a variety of lizards seem to show sinister intent when they deliberately push beakers of poison off tables onto the floor, asphyxiating the man inside. As a flock of seagulls "attack" the fleeing household help and a fashion model, they merely flap about in the air and squawk. When the gulls are superimposed over the retreating humans, they mysteriously turn black in color and then look like crows. Not one human gets so much as a peck.

The single sustained sequence that works at all is when vague, somewhat dotty Iris meanders into the woods on a hunt for butterflies. Iris gets into deep shit the deeper she gets into the woods. She almost grabs a snake that dangles from a branch, backs away in terror from a deadly coiled rattlesnake, falls into a puddle of mud and climbs out covered in leeches that she laboriously picks off in disgust, and eventually succumbs to her injuries. The scene has some suspense to it and isn't badly shot and edited. The scene when Iris' husband wrestles with a clearly comatose gator provides some comedy relief.

There are numerous shots of dumb, impassive bullfrogs as they stare at the estate — giving orders to the other creatures, one supposes — but not for one second are they remotely frightening. At what passes for a climax, they descend upon the house by the hundreds and converge on Ray Milland, through it's not quite apparent what they planned to do — or *could* do — to the man. Smother him? Thump him to death? In any case, he keels over before anything can happen. The most beautiful animal in the picture is Jason's Irish Setter, who never reacts in any way, shape or fashion to the various critters that are all around it. Irish Setters may not be the smartest or most ambitious breed of dog, but even they would react to the smell of a *critter*!

Les Baxter's musical score, which consists mostly of jangling electronic noises meant to wake up the audience, is no help at all, doing nothing to create suspense or tension or even interest in the proceedings. Director George McCowan also seems to have had little interest in the proceedings.

For its killer critters, *Dogs* (1976) focused not on packs of wild dogs but rather domesticated, cuddly pets who strangely band together and attack people for what seems like the sheer pleasure of it. Harlan Thompson (David McCallum) is the head of a biology department for a California university which is home to a top-secret experiment involving a "linear accelerator." (Few details are forthcoming about this project.) Thompson learns that livestock, and then people, are being mutilated — but not eaten — by animals who seem more interested in killing than in feeding. He has trouble convincing the dean that domesticated dogs are responsible for the slaughter, which culminates in an attack on the campus which leaves dozens of students dead. Thompson takes off with his girlfriend and colleague Caroline (Sandra McCabe) — one of the few survivors — as cats now begin to be affected.

Some of the animal actors in *Dogs* are too cute or small to be especially scary, but the larger breeds are another matter. The dogs let out a howl in the night that reverberates throughout the town and is truly nerve-wracking. In the first half of the film there are some well-handled sequences, such as when the pack attacks a young motorcyclist and drags off an elderly woman who comes out to investigate. There is a chilling scene at a kindergarten dog show when the children's beloved pets begin to act in a menacing manner. When Linda Gray, as a flirtatious colleague of Thompson's, is cornered in her shower, the Doberman pinscher doesn't really seem to be "attacking," however. Screams and shots of blood don't quite create the proper illusion. The climactic massacre of college students also doesn't have the impact it should have, and there are indications that in general the film is better edited (by John Wright) than directed (by Burt Brinkerhoff).

Dogs initially creates a sense of impending menace but isn't able to sustain it. One big tension-killer is a sequence when obese student Howard (Barry Greenberg) runs off to the kitchen to get a snack and encounters some snarling critters. Howard is clearly (and somewhat offensively) meant to be a comedy relief character and the movie never quite recovers from the switch in mood. (When a professor tells him to throw the dogs some of his food, he seems reluctant to part with it.) None of the attack scenes have any particular directorial style to them, and the film has no real explanation for the dogs' behavior (the linear accelerator, one assumes, whatever the hell that is) and no resolution. *Dogs* starts off well but never really amounts to that much. Alan Oldfield's opening theme is all wrong, too "pretty" and bucolic, but later on the music becomes appropriately creepy. But for the silly business with Howard, O'Brian Tamalin's script is perfectly workable.

The star of the film may have been David McCallum, but the acting honors go to George Wyner, who plays Michael Fitzgerald, another scientist and teacher. He holds the film together with his solid professionalism and has a particularly strong moment reacting with numb shock when he realizes he inadvertently shot a man he was trying to save instead of the dog who was attacking him. McCallum is by no means bad in the film, although at times he seems as vague and dithery as he sometimes was as Illya Kuryakin on *The Man from U.N.C.L.E.* Linda Gray is decidedly sensual as Miss Engle, and speaks her lines in the same sexy whisper that she used on *Dallas*. Sanda McCabe is competent as Caroline, the nominal heroine who seems like a female throwback. She doesn't seem to do anything but wail and screech when the dogs arrive. When one pokes its head through the doggy door in her garage, she doesn't even have the presence of mind to kick it or throw something at it — she just screams. She only moves to action when Thompson cries out for help when one dog gets his fangs in him. Holly Harris makes an impression as the dean's wife, who grabs the phone out of his hand in no-nonsense style when he has trouble explaining the situation to the governor.

But *Dogs* was a masterpiece compared to the next killer canine movie, *The Pack* (1977), which came out the following year. Jerry (Joe Don Baker) is a marine biologist — and apparently the sheriff— stationed on Seal Island. Most of the island is deserted, but a fishing party arrives just as some dogs abandoned by their owners have banded together. Although they may have been domesticated at one point, most of the animals have become feral and attack their prey — unlike the pack in *Dogs*— because they're starving. After several deaths, Baker traps the dogs in a shack and sets it on fire, ending their menace for good.

The Pack was loosely based on the far superior novel of the same name by David Fisher. Robert Clouse, who wrote the screenplay in addition to directing, puts a little too much emphasis on a truly dumb subplot in which one of the men in the fishing party brings along a sexy young gal, Lois (Sherry Miles), in the hopes that she'll draw out his "geeky" son Tommy (Paul Willson), who seems completely uninterested in her. Whether this is because he realizes that she's way out of his league, is possibly gay (although this aspect goes unexplored) or — as he puts it — hates being pressured by his father, is never ascertained. About halfway into the running time, Tommy is chased by dogs and falls off a cliff, making one wonder why the character was even introduced in the first place. It would have made sense if, for instance, Tommy turned out to be more capable in dealing with the dogs than his supposedly macho father, but his death puts an end to any ironic points Clouse might have been trying to make. It's almost as if he's killed just because, well, geeks gotta die. (Like "Howard" in *Dogs*, Tommy is also overweight.)

The dogs in *The Pack* are well-trained but as monsters they fall behind the canines in *Dogs*. Even when they're being ferocious, they're not exactly terrifying. In one scene that should have been left on the cutting room floor, the leader of the pack (who *is* a bit creepy when it reveals what seem to be two extra-long fang-like appliances in its grinning maw) apparently runs right into a branch, yelps (just like a "real dog") and backs up nervously like the frightened puppy it probably was. This happens in the middle of an "attack" scene no less. But *The Pack* in general is ineptly edited and directed, meandering when it should be building tension, and it has the feel and appearance of an instantly forgettable made-for-TV movie.

An attack on Jerry's girlfriend Millie (Hope Alexander-Willis) with the dogs climbing all over her car falls flat; in fact, most of the "action" scenes are pretty dull. Lee Holdridge's score is mediocre, but it does try to summon up some excitement during the scene when Tommy and Lois run out of the woods because the former is freaked out and thinks the dogs are coming after them. Unfortunately the music can't disguise the fact that nothing is happening — the two are just running aimlessly — and there's no suspense because the dogs don't even show up until the sequence is nearly over. At least this scene features some striking scenery as Tommy runs out onto a cliff overlooking the sea into which he falls moments later.

Similarly there's no suspense in a scene when Jerry rescues a man who nearly got chomped on by the dogs. The man falls into the water but doesn't know how to swim, so Jerry reaches down off the dock and begins to pull him up. But no one is in any danger because the dogs have already run off, so there's no reason for Clouse to give so much time to this business. If the director had at least included a shot of the dogs looking back, suggesting they might return any minute to tear Jerry and the other man to pieces, the scene could have had some tension. No such luck.

There *are* a couple of decent moments. It's almost touching when the latest dog to be abandoned on the island by its owners finds the pack and is accepted into their ranks. (This dog remains domesticated to a large degree and Jerry bonds with it at the film's conclusion.) There's an infrequent chilling moment when Lois takes refuge in the very barn the dogs have been using as a shelter and wakes up to find them all anxiously waiting to snack on her. And the pyrotechnics at the end when the cabin and the dogs caught inside it go to fiery blazes are well-done. For the most part the actors in *The Pack* are bland and the characters uninteresting. Clouse covers the action but little else.

Talk about the deteriorating ozone layer and the dangers it represented was bound to result in a movie like *Day of the Animals* (1977), the premise of which has all animals (including some people) that are 5000 feet above sea level going on the rampage due to an excess of ultraviolet radiation. Steve Buckner (Christopher George) leads a group of backpackers into the mountain wilderness just as reports are coming in of strange animal attacks. After one woman in the party is mauled by a wolf, panic sets in and the group separates into three parts. Advertising executive Paul Jenson (Leslie Nielsen) leads one group but succumbs to madness, murdering one young man and nearly raping his girlfriend. The injured woman is attacked and killed by eagles; and her husband tries to protect a traumatized little girl he comes upon before being dispatched by rattlers hiding in an abandoned vehicle. Buckner and the rest are beset by mountain lions and chased by a pack of killer dogs. Eventually the affected animals all drop dead as the shift in the ozone layer corrects itself and life returns to normal.

Day of the Animals is an improvement over director William Girdler's previous creature feature *Grizzly*. The picture is often quite harrowing and exciting. There is a very effective eagle attack on the young lady as she clings to the edge of a cliff, and a well-done if brief wolf attack on a sleeping camper. In another credible sequence, a pack of wolves attack a helicopter. Later on, what seems to be another pack of wolves attack a cabin into which some of the cast have taken shelter, but these animals are referred to by the characters as "dogs." In truth both wolves and dogs were played by Siberian Huskies, who generally stand in for wolves in movies because they are much easier to train. The dogs even jump onto a makeshift raft that the survivors build to try to get away from them. A scene where mountain lions attack the camp at night is less effective and too darkly lit.

A darkly amusing and suspenseful sequence occurs when Ranger Tucker (Walter Barnes), back down in the town, goes to the kitchen to get a snack, turns his back, then turns around again only to see rats scurrying all over the food on the table. The rats then proceed to jump onto his face and bite him, looking as if they're being launched one by one off a trampoline. One of the most memorable scenes has Leslie Nielsen wrestling a six-foot grizzly bear in a lightning storm after the ozone rays have affected his mind and turned him "invincible." The equally maddened bear has a different opinion.

Dogs go on the attack along with numerous other beasts in *Day of the Animals* (1977).

In the aforementioned cabin attack scene, Girdler pays homage to *The Birds* by inserting quick close-ups of the actors, shot from below, walking into camera range during a lull in the attack as Hitchcock did with his cast during a lull in the bird attacks. Directors should always be careful about reminding the audience of a much better movie, although *Day of the Animals* is not without merit. A more original — and disturbing — scene has the traumatized little girl (Michelle Stacy) watching helplessly from a car in which Frank placed her for protection as the latter is attacked and killed by rattlesnakes as he opens the door of another car a few feet away.

Christopher George and his wife Lynda Day George are no better or worse as the leads than they ever are. Richard Jaeckel is cast against type as a professor and makes less of an impression than usual. Leslie Nielsen steals the picture as the blustering, obnoxious businessman who keeps referring to a Native American (Michael Ansara) as "Kemosabe" and calls Ruth Roman — another cast stand-out — "Miss Beverly Hills Bitch!" Jon Cedar is also excellent as the ill-fated, compassionate Frank. The editing by Bob Asman and James Mitchell is first-rate, but Lalo Schifrin's musical score generally provides pretty sight-seeing music instead of something sinister.

Wolfen (1981) was based on an excellent first novel by Whitley Streiber, who later claimed in his non-fiction volume *Communion* that he and his family were bothered by alien creatures (who in part inspired the wolfen). While that claim is debatable to all but the gullible, it is a decided fact that the makers of *Wolfen* the movie should have stuck with the book's storyline and not mucked it up with the Native American references that were fashionable at the time. Homicide detective Dewey Wilson (Albert Finney) and police psychologist Rebecca Neff (Diane Venora) team up to investigate the mutilation murders of a wealthy couple, the Van der Veers, in Manhattan's Battery Park. They discover that the culprits are not maniacs or terrorists but a sub-group of wolf that uses the tenements of the Bronx as a hunting ground. Van der Veer was planning to renovate this area with an urban renewal project, cutting off the wolves' food supply. After many more murders and a tense confrontation in Van der Veer's office, Dewey placates the wolves by destroying the model of the housing project and, incredibly, lets the creatures go on about their business.

In the book the wolfen were actually a separate species from wolves, wolf-like but different in size, shape and capabilities. In the movie they are simply large wolves who became separated from their country cousins and went underground in the big city, preying on the drunk and homeless. To the Native Americans who know about the wolfen — and apparently Wilson as well — these animals are just "doing their thing" and shouldn't be looked upon as enemies. Jeez — try telling that to all the poor, disaffected, generally African American people dying horrible, painful deaths at the teeth and claws of the wolves as they're being devoured! The film feigns a liberal slant by awkwardly exploring stereotypical attitudes toward Native Americans, but it seems incredible that no one connected with the film saw the vile, even racist hypocrisy of David Eyre and Michael Wadleigh's screenplay.

Realistically there may have been little for Wilson to do in the climactic confrontation with half a dozen snarling wolves, but it is made clear that he is not going to pursue the matter further, *accepting* the presence of the wolves in his city instead of seeing them as the menace they really are. (Of course, the movie seems to say, their victims are only poor, black, alcoholic or addicted to drugs — so who cares? Similar to some people's attitude on AIDS, which to their mindset "only" affects gays, blacks, and drug addicts.) Van der Veer and his wife may not be as sympathetic as the other victims (which include a perfectly nice professor who studies wolves), but they're only killed because Van der Veer wants to clean up the Bronx and provide housing for the under-privileged residents. There's an added irony in the fact that writer-director Wadleigh's only previous film credit was *Woodstock* (1970)!

Before we actually see the wolfen, their presence is made known by "wolfen vision," a kind of shimmering, pastel-colored, double negative image — accompanied by speeded-up tracking shots — that represents their subjective viewpoint. This is certainly colorful and initially effective, but after a while it becomes tiresome. As previously noted, wolves in the movies are generally portrayed by Siberian Huskies, but these wolves look like *wolves*. They are ferocious and frightening and never resemble cuddly old canines at all.

The film will never get points for intelligence but it does have some good scenes, although the opening depicting the murders of the Van der Veers and their security guard, while suspenseful, doesn't quite work. One memorable scene has Wilson and Neff discussing the types of mutilations performed by various political factions as they buy hot dogs from a vendor portrayed by character actor Robert Dahdah. Dahdah's facial expressions as he listens to the two cops continue their distasteful discourse are priceless. A mild *frisson* is generated by the sequence when Professor Ferguson (Tom Noonan) is cornered and killed by the wolves in Central Park at night. Instead of giving the *de rigueur* speech about the

Deadly wolves were the sinister nemesis in the interesting if unsatisfying *Wolfen* (1981).

formidableness of wolves, Ferguson actually defends the animal, unaware that he's soon to be killed by a rogue pack of wolfen. The final confrontation between wolfen and police in the office is taut, with an interesting shot of the many wolves reflected in mirrors that make it look as if there are hundreds of them when there's only about half a dozen — more than enough.

By far the most horrifically memorable scene is set up early in the movie when Whittington the coroner (Gregory Hines) notices that Mrs. Van der Veer's head is nearly severed. He tells Wilson that during the French Revolution every fifth head was still alive for a brief time after being guillotined; according to him the brain can live for about a minute without oxygen (this doesn't mean the person would be conscious, however). "Imagine having to see your own body and know you were dead," he says. In the climactic Wall Street confrontation, one of the wolves jumps at the police inspector (Dick O'Neill) and *tears off his head*, which then plops to the ground where we can see it, eyes wide open, still opening and closing its mouth in shock. The wolfen in the novel may or may not have been able to tear off a head with one bite, but frankly these "normal" wolves do not seem capable of it, and the grisly effect, while "bravura" in one sense, isn't entirely convincing.

Albert Finney is completely miscast as a New York City homicide investigator. He gets across the world-weariness of his character well enough, but affects an inappropriately flamboyant hairdo never, ever seen in the N.Y.P.D. Even the coroner tells him, "You could use a haircut." Diane Venora is low-key but solid as Neff, displaying a strong, utterly realistic reaction to the above-mentioned decapitation. Gregory Hines plays the role of the ghoulish Whittington strictly as — no pun intended — black comedy relief. Edward James Olmos as the "Indian" radical Eddie Holt has an impressive scene where he gets bare-assed and runs around in front of Wilson doing a highly convincing interpretation of a wolf, for a moment suggesting to the cop and the audience that maybe the fiendish killer of the Van der Veers could be human.

The film has an extremely handsome look to it due to George Fisher's outstanding photography of everything from derelict buildings and weed-filled lots to those stunning shots overlooking Manhattan as Wilson confronts Eddie Holt on the bridge where he works. The distinctive special visual effects were by Robert Blalach. James Horner's music contributes greatly to the film's undeniably eerie atmosphere. Besides *Woodstock*, Michael Wadleigh directed two other documentaries in the 1990s, but made no other fiction films, which is just as well. No amount of visual tricks can disguise the fact that *Wolfen* is too slow and disjointed to really work.

A rat that certainly acts in an unnatural manner is at the heart of the Canadian *Of Unknown Origin* (1982), which was based on a novel called *The Visitor* by Chauncey Parker III. Bart Hughes (Peter Weller) and his wife and son live in a beautiful renovated brownstone in Manhattan. Bart is essentially a self-satisfied yuppie with a minor social conscience who figures he'll not have too much trouble disposing of this one troublesome rat that's moved into his abode. But the rat proves extremely difficult to get rid of. In addition the rodent begins to act in an extremely aggressive manner. It attacks Bart on more than one occasion, eats through cables so that the lights go out, and even kills the cat that was supposed to take care of *it*. Bart becomes obsessed with killing the rat, and his appearance and job performance begin to suffer. He sleeps in a hammock to keep the rat off of him at night, and virtually destroys his living quarters in his attempts to get at the creature. Finally he's able to bludgeon it to death and his nightmare is over.

Although it is not really a black comedy, *Of Unknown Origin* is actually more amusing than frightening, primarily because of the rat's distinctly peculiar behavior. It acts as no rat has ever acted before or after. One highlight is when it jumps out of the toilet bowl just as Bart is about to take a pee! (The rat may have merely wanted a drink of water, but it *does* seem to be "hiding"—although you have to wonder how it managed to pull down the toilet seat cover behind it.) There's an even funnier scene when we see the movement of the rat under the blanket just beside Bart's sleeping body. The rat not only kills the cat (off-screen) but leaves its bloodied carcass on top of the refrigerator where Bart is sure to find it.

Many of the other curious scenes are actually dreams or fantasies that Bart has of the rat, such as when it smashes out of a birthday cake. This last sequence and many others employ an unconvincing rat puppet that we fortunately get only glimpses of. Somehow the shots of the clawed pink feet of the creature—a real rat this time—are just as disgusting as close-ups of its dribbling incisors gnawing on wiring and the like. The rat appears to be much larger than usual (if not exactly gigantic), about two feet long, probably by using a puppet in some scenes and special props in others.

Preparing to destroy the beast, Bart gets a book on rats from the library and leafs through it, muttering out loud some of what he reads, in a scene that is the equivalent of when the scientists in 1950s films lectured on the formidableness of the various insects and critters playing the starring roles. Hence we and Bart learn that there are over 24,000 rat bites a year, that rats have chisel-like teeth which can bite through metal, and that rats—who are "of unknown origin"—carried the bubonic plague that wiped out a third of the world's population. The only really chilling scene is when we see truly gruesome photographs of the victims of rat bites.

Peter Weller holds the picture together with his charisma and sense of humor. He never descends into camp or parody but recognizes that the proceedings are absurd and has a lot of fun with the role. Unconventionally handsome, Weller has always been an excellent actor. Lawrence Dane and Louis Del Grande are also notable as Bart's boss and super, respectively. A subplot, where Bart seems drawn to a pretty colleague, Lorrie (Jennifer Dale), whom he kisses, seems dragged in to add to the running time and goes nowhere. Lorrie seems like an instantly disposable victim, but she never even gets bitten. Director George Cosmatos, with the help of editor Roberto Silvi, keeps things moving.

1982 also brought the film adaptation of Stephen King's novel *Cujo*. Dee Wallace stars as housewife Donna Trenton, who is married to Vic (Daniel Hugh-Kelly) but having an affair with the "local stud," Steve (Christopher Stone). Unbeknownst to all of them, the St. Bernard pet of car repairman Joe Cambers (Ed Lauter) suffered a bat bite and developed rabies. The dog dispatches a friend of Joe's, then Joe himself. Donna decides to take her car into Cambers' shop, her little boy Tad (Danny Pintauro) in tow. Vic believes that Steve—with whom Donna just broke it off—has kidnapped his wife and child, but they are actually trapped in their car by the crazed St. Bernard who waits just outside. In order to save her boy, who is seriously ill, Donna manages to outwit and defeat the "monster."

Despite its cuddly appearance in the opening scenes, the St. Bernard is a terrific performer and manages to be quite menacing and horrific throughout the movie; its sheer bulk and size doesn't hurt at all, of course. Nothing the dog does is out of the ordinary — especially considering it has rabies — at least until the very end of the film when it seemingly comes back from the dead after Donna brains it. This kind of one-last-chance for the bad guy or beast to get the heroine became obligatory for horror films regardless of how dead-looking and utterly defeated the man or monster might have been. In *Cujo* the scene is just as illogical as ever.

One of the best scenes (the dog's attack on Gary, Joe's associate, in his home) is briskly edited for maximum impact. Immediately following the deadly attack, that fine character actor Ed Lauter gives a thoroughly realistic reaction of shock and disgust when he discovers his friend's torn-up body (which is not shown to the audience). Too often in movies of this nature the characters come across mutilated corpses — especially of *people they know*— and react with an almost comically mild brief grimace or something equally inappropriate. The protracted scenes with the woman and child cornered by the dog can best be described as harrowing.

Director Lewis Teague (of *Alligator*) and editor Neil Travis do an exemplary job of holding the audience's attention. Even the early scenes of domestic strife, the arguing over the wife's affair, and other familiar stuff is absorbing due to the fast pace and fine acting. In an early sequence when young Tad rushes to his bed and imagines there's a monster in his closet, the camerawork, angles, etc., get across how big the bedroom seems to a small child and emphasizes the lad's abject fear of the dark. Jan de Bont's photography is first-rate. Charles Bernstein's jangling score adds to the tension, but on top of the kid's wailing and the dog's growling it also gives you a headache.

Dee Wallace gives a fine performance as the desperate mother. Although their roles are not as dramatic or showy, both Hugh-Kelly and Stone (Wallace's real-life husband) give solid support. Danny Pintauro is excellent as the child. In addition to the aforementioned Ed Lauter, Kaiulani Lee and Mills Watson stand out as Joe's wife Charity and friend Gary, respectively. But when all is said and done, *Cujo* is very well-done but repellent. Watching a mother and her little child being terrified for an extended period of time isn't exactly "entertainment" no matter how well photographed and directed.

In the Shadow of Kilimanjaro (1986) was said to be inspired by true events. On an animal preserve in Kenya, a drought kills off the baboons' natural food supply. Although they would normally start attacking and consuming one another, for unexplained reasons they begin devouring the local people instead. Jack Ringtree (Timothy Bottoms), a game warden, tries unsuccessfully to get the authorities to evacuate the populace. The baboons advance from attacking lone victims to going after groups of schoolchildren and workers. They launch a full-scale assault on Ringtree and his companions at their headquarters, but a sudden downpour ends the drought — and the threat of future attacks.

The attack scenes, with close-ups of gore inserted at regular intervals, are reasonably exciting. While the baboons are marvelous, well-trained actors, they at all times seem to be merely rushing about instead of mounting a true offensive. It is obvious that director Raju Patel was concerned with filming everything as quickly and economically as possible without regard to such niceties as camera movement or composition, giving the whole film a slapdash appearance. The only halfway striking shot occurs when the baboons attack a man working on his stalled Jeep in the desert. Sitting on the rocks nearby, the animals suddenly rush down off them in a long, scurrying line, swerving en masse toward the unwitting victim. This is the only real attempt made to create fear or suspense.

A subplot has to do with Ringtree and his wife, who's come to Kenya in the hopes that he'll return home and to her, but this doesn't amount to much. The characterizations of the supporting roles are sketchy, relying strictly on whatever impressions the actors themselves care to or have time to give. Generating few thrills or tension, *Kilimanjaro* is a misfire.

Rats figure in *Graveyard Shift* (1990), which was based on a short story by Stephen King. The story takes place in a New England mill which has a serious rat infestation. The rats come out one night and manage to sort of push one poor guy into a machine which mushes him into a paste; this is the prologue. His replacement, John Hall (David Andrews), shows up to irritate some of the employees with his strong, silent manner, and to intrigue at least one of the women, Jane (Kelly Wolf). Hall seems much too intelligent to resort to this kind of low-level desperation job, and if he has an interesting back story, the audience is never let in on it. An exterminator named Cleveland (Brad Dourif) is one of the early victims of a much larger, mostly unseen creature that skulks around in the mill and environs. The nasty foreman Warwick (Stephen Macht) takes a group, including John and Jane, down into the basement for a major clean-up; everyone winds up falling through the rotted floor into sub-basement levels lorded over by the large creature, which turns out to be a rat slightly bigger than a man. Killing off most of the cast, the rat pursues John to an upper level where it gets pulled into the same machinery that pulverized the worker in the prologue. Despite the climactic appearance of the big rat, this is more of a nature-gone-berserk feature than a giant monster movie.

John Esposito's script and Ralph S. Singleton's direction are only serviceable; where the picture excels is in its realistic capturing of mood and place. Many of the supporting actors seem like actual mill workers (and may have been) and both the scenes above ground and in the sub-basements are richly atmospheric. The below ground sets are good and creepy, especially an excellent cavern full of hundreds of skeletons. This appears to be a matte painting combined with a studio set. High on the wall of the cavern there is a shaft of light which shows the exit through which John escapes to the surface.

The smaller rats, which are real, do their usual fine job of interacting with a squirming cast and staring at them with more intelligence than is comfortable. The big rat, whose origin is never revealed or discussed, is more problematic. For one thing, the full-scale puppet never seems alive. Close-ups of its twitching ears and scraping claws are effective, but when seen in full shot the big rat is never convincing. When it shakes its head it simply looks as if an off-camera prop man is shoving it this way and that. With its mutilated and somewhat unformed appearance it somewhat resembles the monster in *Prophecy*.

Brad Dourif offers his usual campy if lovable performance as the exterminator. Stephen Macht is flavorful as the bestial Warwick. Although not beautiful in the Hollywood sense, Kelly Wolf is very appealing as the warm and gritty Jane. Ilona Margolis is vivid as Nardello, who is dumped by the foreman and takes an ax to his car in one amusing sequence. David Andrews plays the brooding drifter in a more than competent manner, but the script doesn't give him much of a character to play. Andrews later played a Ted Kennedy type in the *roman à clef* series *The Monroes* and appears frequently on television.

Graveyard Shift was excoriated by the critics, many of whom found it a rehash of recycled ideas, which it is. But it does manage to get across the depressing bleakness and fragile hopes of the mill workers' lives, especially John, who seems fated for better things.

Willard (2003) was a remake of the 1971 film of the same title. Willard (Crispin Glover) is a lonely, antisocial geek who is told by his elderly sick mother to get rid of the rats in the basement but winds up bonding with them — especially one he dubs Socrates — when he rescues the squealing white rat from the trap he put out for it. "You're my only friend," he tells Socrates. A big brown rat that is twice the size of the others makes his presence known and is christened "Ben." Willard is humiliated and tormented by his boss, Frank Martin (R. Lee Ermey), who stole his business from Willard's father and is trying to put Willard out of his house as well. When Martin kills Socrates, Martin enlists Ben and the rat army to attack and kill Martin. Willard hopes to rid himself of the rats but they follow him back home and try to make a meal of him. Willard winds up in a mental institution where he makes friends with another white rat.

The 1971 film, based on Stephen Gilbert's novel *Ratman's Notebooks*, had the same basic plot, with Bruce Davison — more of a "normal" boy-next-door type than the quirkier Crispin Glover — as the nominal hero, Elsa Lanchester (*Bride of Frankenstein*) as his mother, and Ernest Borgnine as the nasty employer, Willard's uncle. All but the last couple of rat mayhem scenes are played for laughs, and Daniel Mann's direction is too routine to make this first version much more than a moderately entertaining time-waster. The film was successful enough to engender a sequel, *Ben* (1972), in which the title rat leads his fellow rodents as they run rampant in the city in scenes that play like something out of the campy *Batman* TV series. Ben (a remarkably trained and expressive rodent-star) unaccountably befriends a young boy (Lee Harcourt Montgomery) with a heart condition who composes the film's theme song and puts on pup-

Bruce Davison (left) introduces his rodent buddies to hated boss Ernest Borgnine in *Willard* (1971).

pet shows in sequences that become increasingly cloying. Director Phil Karlson imbues the poor film with virtually no tension aside from some moments during the sewer climax, and *Ben* emerges as even weaker than its predecessor. Rosemary Murphy, Arthur O'Connell and other cast members do the best they can with mediocre material.

The 2003 *Willard*, written by director Glen Morgan, is much better, more entertaining, and decidedly much more stylish than the original. It is essentially a black comedy bolstered by the bizarre and intense performance of Glover as Willard Stiles. Glover gets excellent support from a large horde of incredible rat actors (all of whom are kind of cute); the film also employs animation and animatronics in bringing these rodents and their dastardly deeds to life. It seems, however, as if Willard is able to train these creatures practically overnight, as they follow his commands without question in a suspenseful scene when Willard has them chew on the tires of his boss' car while it's parked in the man's garage. The boss gives chase, along with a dog that nearly winds up as the rats' blue plate special.

The best scene is a darkly amusing moment when one of Willard's kind co-workers — fearing that Willard is lonely after the death of his mother — shows up with a cat for a present, the last thing Willard wants. Leaving to have a snack with the woman, Willard quickly throws the cat through the front door into his house, which is now overrun with rodents. As the theme song from *Ben*, sung by Michael Jackson, plays in the background (because the cat accidentally presses a button that turns on the TV), the rats pursue the frantic animal all over the house, back and forth from room to room, stopping only to nibble at the legs of a high piece of furniture in order to get at him as he stares down at them in confusion from the top. Finally the cat falls into the rats' midst and is never seen again, a development that probably did not sit well with the average cat fancier. The death of Willard's boss at the teeth of the rats frankly could have used some shots of those teeth tearing and rending — a lot more gore — especially given the utterly vile nature of the victim. There was hardly a soul in the audience who didn't want to see this guy get what was coming to him, an illustration of the cathartic quality of the movies where bad guys can "get theirs" as they rarely do in real life.

R. Lee Ermey plays Frank, the boss, in a much too broad and caricatured style, even for this picture. Ernest Borgnine got the miserable nature of the character across without making him seem almost non-human. Laura Elena Harring isn't given much to do but she's fine as Cathryn, Willard's initially sympathetic co-worker. (In the original, Willard seems to fall for his co-worker but in this version it is never made explicit.) Jackie Burroughs, who played Dr. Treger in *Gnaws: Food the Gods 2*, is on the mark as Willard's aged, bedridden mother. It could be argued that this version of *Willard* presents a kind of mockery of old age, senility, and elder care with its portrait of the mother and her relationship with Willard, although that was probably not the intention.

With an assist from editor James Coblentz, director Glen Morgan makes sure that the audience's attention never flags. Robert McLachlan's photography is first-rate. Shirley Walker contributed a notably quirky and appealing musical score. The original Willard, Bruce Davison, was cast as Willard's father, but can only be seen in old photographs and in a portrait that hangs on the wall. Stephen Gilbert's novel, which started it all, is only mentioned in the interminable scrawl of credits at the end.

SEVEN

The Indefinable — Blobs, Things, and Other Oddities

While dinosaurs, mythological monsters, big insects, and nature-gone-amok films seem to have dominated the creature feature genre, over the years there have been plenty of movies with monsters that were much less clearly defined. Some of these were weird creatures from space; others had a terrestrial origin but were no less bizarre. As we will see, some were outright outré.

William Cameron Menzies directed and production-designed his 3-D thriller *The Maze* (1953), which certainly had horror fans talking when it was released and afterward. Gerald MacTeam (Richard Carlson) is happily engaged to Kitty (Veronica Hurst) when he receives a message from the ancestral Craven Castle in Scotland and rushes off. Weeks later he sends word that Kitty is to forget all about him. but she decides to go to the castle with her Aunt Edith (Katherine Emery). MacTeam receives them and other visitors coldly, and it isn't long before it's clear that something strange is happening in the castle. It turns out that to MacTeam, the new baronet, has fallen the task of following the orders of a 200-year-old ancestor, an evolutionary freak who stopped short at the amphibian stage, who falls from a window and frees MacTeam to marry.

The Maze is well-paced and manages to work up a great deal of suspense over the secret of the castle and the nature of the strange being that can be heard literally sloshing down the hallways after the bedroom doors are locked at night. With the help of Gerald and the servants, this thing makes its way down to the maze outside the castle every evening. At the eerie climax, Kitty and Edith follow the procession down to the maze and get lost inside it, whereupon they come upon the dread being that the audience has been waiting for with breathless anticipation for the past 70 or so minutes. They discover....

A big frog.

Yes, a big frog about two or three feet high squatting on the ground, radiating as much menace as a rubber chicken. This was all the special effects people could come up with. MacTeam explains at the epilogue how a human fetus goes through different stages and that his ancestor — Sir Roger Philip MacTeam (1750–1953) — never got past the amphibious stage, so someone got the idea the guy would simply look just like a man-sized frog. Even Paul Blaisdell, monster creator for a lot of cheap creature features, could have come up with something more original and repulsive than the comical *Princess and the Frog* prop employed for the not-so-dramatic climax. It looks like a child could just about fit inside

167

the frog and make it move about, and indeed it looks like something you would see in an elementary school play. Although Kitty and Edith scream in terror when they see the frog — which actually roars — the audience only guffawed. What a crock!

The shame of it is that *The Maze* is not a bad picture for most of its length, and deserves a better "monster." A gifted FX person with a little money could have come up with a half-man, half fish curiosity that might have chilled the bones and brought forth a measure of disgust. The frog in *The Maze* is much worse than the big bird in *The Giant Claw* or the "giant salami" of *Prophecy*. At the end of the film we learn that far from being a monster, Sir Roger was highly intelligent and perfectly capable of running the affairs of the family. Therefore it makes little sense that Gerald would give up the woman he loves and his whole life to serve Roger (even if it is traditional to do so), and even less sense that he would be so utterly miserable to Kitty when she arrives. His behavior adds dramatic tension and mystery, of course, but it's illogical.

Despite its ludicrous moments, the film ends on a quietly pathetic note as we are asked to ponder Roger's long existence during which he was well aware that he was a freak. "He wasn't going to hurt you," Gerald tells Kitty, "he was only trying to hide." A highlight of the film is when Kitty finds a hidden passage in her bedchamber and climbs up stairs full of cobwebs and bats to look out a window overlooking the maze. This is a very creepy scene that makes good use of Menzies' talents as a designer.

The actors in the film are professional. Martin Skiles' music helps add to the jitters felt by the viewer during the final moments before the big, utterly disappointing revelation.

Professor Quatermass was a brilliant, peppery, and popular character in British television serials. Four of his adventures were turned into films, and the first two — Hammer Films' *The Quatermass Xperiment* (1956) and *Quatermass 2* (1957) — definitely fall into the category of creature feature. It is hard to imagine that the makers of such films as *The Blob* and *Caltiki, the Immortal Monster* weren't aware of *Quatermass Xperiment*, as the movie presented the first real "blob" of the movies. The film was retitled *The Creeping Unknown* for the American market because the Quatermass character was virtually unknown in the U.S.

Without waiting for official permission, Professor Quatermass (Brian Donlevy) launches a spaceship with three men aboard. When the ship returns, two of the men are missing and the third, Victor Caroon (Richard Wordsworth), is in a terrible state. Caroon's wife Judith (Marsia Dean) agonizes over his health and shattered demeanor, while Quatermass seems more interested in learning from the ailing man the secrets he may have uncovered in space. It develops that an alien organism has entered Caroon's body (it turned the other men to jelly) and is slowly transforming him into a monster that can absorb living matter, including human tissue. After digesting several zoo animals, the completely inhuman Caroon becomes a tentacled monstrosity that displays itself to television cameras at Westminster Abbey before being electrocuted by Quatermass, who's determined to continue his "Xperiments" come hell or high water.

The special effects of *Quatermass* vary in quality. The Caroon-monster, while still at a smaller size, looks like a starfish made out of drying waffle batter. The full-size creature, which looks like carpeting with bladders but is made up of cow guts, tripe and wires, is made to look about twenty feet wide with a mushroom cap on top. There's an interesting moment in the spaceship when Quatermass finds a little bit of the organism and says "it's alive," but we never see what he sees before he puts it into a box. The rubbery corpses of the creature's victims are serviceable, but much more impressive than the monster is the grim, cluttered, claustrophobic spaceship that picked up the malevolent organism that transforms Caroon and absorbed his colleagues.

The opening with the spaceship nearly crash-landing on top of a spooning couple and an old man is splendid. There is a creepy scene when Quatermass and others watch the film taken from a special camera in the spaceship, which shows the ship impacting with some mysterious force and some of the consequences of this "collision." The low-tech quality of the film-within-a-film and the old-fashioned projector via which it's viewed somehow add to the spookiness. There are effective moments once Caroon begins to transform, such as when his hand absorbs a cactus plant and he uses the disfigured paw to club a man to death. These scenes are abetted by the expressive pantomiming of Richard Wordsworth. The makeup around his eyes may give him that haunted look, but its his acting that clues us in to the man's inner torment, terror, and confusion. In one sequence set against the backdrop of an ugly canal, Caroon backs away from a little girl at play after an obviously intense internal struggle.

Quatermass Xperiment has a documentary feel to it and was undeniably an influential picture, leading into a boom in British horror film production and helping to put Hammer on the map — not to mention engendering a subgenre of "blob" movies. Unfortunately, *Quatermass* becomes increasingly ridiculous, its "science" on a comic book level, once Caroon leaves the hospital. Everything about the movie is more or less reasonable until we learn that Caroon is ingesting people and animals and has in fact become a form of alien invasion all on his lonesome. Worse, *Quatermass* becomes talky, silly, schlocky and a bit dull. Even the hoped-for exciting climax at Westminster Abbey is drawn-out. A camera crew is doing a report about the restoration of the abbey. After the discovery of a body of a crew member killed by the creature, there's a bit of black comedy as they decide to continue the program "in another part of the abbey." The announcer is so unconcerned about the man's death that he reminds one of the callous Quatermass.

The script makes Quatermass virtually seem like a caricature of a mad scientist, completely devoid of human feelings. If he expresses any concern over Caroon it's because he wants the knowledge trapped in his crazed, disintegrating brain, not because he cares about the man or his wife, Judith. He shows absolutely no compassion for Judith (we never see the families of the dead men). Quatermass seems especially loathsome in his attitude because it's impossible for the average viewer not to feel sorry for Caroon, Judith and Caroon's victims. Quatermass believes that "every experiment is a gamble" but it isn't his life on the line. He believes mankind must be willing to accept the consequences of experiments meant to better the world, but it's hard to believe he cares about "mankind" when he can't even summon up any sympathy for Caroon. On the other hand, his persistence in reaching for the stars is almost admirable. The film's last line has him snarling "Gonna start again" as he walks away from the mess he helped to create. He has absolutely no guilt or sense of responsibility.

Although British films often hired Americans as leads to increase their appeal in the

U.S. market, Brian Donlevy was an odd choice for the role of Quatermass Donlevy is good, even if he plays Quatermass in one note—all bristling impatience and obnoxious arrogance. Devoid of British class and gentility, he makes Quatermass seem less a scientist and more of a racketeer in a Hollywood *film noir*. His obvious non–Britishness is never referred to. Marsia Dean is miscast as Caroon's wife, coming off more like a mildly concerned cousin than someone in agony over the fate of a beloved husband. Richard Wordsworth's portrayal of Caroon, as noted, is on the money despite it being a mostly silent performance. Jack Warner and Lionel Jeffries are fine support as, respectively, Inspector Lomax and Blake of the Ministry of Defense. Thora Hird nearly steals the picture in her bit as a drunken old lady at the police station who's seen the monster and is hoping it's an hallucination, although this moment of comedy relief severely dampens the tension. "What's a young lady to do with creepy crawlies about?" she wonders. Walter Harvey's photography is a bonus. Director Val Guest does a competent enough job but doesn't prevent the film from sinking into tedium long before the closing credits.

Quatermass 2 was retitled *Enemy from Space* for American release. Quatermass is in a lather because the government won't give him funding for a moon base colony he wants to build. He is then astonished to discover by chance that his moon base is being erected near the English town of Winnerden Flats. Although told that the "moon base" is actually a refinery for artificial food, he uncovers a vast conspiracy that reaches high into the government. Aliens who want to take over the world have fallen to Earth in small rocks and taken over the minds and bodies of Earthlings. They are able to mass together to form huge creatures inside the 200-foot domes of the refinery. Quatermass manages to destroy the asteroid whence come the alien-rocks; the huge monsters fall apart and the mind-controlled humans return to normal.

The effects in *Quatermass 2* are low-grade but serviceable. The big monsters that break out of the domes at the climax, photographed against miniatures, look like shapeless mounds or wet living hills of rubber covered in sheaves of seaweed. The powerful windstorm that accompanies their destruction and overturns cars is credible. The makeup jobs done on various actors to show that they have been burned by the rocks and are now possessed by the aliens inside those rocks, are suitably weird-looking.

Quatermass 2 has its memorably gruesome moments, such as when an associate of Quatermass' stumbles out of one of the domes he was inspecting, horribly burned and disfigured, and weaves his way down the outdoor steps outside the dome, desperately urging Quatermass to stay away from him. During the climactic battle, the pipes that carry oxygen to the domes are turned on full in the hopes that the gas will destroy the monsters. Several men go out to talk to the supposedly conciliatory aliens but never return. Later, it is noticed that blood is seeping out of the oxygen pipe, which has been stopped up by something. "It's been blocked with *human pulp!*" cries Quatermass. The mind-controlled humans revert to normal at the end of the film, but it's interesting to contemplate how some of them will feel when they learn they killed possible friends and family members under orders of the aliens.

Donlevy, reprising the role of Quatermass, makes the scientist a little mystified and confused at times, as well as kinder and gentler. He apologizes for "jumping on" a staff member, and shows genuine concern for another colleague who has been burned by the rocks. John Longden plays Inspector Lomax in this edition and is fine. As in *Quatermass Xperiment*, the pace drags a bit at the end — Val Guest was again the director — but the movie is more entertaining than its predecessor. Gerald Gibbs' photography and James Bernard's musical score are definite assets. Like the television serial it was based on, much of *Quatermass 2* was filmed at the Shell Haven Refinery in Essex. With its huge pipes, towering domes, large drums and general feeling of vastness and sterility, this choice of locale adds immeasurably to the film's impact.

But *Quatermass 2* never answers the basic question that hangs all over the film: Why on Earth would the scientist expect the government to fund his moon base colony project when Quatermass hasn't even gotten a man on the moon yet? And considering the disastrous events in the first film....

X the Unknown (1956) was another Hammer horror thriller featuring a blob-like monster. A fiery fissure opens up on Army property in Scotland during a field exercise, burning two soldiers. A series of mysterious deaths occur which point to the existence of some sort of deadly unknown creature. Dr. Adam Royston (Dean Jagger) investigates and theorizes that an ancient life form of pure energy is issuing from the fissure in search of the radiation it feeds upon. When the monster — a huge, shapeless mass of shiny stuff — shows up to ingest some cobalt at a government plant, Royston's "theory" is proven. As the creature oozes across the countryside, Royston comes up with a way to destroy it and, after some doubtful moments, finally succeeds.

The monster appears as a thick, viscous, glistening liquid and there are some striking shots of it spreading across a field in the moonlight, and pouring down a narrow country lane between quaint old buildings like a malevolent porridge. Slow motion is employed to make the mass seem a little more gooey and oozy as it comes over and plops down off a miniature wall. At the climax when the creature is destroyed, it resembles a moldy, glowing carpet. Although devoid of personality it exudes a certain quiet menace. (This life form might be considered outside the scope of this volume as it isn't a biological "creature" in the usual sense, but as its movie influenced later films it is included.)

X the Unknown proceeds as a mystery, almost a "locked room" thriller, as people die in horrible ways and in places where there seems to be no entrance for a killer — unless it can seep through the grills in a ventilation plate. The film is full of creepy scenes such as when a little boy enters a forest on a dare and comes across the smoldering off-camera creature. A scene in a hospital radiation room where a medical Casanova and a pretty nurse have come for an assignation is certainly memorable. As the creature enters the room, off-camera, the doctor's flesh begins to burn. His thumb twists and grows to twice its normal size. After the poor fellow collapses, his flesh literally melts and drips off his skull in a grisly shock scene that was cut for TV showings in the years after the film's release.

There are tense moments, especially at the climax, when one character volunteers to lure the creature out of the fissure by backing up a Jeep containing radioactive material. The Jeep's wheels get stuck in the mud just as the monster begins to poke its wet mass out of the crack in the mud. The film is not "sensational" for the most part like *The Blob*; it's often talky, "serious," and a bit dull, but it does hold the attention and work up some shudders. In fact, the serious tone of the film gives it a veracity that similar films often lack.

Although there have been reports that the script was originally to be turned into another Quatermass movie, it is more likely that it was simply an imitation of the Quatermass series. Further films with the Adam Royston character did not materialize. Dean Jagger, who is quite good in the film, objected to the original director, Joseph Losey, because he had been blacklisted and Jagger refused to work with an alleged "Communist sympathizer." Losey went on to direct several movies, some of which were in the science fiction genre. The work of his replacement, Leslie Norman, is professional and workmanlike; Gerald Gibbs of *Quatermass 2* was responsible for the crisp black and white lensing. The prolific Jimmy Sangster contributed the screenplay. Leo McKern, who plays Inspector McGill, would later show off his comic talents in *The Adventure of Sherlock Holmes' Smarter Brother* and played in *Rumpole of the Bailey* for British television. Anthony Newley, who plays a charismatic soldier named "Spider" Webb, had a big hit with his show *Stop the World, I Want to Get Off* some time later. Jane Aird and Michael Brooke offer the only humanistic touches in the film as the grieving parents of the boy in the woods who dies of his injuries.

The Unknown Terror (1957) had enough eerie and distinctive scenes for it to make an impression on young creature feature fans. An expedition consisting of spelunker Dan Matthews (John Howard), his wife Gina (Mala Powers) and old friend Peter Morgan (Paul Richards) travel to South America to search for Gina's brother, who disappeared while trying to find a legendary cavern known as Cuervo Muerto, the Cave of Death. The trio stay with the secretive Dr. Ramsey (Gerald Milton) — who experiments with fungi, supposedly to extract antibiotics — and his beautiful Indian wife Concha (May Wynn). Matthews and the others enter the cave only to discover that Ramsey has filled it with transformed Indians and a giant fungus, which if unleashed "will destroy the world!" Morgan uses explosives to trap the spreading fungus, Matthews and Ramsey are killed, and Gina is free to be with the man, Morgan, that she has apparently always loved.

The special effects are cheaply done but effective. Much fun has been made of the so-called "soap bubble" effect of the spreading fungus — it's certainly some kind of foamy liquid — but it looks just like what it's supposed to be, a spreading, viscous material that seems slimy and dangerous. The cave creatures who have been exposed to the fungus are humanoid monsters (tribal sacrifices, one assumes) with long black hair and disfigured faces that are barely glimpsed. They remind one a bit of either Morlocks from *The Time Machine* or the Boogey Men from Laurel and Hardy's *Babes in Toyland* (aka *March of the Wooden Soldiers*). The cave setting in the film — designed by James W. Sullivan — is wonderfully creepy, with a pool of boiling liquid, and spores and mold covering the rocks, although it's hardly as large or awesome as something that the locals think of as purgatory should be.

The movie is good comic book fun. The climax with the fungus pouring down from the outcroppings and threatening the cast is exciting, and it's a kick to see Morgan discovering that there's a *door* in the cave that leads right into Ramsey's home (especially as it takes the group a long time to even find the cave, which is directly below them all the time). The movie pulls you in right from the start with the prologue involving the missing brother coming upon something terrifying in the cave and by positing several other mysteries — the past history of Mr. and Mrs. Matthews and Morgan, for instance — and taking its time to explain them. Screenwriter Kenneth Higgins' dialogue is often unconvincing, however, with the characters never quite saying what they would probably say under the circumstances. When after the first trip Morgan returns from the cave without Matthews, you can't imagine that Matthews' wife wouldn't cry out, "You mean you just *left* him there?!" In addition, the mad doctor Ramsey is given absolutely no motive for wanting to create a fungus that could "destroy the world!"

The actors are adequate but often perfunctory, such as when Morgan and Matthews come upon the body of a young Indian man who helped them and have so little reaction to his death that they seem like cold-blooded monsters. Raoul Kraushaar's music adds to the atmosphere and there's even a pretty theme for Concha. There's also a snappy Calypso number, "Suffer to be Born Again," which intrigues Matthews because the grim lyrics (set to a bouncy beat) actually describe the Cuervo Muerto. Director Charles Marquis Warren, a busy helmsman of low-budget features and TV episodes, keeps things moving; this was his only genre credit. An interesting aspect of *The Unknown Terror* is that it presents yet another "blob" that predates *The Blob.*

Although obviously not the first movie to deal with a "blob" or shapeless monster, *The Blob* is the most famous and financially successful of the bunch. It was one of the few creature features of the period to be released in widescreen format and in Technicolor with a huge publicity campaign. Steve (Steve McQueen) and Jane (Aneta Corsaut) are driving home from a date when they come upon an elderly man (Olin Howlin) stumbling across the road. The old man happened across a small meteorite containing an unknown substance that crawled up on his arm. At the doctor's office, the substance completely consumes the old-timer, then makes quick work of the doctor and his nurse. As the creature absorbs other townfolk, Steve and Jane try to warn the cops of the danger, but they think it's a practical joke. Finally the now-massive blob invades a move theater, and then traps Steve, Jane and others inside a diner. The creature is defeated by freezing it with CO_2.

A variety of techniques were used to bring the Blob to life. In some shots it's merely a tricked-up weather balloon. In others it's silicone gel and maneuvered with air pressure. The Blob looks surprisingly good and realistic for the most part. There's a wonderful bit when it slips under the door of a supermarket freezer and briefly looks just like a huge, hungry tongue. The red gelatinous growth covering the hand of the old man is effectively disquieting, and the Blob emits a yellowish glow when the nurse hits it with hydrochloric acid. Cartoon animation is employed to show high-tension wires falling onto the Blob once it envelops the diner. When the Blob oozes onto the diner it's actually attaching itself to a *photograph* of the building, a technique also employed by Bert I. Gordon in the previous year's *Beginning of the End.*

A major flaw of *The Blob* is that there isn't enough of the monster, with much of the running time devoted to Steve and Jane, their teenage hot-rodder pals, the exasperated police, and so on. In spite of this, the film manages to work up some chills and suspense of a minor variety. There's a creepy bit when the doctor, calling his nurse on the phone, sees the blanket covering the old man in the next room rising and *rising* as if something is under there. At the movie theater, the Blob somehow rears up from the floor and attacks

The deadly fungus of *The Unknown Terror* (1957) erodes the flesh of a victim.

the projectionist like a club, then squeezes through the apertures in the front wall of the projection booth. Nothing much else happens however; we just see screaming teenagers running from the theater.

Nearly thirty at the time of filming, Steve McQueen displays star quality in *The Blob*, but so do some of his less-famous buddies. Whether she was playing a prim and proper, very dull teen like Jane, or "Helen Crump" on *The Andy Griffith Show*, Aneta Corsaut was always one of the most sexless of Hollywood leading ladies, although her performance in *The Blob*, her first credit, is not bad. Corsaut later appeared in *The Toolbox Murders* with Cameron Mitchell. Olin Howlin, the first victim of the Blob, also played the crazy old coot in the alcoholic ward who sees the giant ants outside his window in *Them!*. He could practically be the same character four years later.

Burt Bacharach composed the awful song that plays over the opening credits. He received no on-screen credit and was probably grateful in his later years. Ralph Carmichael's score is no world-beater, but it's sufficiently spooky when it needs to be. Irwin S. Yeaworth, Jr., directs with efficiency if little flair. In 1972, Larry Hagman of *Dallas* fame directed a campy comic sequel to the film, *Beware! The Blob*, and there was a more elaborate remake in 1988.

339-A- "THE BLOB" #1

The ever-delightful Olin Howland comes across the meteroid that contains the jelly creature in *The Blob* (1958); shortly afterward he'll become its first victim.

The remake has the same essential storyline as the original but suggests that the Blob comes not from outer space — although it still descends from the sky like a meteor — but is a bacteriological warfare experiment gone haywire. Much of the running time deals with the arrival in town of a "biological containment team" that hopes to use the Blob as a weapon and affect "the balance of world power." The Steve McQueen character has been divided into two young men, a nice boy-next-door type, Paul (Donovan Leitch), and a bad-boy, reform-school (but really okay) type named Brian (Kevin Dillon). After Paul and his date Meg (Shawnee Smith) come across the old man with the stuff on his arm, Paul is killed and Brian and Meg team up to save the town. Meg takes a much more active role in the proceedings than the female lead in the first film.

When we first see the Blob coming out of the meteor and plopping onto the man's arm, it looks just as it did in the first film. Although it may seem to make sense that the Blob has an acidic quality, the first film didn't show us this aspect of the monster and the second does, as the Blob (like the monster in *Alien*) drips acid. This acid eats away the lower half of the old man's body. (It could be argued, however, that acid *destroys* tissue while the blob is supposed to *absorb* it, or how else could it grow so large?) Afterward the Blob generally looks like some red, slowly drying mass of rubber cement. The monster is brought to life via air bladders, animatronics, and even a flock of puppeteers making it move from within. Purple rock salt was used to form the frozen Blob at the end of the movie.

This Blob is more "creative" than the first one, at various times forming into a giant tower, opening up a maw-like orifice as it tries to engulf a few victims, and smacking one poor man into the sidewalk with a tentacle, then pulling the appendage up to show the man, crushed, stuck to the bottom. Unlike the first Blob, this smarter, more diabolical Blob spends a lot of time lurking on ceilings, dropping down on unsuspecting Paul in the hospital, and snapping out its tentacles to grab at the very surprised people below once it's grown much larger. A scene that was appreciated by many movie fans occurs when a man yakking through the movie showing at the local bijou is yanked right out of his seat by the Blob. The Blob also yanks a dishwasher *through* the tiny drain at the bottom of the kitchen sink, and engulfs a phone booth and the waitress inside. Occasionally we see its victims swimming inside the goo, half-dead or screaming.

The movie takes too long to get going, however. The opening scenes involving assorted high schoolers play like a teen comedy and almost give *The Blob* a slasher film sensibility. At least this leads to one genuinely hilarious scene when Scott, one of Paul's friends, buys condoms at the pharmacy. Because his priest is hovering nearby, Scott tells the pharmacist that the prophylactics are actually for Paul and his date. When Paul goes to pick up Meg, her father turns out to be the pharmacist!

Although there are some effective scenes sprinkled throughout the movie, *The Blob* suffers from Chuck Russell's slack direction and pacing. The expanded storyline involving the biological containment team makes the film lose its focus and even become dull. Perhaps the ultimate Blob film has yet to be made.

Caltiki the Immortal Monster (*Caltiki, il mostro immortale*), made in 1958, is an interesting variation on *The Blob*. An expedition to Mayan ruins discovers a strange living creature that can grow and absorb human flesh. Professor John Fielding (John Merivale) destroys it with fire but not before it infects the arm of his friend Max (Gerard Herter), who eventually goes mad. Fielding learns that the creature is a unicellular animal over 20 million years old. Fielding also learns that the creature's outbreaks — the last of which apparently was in 607 AD when the Mayans disappeared — coincide with the appearance of a radioactive comet that is now again approaching the Earth. In Merivale's home laboratory, a portion of the creature divides into many monsters — one of which is several hundred feet tall — and threatens his wife and child until the Army use flame throwers to blast them out of existence.

This Italian production is bolstered by a good story by Filippo Sanjust (Philip Just) which proved rather influential; a similar premise was used for Dean Koontz' novel *Phantoms* and the subsequent film version, among others. If there is any major problem with the movie it's the monster itself, which is brought to life with very mixed results. In general Caltiki looks like a writhing carpet or a shapeless piece of rubber or vinyl. Supposedly rising out of an underground lake, it actually looks as if someone off-screen and in front of the lake is pushing it up from below into camera range. Air is pumped into the "carpet" to make it wiggle and grow in size. It looks like stretching taffy covered with soap bubbles in the scene when it splits into two (which may be why the pseudonym "Foam" was used for one crew member). Shot against the backdrop of miniature props such as furniture, it resembles a giant mottled tongue poking into corridors that can barely contain it.

Another problem is that Caltiki doesn't appear very much until the finale. Far too much of the running time is devoted to the psychotic antics of Max, a sleazeball who treats his lover Linda miserably, and comes on to his friend Fielding's wife, Ellen. Affected by the monster invading his brain, he goes completely insane and breaks out of the hospital, terrorizing Linda and Ellen at Fielding's home before being dispatched by Caltiki. The shot of his head being engulfed by the blob, re-emerging as a fleshless skull, was a memorable shock scene of the '50s. We also see another victim of the monster, only in this case his eyeballs are still intact inside his skull, a nice macabre touch.

Among the better aspects of *Caltiki* are the atmospheric scenes in the underground Mayan temple with its stone steps, spooky caverns, big statues and that sinister pool that hides many skeletons and of course Caltiki itself. Some outdoor scenes seem to have been shot on actual ruins while others employ matte paintings. The most exciting and suspenseful scene occurs at the climax when Fielding tries to get his wife and daughter out of the house, which is in flames. As he places a ladder below the second story window where they wait, one of the blobs begins to enter the bedroom behind them. Fielding realizes another blob is quickly approaching the ladder under his feet. He manages to get his family out before they can be burned or eaten alive.

The film is so heavily dubbed that it's difficult to judge the actors' performances. John Merivale makes a stalwart, intense hero, while Gerard Henter seems to play Max over-the-top before he's even out of the starting gate. Didi Sullivan and Daniela Rocca are at the least decorative as Ellen and Linda respectively, and Rocca seems rather vivid. Director Riccardo Freda (Robert Hampton) doesn't give the film too much style but he keeps things moving. He later claimed that much of the film was actually directed by the cinematographer, Mario Bava (John Foam). Bava also contributed to the special effects under the pseudonym "Marie Foam."

England's *Fiend Without a Face* (1958) was based on a notion also used in *Forbidden Planet* (1956) but also provided creature fans with some highly original and unusual monsters. On and around a U. S. Air Force base in Manitoba, people are killed by a deadly unseen force. Their brains and entire spinal columns have been sucked out "like an egg" through two holes in the skull. Major Jeff Cummings (Marshall Thompson) investigates and meets the sister, Barbara Griselle (Kim Parker), of the first victim. Cummings becomes suspicious of Barbara's employer, Professor Walgate (Kynaston Reeves), who has written about psychic phenomena. Eventually Walgate confesses that he is inadvertently behind the murders. Using a thought materialization device, he created an invisible being to contain his detached thoughts. Drawing on radiation from the base's atomic plant, the being has multiplied. Becoming visible as they draw more power, the monsters — brains that slither along on their spinal columns — attack en masse but are defeated when Cummings runs to the plant and sets an explosive which destroys the building.

Fiend Without a Face proceeds as a perplexing mystery for its first half, unlike films whose titles scream out the identity of the mysterious creatures before you've even entered the theater (*The Deadly Mantis* and *Attack of the Crab Monsters*, for example). Unfortunately the film's poster art shows one of the brain monsters, so no one in the audience could have been very surprised by what they saw during the climax. Although a bit silly-looking, even "cute," the lively living brains are inventive and unique. They use their spinal cords to strangle victims, push themselves forward across the floor, and even to propel themselves into the air. They have antennae coming out of the "head" (the brain itself) and two thin slithering, arm-like tentacles on either side of the spine. The sounds they make are unnerving: thumping heartbeats accompanied by somehow "angry" sloshing, crunching, liquidy noises.

The brains were brought to life via stop-motion animation by the team of K. L. Ruppel and Florenz Von Nordhoff. Not only are the monster models well-designed, but the animation itself is very fluid. Some of the brains even have a bit of personality, such as when one lands on a couch in the professor's living room and sort of cocks its head like a curious dog. With their creations' antennae, spines, and tentacles all going in different directions, Tuppel and Von Nordhoff must have had quite a time keeping the frame-by-frame movements of the creatures straight (although not as hard a time as Harryhausen did keeping track of the Hydra's many heads in *Jason and the Argonauts*). There is some excellent time-lapse photography showing the dead brains dissolving into bubbly goo, backed by "plopping" sounds.

Early attack scenes, when people are killed by noisy invisible creatures, are well-handled. The climax after the brains become visible has an almost unavoidable black comedy aspect to it, especially as the brains seem to continuously launch themselves at the very shapely screaming heroine instead of the men. When one cowardly character panics and refuses to help the others board up the doors and windows, there is little surprise when one of the creatures drops down into the fireplace and gets him. The brains themselves are probably better actors than most of the cast but they're just a little *too* bizarre to take seriously.

There are similarities to *Forbidden Planet* (but one must keep in mind that *Fiend* was based on a story that predated *Forbidden Planet*). The flashback showing Walgate trying to create matter out of thought with his device instantly reminds one of the scene in *Planet* when the astronauts use a similar (if more elaborate) kind of device in the Krell laboratory. Walgate's device even gives him a shock, as the Krell device does the Earthlings.

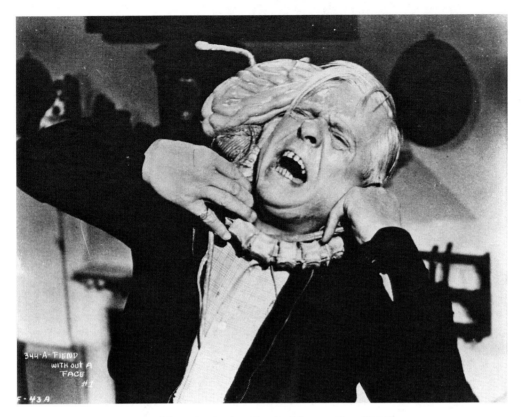

A pitiful victim in the *Fiend without a Face* (1958).

The monster in *Forbidden Planet* is a materialization of Morbius' thoughts, just as the brains in *Fiend* are the materialization of Walgate's thoughts.

The pseudo-science of *Fiend* is particularly of the old comic book variety. Walgate states that his brain-creatures are using the stolen brains of the murdered townspeople to move around in, but this simply isn't possible, as there are *dozens* of monsters and only a very few people have been killed. Besides, Walgate also claims that the "fiends" reproduce by using the energy from the atomic plant; as they are already the *solid* materialization of thought, why would they even *need* a human brain to reside in? There are other problems as well. Constable Gibbons goes out to hunt the monsters and comes back a jibbering idiot but we never learn if he's in shock, has had his brain removed but still lives, or what ultimately becomes of him. At the climax when Cummings rushes through the woods to the atomic plant, Barbara says "Jeff's been gone for hours!" but there's absolutely no sense of the passage of time. To the viewer it only seems as if he's been gone for a few minutes.

Leading man Marshall Thompson with his baby face and bland demeanor at first seems an unlikely hero but he's able to work up some amusing petulance at times. Kim Parker is not only decorative but is a competent enough actress. Previously she had appeared in *Fire Maidens of Outer Space* (1956) but would make only one more film after *Fiend*. There are a host of effective character actors in the movie, including Kynaston Reeves as the professor.

Buxton Orr's score makes absolutely no impression. Arthur Crabtree would direct one more horror item, *Horrors of the Black Museum*—his last directorial effort—the following year. Despite its flaws, *Fiend Without a Face* is well-paced, suspenseful, and very entertaining.

The Crawling Eye (1958) was a British terror film based on the television serial *The Trollenberg Terror*, which was the film's U.K. title. Mysterious disappearances and deaths occur on the Trollenberg mountain in the quaint Swiss village of the same name. Scientist Alan Brooks (Forrest Tucker) arrives in the village at the urging of Professor Crevett (Warren Mitchell), who runs an observatory at the top of the mountain. Crevett sees warning signs that remind him of an alien infestation in the Andes a few years before, such as a radioactive cloud that never moves. The aliens want to kill Anne Pilgrim (Janet Munro), one-half of a sister mind-reading act, because of her telepathic abilities, and they resuscitate a murdered man, Brett (Andrew Faulds), for that purpose. The aliens—big cyclopean, brain-like horrors with tentacles—make their move under cover of the cloud and attack the observatory where the villagers have taken refuge, but bombs from fighter planes blow them to pieces.

The "crawling eyes" of the movie are scary, well-designed, bus-sized horrors with pneumatic tentacles that become quite thin at the ends while still looking strong enough to yank various people off of the ground. What makes these critters especially unnerving are the eyes set in the middle of their bodies (they have no faces to speak of). Generally FX men just plop a big round frozen prop eyeball in their assorted monsters, but effects man Les Bowie was wise enough to surround the aliens' eyeballs with membrane-like tissue, so that when the eyes move from side to side they have a much more realistic appearance. The creatures will seem ludicrous to monster fans weaned on computer imagery, but on their own terms they are very effective. The brain-bodies of the aliens are lined with veins and are white in color.

The other effects work in the film may be cheap but it all works. Bowie was embarrassed by the alien cloud on the mountain, which is simply a piece of cotton tacked to a photograph, but it looks just fine and even glows on and off as if from inner activity or radiation. A dead man's arm dissolves in a puff of smoke and becomes skeletonized in a nifty bit of superimposition. The miniatures of the village and the observatory on its cliff face are all well-done.

The film gets right into the thick of things with a prologue in which a student climber has his head torn off in an accident. A lot of horror surrounds the character Brett, another climber who is killed by the aliens but returns to do their dirty work. He deposits the head of his friend in a knapsack and takes a pickaxe to two members of a rescue party who get too close to the cloud. The scenes when he comes back to the inn—now an alien struggling to pretend to be human—and tries more than once to murder Anne are exciting and creepy, although it's almost comical to see Anne's sister Sarah screaming repeatedly for Alan instead of doing *something* herself when Brett storms into Anne's bedroom with a cleaver; Sarah could at least have thrown something at the guy until Alan arrived with his pistol. Our first sight of the alien as it knocks down the door of the hotel and plays peek-a-boo with its big eyeball is a highlight, as is the business with the cables beginning to freeze as Alan and the others escape by cable car to the observatory far above.

180

The film has been criticized because when Alan saves the reporter Phillip (Laurence Payne) from one of the monsters right outside the observatory's front door, his actions are captured by a closed circuit camera. How can this be when the rooftop cameras always seem pointed at the mountain and the cloud that covers it? But there's no reason why there couldn't be a camera just outside the front door as well, one that will reveal who visitors are before allowing them entry. However, there are a couple of "impossible" moments elsewhere in the film. The first of these concerns the death of the climber Dewhurst. His companion, Brett, has left the hut they are staying in and disappeared. Dewhurst opens the door, looks out, sees only snow, and closes the door. We can see that there is no one else in the cabin, and no one, Brett included, has walked in through the door. Yet after he closes the door, Dewhurst looks toward the camera and starts to scream — but at what? The next day his headless body is discovered in the hut. There are a number of decapitations in the film, most performed by Brett, but it is also likely that the tentacles of the aliens could tear off a person's head. But who got Dewhurst? Brett is clearly not in the cabin, and there is no crashing noise to suggest the aliens have smashed their way into the hut, whose door (bolted from the inside, no less) and walls are completely untouched the following morning. The only explanation is that one of the monsters managed to open a window with its tentacle, tore off Dewhurst's head, and then closed the window behind it, creating a mystery and hiding evidence of its existence. But the movie never makes this clear.

Another problem arises while Alan and the rest of the villagers are waiting for the cable car to take them up to the observatory. It makes sense that the cable car station wouldn't be far from the inn, probably next door, but an insert shows the village and inn far, *far* below the station. Not only does it make it ridiculous that a small child would be able to go all the way back down to the inn for her missing ball, but even more implausible that the mother would never notice she was gone during all the time it would take her little legs to descend. Clearly the inn is not such a great distance from the cable car station as is shown, and just as clearly this is a case of the filmmakers using what they had at hand — those long shots of the village — without stopping to realize how it would look.

As in *Cosmic Monsters*, Forrest Tucker makes an acceptable lead, but he hardly reacts to the incredible nature of the aliens once he sees one of them outside the hotel lobby. Janet Munro plays the part of the confused telepathic Anne with more conviction. *The Crawling Eye* is one of the creepiest and most entertaining British creature features ever, but one sometimes wishes that director Quentin Lawrence had sometimes picked up the pace, and that the film had a more memorable and exciting musical score than the one provided by Stanley Black.

The relationship of *It! The Terror from Beyond Space* (1958) to *Alien* will be discussed shortly, but for now we'll concentrate on *It!* which deals with a rescue mission to Mars — in 1973!— to pick up the only survivor, Colonel Edward Carruthers (Marshall Thompson), of the first expedition. Carruthers insists that everyone else was killed by a barely seen creature — said creature sneaks aboard the flight going back to Earth, of course — but the others, especially commander Van Heusen (Kim Spalding), think he killed his companions so that the supplies would last longer (their ship developed technical problems, stranding them). It isn't long before bodies begin turning up on the ship and the creature makes its presence known. The alien sucks out every bit of liquid in the human body through osmosis. Van Heusen's girl, Ann (Shawn Smith), falls for Carruthers, while Van Heusen picks up a space germ from the monster and conveniently dies. The monster itself is killed when the astronauts draw all the oxygen out of the ship, effectively suffocating it.

It! is an easy movie to belittle, but the fact is that it's a taut, fast-paced, entertaining B picture that holds the attention and on its low-budget level is rather well done. The monster, essayed by Ray "Crash" Corrigan, who starred in the serial *Undersea Kingdom* decades before and had been playing gorillas and the like ever since, has a bony, ridged, ghoulish face with big teeth and clawed, grubby hands; the suit was designed by Paul Blaisdell. The script was by Jerome Bixby, best known as the author of "It's a Good Life," about a little boy whose mental powers hold his entire town in thrall. The characters are more likable than the ones in the later *Alien*, and Bixby even adds some humanistic touches and dialogue that gets across the innermost feelings and fears of the crew members.

Van Heusen is a touching figure, watching the woman he loves fall for somebody else as he lies helpless and dying. (At the end of the film, after he's collapsed and died after saving the others by opening the air lock, Ann *completely ignores him* and runs over to hold hands with Carruthers!) Van Heusen is made all the more poignant a figure because there's just something about the actor portraying him, a certain world-weariness or defeatist attitude that he somehow emanates. Spalding didn't do much acting thereafter. *It!* was Corrigan's final film.

There are some very good scenes in *It!*, such as when a crew member tries to rescue another fellow who's stuck in a claustrophobic air shaft with the monster. Although it usually garners laughs at film festivals, the shot of two men walking up the outside of the ship is perfectly serviceable and even effective. The acting, from some new young players and reliable character actors, is good as well. Edward L. Cahn probably never directed another movie with such surprising staying power. Paul Sawtell and Bert Shefter, who would go on to bigger projects, contributed the spooky musical score.

The Horror of Party Beach (1964) was a combination monster flick and beach party movie. Radioactive waste dumped offshore mutates skulls in a shipwreck into humanoid monsters — essentially giant protozoas — that feed off human blood. Their first victim is wild and crazy Tina (Marilyn Clarke) whose bloody body washes up on the beach. As the attacks continue, Tina's boyfriend Hank Green (John Scott), his boss Dr. Gavin (Allan Laurel), and Gavin's daughter Elaine (Alice Lyon) try to come up with a way to destroy the creatures even as they track them to their lair in an abandoned quarry. Elaine is nearly killed by the monsters before her father and Hank show up to vanquish them with sodium bombs.

The "horrors" of Party Beach are men in tight costumes with big frog-like faces (outsized head pieces) and what looks like seaweed clinging to their bodies. They have big white round eyes set deep in well-like bony sockets. They have clawed, slimy fingers, and their mouths are full of what appear to be phallic-like sausages but which are possibly meant to be some kind of weird teeth or tongues. The actors playing the "horrors" move with an odd, sideways shuffle, wiggling their behinds, and are often rather hammy in their pantomiming. The monsters make noises like metallic burps or gurgles. Some people think the creatures — who multiply as if by magic as the movie proceeds — resemble sea horses. Time lapse photography is used to show tissue growing on a skull and forming into a monster, with somewhat transparent fish swimming by. There is one not-bad shot showing the first creature, the skull beneath the new tissue still apparent, beginning to come to life. The explanations for the origin and behavior of the monsters are so much gobbledygook.

There are several attack scenes in the movie, none of which are done with any particular style. When the monsters invade a slumber party and kill twenty young women, we see quick shots of girls with torn disfigured faces, fingers being stuffed into the creatures' mouths, close-ups of screaming bloody teenagers, all very frenetic (and disturbing at the time) if not impressive in the cinematic sense. There is some suspense in a scene when the monsters trail two women down the street and are just on the verge of grabbing one of them when the girls' ride arrives to pick them up and they're spared. There is even more suspense at the climax, when Elaine has her leg caught between rocks at the quarry as night falls and the monsters begin to emerge from the water.

Although the main targets of the monsters are nubile women — considering that the target audience for the film was teenage boys — some men get killed as well, such as two drunken pals who encounter the creatures and a young man who is found clawed to death in his car. However, one does get the feeling that the first victim, Tina, is almost being punished for her licentious, "shocking" behavior on the beach, flirting and dancing shamelessly with the guys and almost baring her breasts at one point. (Talk about *Girls Gone Wild*!) "You ain't seen livin' till you've seen Tina swing!" the young lady says. Tina seems almost innocent by today's standards. She is a very recognizable type, however: the young woman who has average looks but attracts men by acting all sexy and by at least appearing to be "easy."

At first Eulabelle Moore seems to be playing a ludicrously stereotypical black maid more of the type one used to see in Hollywood films of the 40s and 50s. She is uneducated, superstitious (she believes the monsters are the result of voodoo) and discovers the way to kill them purely by accident (knocking something over onto the severed hand of one of the creatures). At the same time she is never deferential nor docile, is highly opinionated, and despite her in some ways simple-minded nature she inspires others to necessary action, such as when Hank seems about to give up on his search for a supply of sodium until she tells him to get cracking.

Director Del Tenney seems to have ambitions to direct something along the lines of *West Side Story*, which was released three years earlier. Tenney has Hank and Elaine approach each other across a dance floor like Tony and Maria in the earlier film. In the opening beach scene there are acrobatic fighter-dancers who remind you a bit of the Sharks and the Jets. The groovy Del-Aires provide several perfectly pleasant rock songs, including "Zombie Stomp," "I'm not a Summer Love," and "Elaine," which sounds like something that made the charts in '64. The uncredited musical score consists mostly of squeaky, jangling noises as well as weird electronic music for the monsters' theme.

The screenplay was by Richard Hilliard, who also did the honors for Tenney's *Psychomania*, a *Psycho* imitation, the previous year. He also did the wide screen photography for *Party Beach*, which is crisp and professional for the most part, but often under-lit. The editing is often very clumsy. *Horror of Party Beach* was the only acting credit for most of the amateurish cast, including hero John Scott, who served as assistant director on Del Tenney's *The Curse of the Living Corpse* that same year. It was also the only acting credit for Alice Lyon and Allan Laurel, although Eulabelle Moore appeared in a couple of TV shows and Marilyn Clarke appeared in one more film and a TV episode. Tenney himself played the gas station attendant some girl customers think is "cute."

The Horror of Party Beach is a well-liked "trash" movie with many devotees — and it is fun at times — but it ultimately fails to sustain tension or interest.

The Flesh Eaters (1964) was one of the most inventive — and gruesome — creature features of the 60s. A down-on-his-luck pilot, Grant Murdoch (Byron Sanders), agrees to fly alcoholic actress Laura Winters (Rita Morley) and her long-suffering secretary, Jan Letterman (Barbara Wilkin), to Provincetown so that the former can make a stage appearance. Forced to land on an isolated island due to mechanical problems, the trio encounter mysterious marine biologist Peter Bartell (Martin Kosleck). Bartell had been a U.S. agent assigned to spy on Nazi experiments in Germany; now that the war is over, he is continuing one of those experiments in the hopes of selling the results — a small organism that eats human flesh — to the highest bidder. Bartell kills a beatnik who arrives on the island, and inadvertently merges his Flesh Eaters into two huge creatures — one about a hundred times larger than the other. Murdock manages to kill the larger of the monsters with human blood, while Bartell falls amidst his Flesh Eaters and, in agony, commits suicide before they can fully consume him.

The Flesh Eaters themselves are little more than dots of light, an inky or phosphorescent circle in the water, and when they are agitated or feasting throw off a kind of bubbly boiling effect that looks like the water they're in has turned to seltzer. There is also a shimmering phosphorescence on the fish skeletons that are lying all over the beach. The first creature (comprised of Flesh Eaters) is about three feet high and is a duplicate of the much larger one, which is about twelve to fifteen feet high. These crab-like creatures have two pincers, mottled skin with large white bumps, a maw surrounded by wiggling, floppy tentacles, and a round nucleus on top of the head. They are neither cute nor pretty but they do generate disgust. They appear to be props with limited mobility.

The other effects are not exactly hi-tech. A huge solar battery that Bartell uses to gather power for his experiments looks like a huge cardboard domino. The skeleton of a victim on the beach, all clean, stark white, with the bones all attached, looks like something you might find in a doctor's office — or a novelty store. At least the hero doesn't buy it when the mad doctor suggests the victim was eaten by sharks that just happened to pick the bones clean!

The Flesh Eaters is full of memorable sequences. The best is a protracted, suspenseful bit when Laura goes out on a jetty to get her suitcase full of liquor that has washed up against the rocks. Laura panics and has trouble clambering over the rocks and getting back to the beach. Grant goes out to save her, balancing precariously on one big slab beneath which the Flesh Eaters are sizzling. As Laura is unable to move, he has to jump to her rock, then jump back, carrying her in his arms. One slip and.... Expert filming employing tight shots and clever angles, as well as adroit editing by Radley Metzger, creates a taut and exciting sequence.

A truly gruesome sequence — in fact, *The Flesh Eaters* is preoccupied with blood — has Bartell feed some of his Flesh Eaters to the beatnik Omar (Ray Tudor), who writhes on the ground, howls in agony, and watches as his stomach seems to dissolve into a pool of blood. Bartell records his death rattle and puts the recorder on a raft with Omar's body. This often censored shot shows what appears to be a completely different actor playing dead with a hole in his chest exposing his ribs. In 1964 this must have packed quite a wallop.

There are other good scenes. A flashback shows the Nazi experiments, with a series of women calmly jumping one by one into a pool filled with Flesh Eaters without a sound or struggle, which somehow makes the whole sequence even more disquieting. A man who arrives at the island in a supply boat has his face stripped of flesh when he plows inadvertently into the flesh eaters. This scene is particularly disturbing because it had earlier been established that this man, Matt (Christopher Drake), is a decent fellow who comes a day early because he's genuinely concerned about Bartell after a sudden storm battered the island. In the finale Grant grabs onto the giant monster's pincer and lets it lift him up to the nucleus so that he can shoot it full of blood (the only thing that can kill it) from an outsized syringe (the black-and-white film turns red for a few seconds).

The actors are all pretty good. Byron Sanders may not be a great actor but he intelligently plays this stuff for all its worth, never suggesting that it's beneath him, which it isn't. Rita Morley offers a striking portrait of a spoiled, childish, petulant, utterly overbearing, but oddly likable woman-child. There's an amusing shot of her kneeling as if in worship at Bartell's feet, part of her ploy to seduce the mad doctor. Barbara Wilkin may have been hired for her great figure — she strips off her blouse to use it for bandages at one point, walking around in her bra until Grant chivalrously gives her his shirt — but she's perfectly professional as Jan. Her apparent non-reaction to the shooting death of Laura has more to do with poor continuity than with any inadequacy on her part. Ray Tudor has fun as the sad, comical, terribly doomed beatnik who intones that "love is the weapon" all the time, but is proved disastrously wrong. Martin Kosleck is perfection as Bartell. Finding the aforementioned skeleton on the beach, he feigns compassion and sympathy — "Some little family is out searching for a mother or a daughter at this very moment," he intones — effectively hiding his sociopathic nature.

Kosleck was born in Germany and was so critical of the Nazi regime that Josef Goebbels ordered his execution by the SS. Kosleck managed to flee the country and emigrated to the U.S., where he became a very busy character actor, ironically cast as Nazi villains in most of his films. When he was 29, Byron Sanders modeled for Salvadore Dali for his painting *Crucifixion*. Years after his role in *Flesh Eaters*, he became a soap opera actor, and then turned to tennis instruction after retiring from acting. Rita Morley also wound up on soaps. Ray Tudor only did one other film. This was the only film credit for competent director Jack Curtis.

Julian Stein's score has a brassy, jangling appeal to it. The lensing is professional and crisp. Screenwriter Arnold Drake created *The Doom Patrol* for DC comics and was a busy comic book writer with a few minor screen credits. There is certainly a comic book–type zaniness and improbability to *The Flesh Eaters*, which is part of the fun. The premise and situations are splendid, and Drake also wrote some choice dialogue, much of it given to

Rita. After Omar shows up, Rita looks heavenward and says, "Now they're all here. Doctor Cyclops, Gunga Din, and now Buster Beatnik. Oh, Lord protect a simple lady lush in a place like this!" After Omar tells her that she has to give up everything that's poisoning her system, including white bread, alcohol, coffee, onions, and sex, she replies, "I can do without all of those things, but you can't expect me to give up onions!"

Island of Terror (1966), a late entry in the British creature feature sweepstakes, has a "'50s" feel to it. In some ways it's almost a remake of *Fiend Without a Face*. On a remote island, scientists try to find a cure for cancer by creating living matter to counteract the cancerous cells. Unfortunately this matter forms into deadly creatures dubbed "silicates" that are not carbon-based but live off the bones of animals and people. Dr. Brian Stanley (Peter Cushing) and David West (Edward Judd) arrive on the island to determine what's responsible for the grotesque boneless corpses being found and discover the Silicates. The scientists inject cattle with strontium 90 in the hopes that the radioactive substance will destroy the Silicates after they've ingested the cattle's bones. The plan works, but not before an attack on the town hall where the island's terrified inhabitants have gathered. An epilogue shows an explosion in a lab in Japan which signals the creation of more Silicates.

The Silicates emit eerie electronic chittering noises like metallic bugs, and make disgusting gurgling sounds — like liquid sucked through a straw — as they suck out their victims' bones. Their physical appearance is disappointing, however. They are flat, about a foot high and five feet long, turtle-like, with a very hard "shell" or external skeleton. Their bodies are black, mottled and shapeless and have a stalk, antennae or tentacle emerging from the front that wraps around victims and begins the ingestion process. In some ways they resemble miniature "Crawling Eyes" without the eyeballs. There is a nice, if weird, effect when the Silicates split in two and issue what looks like very thick spaghetti strands in a viscous broth.

Unfortunately, the Silicates' victims, all shriveled, shrunken and flattened, look a bit comical. When Stanley and West see their first de-boned corpse in the autopsy room, Peter Cushing's droll, understated delivery of "not a very pretty sight" is absolutely hilarious, especially when combined with a shot of the corpse itself, the face of which is almost laughably twisted and grotesque (like one of the masks in the classic *Twilight Zone* episode where the wealthy man makes his anxious heirs put on hideous masks that actually transform their faces). A lot of rubber limbs and heads are employed to portray the pitiful corpses.

There are moments that give one pause in *Island of Terror*. Their tentacles may explain how a silicate can wind up in the branches of a tall tree, but it doesn't explain how one would manage to climb on top of the smooth surface of a car roof — nor why it would want to go up there in the first place. One also has to wonder why the Silicates bothered closing the laboratory door behind them. No one ever makes much of an effort to save the victims — people just stand there and watch as their friends are being killed — until West picks up an axe when a tentacle wraps itself around Stanley's wrist. Instead of hacking at the tentacle first to see if that will make it let go, he *chops off Stanley's hand* — at Stanley's urging no less. The scene is nonsensical, but it does deliver a quick, very realistic shock for the viewer, a memorable '60s "gross-out" sequence.

Although *Island of Terror* is a low-budget production, it has an attractive look, thanks to Reginald H. Wyer's crisp photography, beautiful woodland settings, and exquisitely decorated old manor houses. Malcolm Lockyer's music is a decided plus, and Edward Andrew Mann and Allan Ramsen's screenplay is first-rate, proceeding for the first half like a very suspenseful mystery. Terence Fisher's direction is taut, fast-paced, and workmanlike. Edward Judd is typically stalwart and a bit stiff as West, but Peter Cushing is as marvelous as ever as Stanley. He etches a convincing portrait of a truly brave man in that he's clearly afraid, isn't afraid to say so, but does what has to be done in spite of it. His sense of humor — "Good Lord! It looks like Wuthering Heights!" he says as they approach the island laboratory where the nightmare began — adds to the picture's considerable charm.

Carole Gray is notable as West's new girlfriend, Toni, who accompanies the men to the island and whom West nearly mercy-kills with a needle when he thinks the Silicates are about to attack (he's a bit premature in every sense of the word). On her first date with West when the trouble erupts, Toni falls in love with him — and tells him so — very quickly. Judging from his uneasy manner when he's being tender with her, one has to hope West isn't commitment-phobic. At the end of the film, West makes a kind of "progress must always claim victims" speech that seems mighty insensitive to the de-boned island residents and their loved ones.

Alien (1979) not only presented a unique monster, but was one of the most influential (if derivative) "creature features" of all time. In outer space, the commercial towing vessel the *Nostromo* is on its way back to Earth when its crew are brought out of suspended animation early to investigate a signal coming from an unknown planet. The signal turns out to be a warning — with good reason, as one of the crew men, Kane (John Hurt), is attacked by an organism that attaches itself to his face, implanting a creature that eventually bursts out of his chest. This creature rapidly grows to huge size and kills off the other crew members one by one. In an escape pod, Ripley (Sigourney Weaver), the only survivor, manages to blast the alien out of existence after destroying the ship.

The alien was designed by artist H. R. Giger, who came up with a sleek, terrible, bio-mechanical monstrosity comprised of flesh and living metal — large black elongated head, a metallic "tongue" that can lash out and kill, claws, serrated tail, an essentially humanoid body. (The "bio-mechanical" theme carried over into the art direction; the derelict spaceship has outer holes that resemble vaginas.) An efficient killing machine and little else, it has acidic blood that seeps through several levels of the *Nostromo* in one of the best scenes. The aliens engendered many imitations, including The Brood or "sleazeoids" of the *X-Men* comic book, and numerous filmic monsters. *Alien* had the same premise as *It! The Terror from Beyond Space* (1958) — monster picked up on planet kills the crew off — but has a different tone and approach, aside from the obvious differences in budget. There were also marked similarities to Mario Bava's Italian space opera *Planet of the Vampires* (1965), which also featured a derelict spaceship with giant skeletal remains, which the characters of *Alien* come across at one point. None of the *Alien* sequels have ever introduced us to this star-spawning race of giants, more's the pity. (Incidentally, the characters in *Alien* have absolutely no reaction to the dead pilot's massive size.)

The production values and effects are first-rate, with superlative models and miniatures of the spaceship, escape pod and so on, and the sets, such as the huge chamber in

Alien (1979) was so successful that Sigourney Weaver battled the monsters in three films; her shaved head look is from *Alien 3* (1992).

which the alien eggs are found, highly impressive. The eggs, the creature that covers Kane's face, and so on, all look realistic because actual animal innards were used in their construction. But when you come right down to it, the alien — however striking it looks — is merely a stunt man in a black outfit and outsized helmet. Carlo Rambaldi was responsible for the "alien head FX," while Roger Dicken constructed the smaller alien creatures with their gooey insides.

Highlights include the once quite shocking business with the alien literally bursting from Kane's chest, and the sequence when the ship's commander, Dallas (Tom Skerritt), has a final encounter with the creature. Also startling is the sequence when the ship's science officer, Ash (Ian Holm), has his head literally knocked off by a punch from Parker (Yaphet Kotto) — Ash turns out to be a robot. There is a lot of suspenseful scurrying through claustrophobic corridors. If slow-paced at times, the picture is generally tense and harrowing.

Whatever its merits, *Alien* never strays too far from its B movie origins. The monster grows to full-size and then some in an incredibly short period, reminding one of a fantasy creature in a comic book or sword-and-sorcery epic. The characters in Dan O'Bannon's script are one-dimensional (one could even say Parker was a "lazy," whining, racist stereotype were it not for the fact that his buddy Brett comes off as his white counterpart), and they show little genuine concern for one another (even *It! The Terror from Beyond Space* is not so cold-blooded). The dead Kane is shot out into space by the unaffected others like so much space trash. Ripley was originally envisioned as a male character, but as a female she is admirably strong and efficient and effectively hides her emotions (which is not to say she is unemotional). Ripley and Lambert (played by *The Birds'* Veronica Cartwright, who was the first choice to play Ripley once it was decided to make the character female) are the yin and yang of

The crew of the *Nostromo* discover a spaceship with the huge remains of a dead pilot in an atmospheric scene from *Alien* (1979).

"femininity." Ripley gets things done while Lambert mostly just acts simpering and hysterical (not that anyone would blame her considering the circumstances). For a film that takes place in the silence of space, there is a lot of dramatic license taken as we hear the spaceship blowing up and many other explosive noises.

Early in the movie, Dallas and others come back to the ship with Kane, who has an alien life-form attached to his head and is in bad shape. Dallas wants Ripley to open the air lock but she refuses, citing the possibility that Kane has picked up a dangerous organism and needs to be quarantined outside the ship for all of their sakes. Ripley is making a good point, but Dallas, more humane if less practical, feels that Kane's chances for survival are nil if he can't be brought to sick bay. (Ripley's attitude might have been different had she had emotional feelings for Kane.) There is dramatic tension to the scene but it's all contrived. Ripley claims that when Dallas is off-ship she's in charge, but considering the fact that Dallas is *right there standing outside the ship* this argument is specious. In reality, she might have protested, but she would not have countermanded — or been realistically able to countermand — his orders. (Ash opens the air lock, because the company he "works" for wants to get its hands on the creature. It is never explained how anyone knows of its existence.) Of course, Ripley turns out to be right, and ironically — but not so surprisingly — she becomes the crew's only survivor.

The acting is serviceable if unspectacular. There is no denying that Sigourney Weaver is very effective in the role of Ripley in this and the three *Alien* sequels (she did not appear in *Alien vs. Predator*), although she has yet to prove her mettle as a "serious" actress, giving second-rate performances in just about every other picture she's appeared in. Playing Ripley has made her famous enough to be sought after, but hasn't given her the experience or sheer talent she needs to shine as anything else. Ridley Scott's stodgy direction takes a back seat to the effects and Derek Van Lint's atmospheric photography. Jerry Goldsmith's score has its moments, but the romantic music that plays over the end credits — and seems distinctly out of place if decidedly beautiful — comes from Howard Hanson's Symphony # 2.

As of this writing, a sequel is being made to *Alien vs. Predator*. Entitled *Aliens* [plural] *vs. Predator* it will be the sixth film in the series.

David Seltzer, screenwriter of *The Omen*, prepared an excellent "novelization" (which actually read like a first-rate horror novel) of his screenplay for *Prophecy* (1979), which arrived in book stores a few months before the film itself hit movie screens. The book was gobbled up by happy monster devotees, who formed a built-in audience for the hotly anticipated screen version. Unfortunately, these same fans spread the word that the film was not on a par with the book, and *Prophecy* sank at the box office. Which is too bad, for the film has much to recommend it.

Maggie and Rob Vern (Talia Shire and Robert Foxworth) are a professional couple — she plays cello, he's a doctor serving the underprivileged — living in Washington, D.C. Rob decides to take an offer from the Environmental Protection Agency to go to Maine to see what is adversely affecting the "O.P.s" (Original People or Native Americans) who live in the area. The Verns discover not only that there is a major dispute between the Opies and the lumber company over who owns the land, but that many people have gone missing, their disappearances blamed on the "Indians." They also discover that the local paper mill is using an outlawed chemical, methyl mercury, to cheaply prevent algae build-up on their lumber. Mercury poisoning is responsible for birth deformities and odd behavior among the Opies, and has also created a huge, hungry mutant monster which some locals think is the god Katahdin. Maggie is greatly alarmed because she has eaten some fish and, unbeknownst to Rob, who wants no children, is pregnant. After several deaths and many misunderstandings, Rob manages to kill the creature as it attacks him and others at his cabin. (The situation with Maggie's pregnancy, Rob's reaction to same, and any possible birth defects remain unresolved.)

Prophecy was excoriated by critics, many of whom had read the book and were just as anxious to see a great film adaptation as everyone else. The shame of it is that *Prophecy* is actually a pretty high-class monster movie, with one highly unfortunate exception — the monster itself, which is understandably a big problem in any creature feature. While the monster in *Prophecy* may not look as ridiculous as the big bird of *The Giant Claw*, it looks nothing like the monster described in the novel or pictured in the advertisements. It's explained in the film that mercury adheres to DNA and freezes the development of the monster-fetus at different stages along the evolutionary scale (all fetuses go through this process). Therefore the beast should be a nightmarish conglomeration of different types of animals in a huge, hulking frame. The animal is huge, all right, but it simply resembles an outsized bear that walked into a propeller; it has red, disfigured skin and the left side of its face looks like bloody hamburger. Most of the time the beast is only seen in very quick shots, which was a wise move on the moviemakers' part, but at the climax the camera lingers over it a little too long. The failure of *Prophecy* can be traced to one absolutely dreadful long shot as the monster rushes at the cast from the ruins of the cabin, looking like nothing so much as a pudgy overgrown Teddy bear played by a man in a ludicrously unconvincing costume.

A shot that lasts mere seconds put paid to a movie that otherwise displays a lot of cinematic veneer and excellent production values.

Special effects were credited to Robert Dawson (who worked on no other creature features) and Thomas R. Burman (special makeup effects), who had previously worked on such films as *Frogs* and *Food of the Gods*, and would work on *Cat People* and others in the future. (It was around this time that monster creation in movies was often considered a more elaborate "makeup" effect.) Didn't anyone bother to read the script? Yes, the monster may have been born of a bear, but it wasn't supposed to look like one. It is possible that corners were cut in the rush to get the film in release, and/or there wasn't enough time to come up with another approach. Director John Frankenheimer also helmed such acclaimed and famous films as *The Manchurian Candidate* (1962), *Seconds* (1966), and *Black Sunday* (1977)—this was a rare occasion of a big name director helming a creature feature. One would imagine that he was horrified by what the FX people came up with—and not in the right way.

The special effects teams were also responsible for the cruddy-looking puppet baby monster, which never looks remotely alive, and for the phony giant salmon and tadpole props. The ominous huffing noises of the monster are well concocted by the sound department, however. And the effects when the creature crashes into the cabin and sends pieces of the walls flying inward are splendid. The monster was played by Kevin Peter Hall (1955–1991), who was 6'5" and, unlike the mutant bear, not pudgy. Hall also enacted the title role in the two *Predator* films and played the bigfoot Harry in *Harry and the Hendersons*.

Despite the insufficiencies of the FX work, *Prophecy* is a well-made and entertaining movie. You're pulled into the highly disquieting atmosphere from the first, with a prologue that shows a search and rescue team being killed by the unseen monster. There is a nice segue from the river with the dead bodies to Maggie playing her cello in the symphony. A confrontation between the lumber men and the Opies at the entrance to the forest, involving a chainsaw and axes, is tense and exciting. The movie works up a lot of suspense and shudders, such as when Rob looks up at a tree to see claw marks from the creature many, *many* feet above his head, or when the mutant bear slowly makes his way across a river covered in a voluminous layer of mist.

David Seltzer's script is one of the more intelligent to make use of a Native American background and Indian legends. Harry Stradling, Jr.'s exquisite photography adds to the chills and makes the most of the striking locations (British Columbia instead of Maine). Leonard Rosenman's score backs up each scene with impact and tension. The entire cast plays with absolute conviction. Talia Shire is particularly impressive once she realizes that she may be carrying a monster inside her, and is even believable when the script sort of asks her to "bond" with the mutant baby. Foxworth is also excellent, a notable portrait of a man who cries for humanity but can't quite see that his own wife is in pain. Armand Assante is striking in his contempt and resolve as Opie leader John Hawks, with fine support from Victoria Racimo as his wife, Ramona. Richard Dysart scores as Isley, who works for the paper mill but eventually wants to make up for his part in the tragedy. George Clutesi plays a more benign part, as the oldest member of the tribe, than he did in a similar role in *Nightwing*.

Frankenheimer and editor Tom Rolf make sure there isn't a boring moment in the movie, even if they are ultimately defeated by that pudgy Teddy bear. Incidentally, the effects of mercury poisoning are more or less as described in the film, and the incident in Minamata, Japan, where thousands died due to mercury ingestion was an actual occurrence. Mercury can be responsible for severe birth defects, but luckily there have been no recorded cases of any actual "monsters."

Dean Koontz's scary 1983 novel *Phantoms* seemed to have as its chief inspiration the film *Caltiki, the Immortal Monster*. Like *Caltiki*, it deals with the sudden disappearance of large groups of people at different times during history. Like *Caltiki*, the creature responsible is a big, bad-tempered blob that comes up from the bowels of the earth. Koontz's storyline and characters are entirely different, however, and his monster has intelligence and a sadistic nature. The film version of *Phantoms* came out in 1998.

Dr. Jennifer Paley (Joanna Going) and her younger sister Lisa (Rose McGowan) arrive in Snowfield, where Paley has her practice, and discover that virtually all of the town's inhabitants have vanished. They discover a few dead bodies and body parts, and hear weird, terrifying noises through the phone system and elsewhere. Coming upon Sheriff Hammond (Ben Affleck) and his sleazy deputy Stu (Liev Schreiber), they discover some kind of horrible, unseen presence is toying with them. Eventually they learn about Dr. Timothy Flyte (Peter O'Toole), who has theorized that mass disappearances down through history have been caused by the same gigantic and unknown creature. Flyte comes to Snowfield to confront this ancient being, a massive shapeless force, and helps destroy it with a bacteriological weapon. Deputy Stu, who was killed, absorbed, and used by the creature, is still on the loose, however.

Computer imagery is responsible for most of *Phantoms'* effects, along with the occasional mechanical prop. There is a big dragonfly-mosquito-bat kind of creature that lifts Stu off his feet, bores into his face, and flings him around the room, but this is seen only in very brief shots as it goes about its business. A "dog" that opens up to reveal black tentacles (the creature can send out parts of itself as well as people and animals that it has absorbed) is reminiscent of the thing-dog in 1982's *The Thing*. When we finally see "the ancient enemy," it appears as a sixty-foot-high swirling cone drawing people up into its mass like a cyclone. It seems to be comprised simply of black shapeless matter. Although this bit of FX work would have to be considered more impressive than anything in *Caltiki* or *The Blob*, it isn't nearly as effective or "icky." There is a protracted scene wherein the dead Stu reappears to turn into another tentacled creature as if his internal organs are uncurling and taking on a life of their own.

The first half of *Phantoms* is mostly excellent and chilling, setting up a bizarre, eerie mystery and pulling the viewer into the women's terror. Like the remake of *The Blob*, the movie brings in a kind of "biological containment team" of its own, and there are suddenly too many people running around for that feeling of petrified isolation to be sustained. The final quarter of the film is drawn-out and slack, ultimately becoming a boring mélange of gooey creature makeup effects that we've all seen before interspersed with a lot of lulls and pauses. In the novel, the big blob had much to do once it emerged from its hiding place; here it makes a brief, if dramatic, entrance and then we're onto an anticlimactic scene showing undead–Stu terrorizing the two women all over again.

Still the movie has a few memorable scenes. Jennifer finds two severed hands in a restaurant kitchen and then looks with some trepidation into an oven after the timer goes off. Instead of body parts we see two cakes in their pans. *Then* the severed heads drop into view from the upper half of the oven. There's a clever moment when a "drone," a piece of the creature shaped like a man, spits into its hand and the liquid turns into a tiny lizard. The best scene is probably when Flyte stands on the empty street and demands of the creature, "Show yourself!" Suddenly the entire street from one end to another is full of the reanimated bodies of all of the missing townspeople. One can accept that this huge, malevolent organism can have absorbed the Mayans and other vanished cultures, but Flyte also claims that it was responsible for the extinction of the dinosaurs, species of which circled the entire globe. There is a big difference between a "disappearance" and an extinction!

Although he looks more like a lacquered, waxy *GQ* model than a small-town sheriff, Ben Affleck is acceptable enough as Hammond on a line-by-line basis, but he doesn't offer much more. Hammond is not the sheriff of Snowfield but has come from another community when a call from the Snowfield sheriff was cut off. But surely Hammond might have friends or family in Snowfield, maybe even a girlfriend or two? It's one thing to be strong and stoic, but he displays very little amazement or fear at the loss of so many people and the odd goings-on in the town. Joanna Going and Rose McGowan as the sisters hardly register much sympathy for Jennifer's dead housekeeper whom they come across, and look at the severed hands in the kitchen as if they were the sort of thing you saw every day (at least Jennifer is a doctor). Peter O'Toole doesn't act is if he thinks he's slumming, but he and the rest of the actors are a bit too "light" in their approach when you consider the tragedy that has occurred and what's at stake — not only their own survival but the survival of the entire planet! Only Liev Schreiber, whose character is established as being a little "off" right from the first, seems to be having much fun.

Richard Clabaugh's photography is first-rate, and director Joe Chappelle has crafted some genuinely suspenseful and absorbing opening scenes. But while this is one of the few non-human monsters in movie history who delights in playing mind games with its victims, its appearances are ultimately too unsatisfying to make *Phantoms* a truly memorable creature feature. Which is too bad considering how great and shuddery the book was.

Filmography

Alien (1979). Twentieth Century–Fox. Director: Ridley Scott. Screenwriter: Dan O'Bannon. With: Sigourney Weaver, Tom Skerritt, Veronica Cartwright, Yaphet Kotto, John Hurt.

Alligator (1980). Group 1 International. Director: Lewis Teague. Screenwriter: John Sayles. With: Robert Forster, Robin Riker, Michael Gazzo, Dean Jagger, Sidney Lassick, Bart Braverman, Perry Lang.

Attack of the Crab Monsters (1957). Allied Artists. Director: Roger Corman. Screenwriter: Charles B. Griffith. With: Pamela Duncan, Richard Garland, Russell Johnson, Mel Welles, Leslie Bradley.

Attack of the Giant Leeches (1959). American International. Director: Bernard L. Kowalski. Screenwriter: Leo Gordon. With: Ken Clark, Yvette Vickers, Bruno Ve Sota.

Barracuda (1978). American General. Directors: Wayne Crawford, Harry Kerwin. Screenwriters: Wayne Crawford, Harry Kerwin. With: Wayne Crawford, Jason Evers, William Kerwin, Bert Freed, Roberta Leighton.

Bats (1999). Columbia. Director: Louis Morneau. Screenwriter: John Logan. With: Lou Diamond Phillips, Dina Meyer, Leon, Bob Gunton.

The Beast from 20,000 Fathoms (1953). Warner Brothers. Director: Eugene Lourie. Screenwriter: Fred Freiberger. With: Paul Christian, Cecil Kellaway, Paula Raymond, Kenneth Tobey.

The Beast with a Million Eyes (1955). American Releasing Corporation (ARC). Director: David Kramarsky. Screenwriter: Tom Filer. With: Paul Birch, Lorna Thayer, Dona Cole, Dick Sargent, Leonard Tarver.

Beginning of the End (1957). Republic. Director: Bert I. Gordon. Screenwriters: Fred Freiberger; Lester Gorn. With: Peter Graves, Peggie Castle, Morris Ankrum.

Ben (1972). Bing Crosby Productions. Director: Phil Karlson. Screenwriter: Gilbert Ralston. With: Lee Harcourt Montgomery, Joseph Campanella, Meredith Baxter, Rosemary Murphy, Arthur O'Connell.

The Birds (1963). Universal. Director: Alfred Hitchcock. Screenwriter: Evan Hunter. With: Tippi Hedren, Rod Taylor, Jessica Tandy, Suzanne Pleshette, Veronica Cartwright.

The Black Scorpion (1957). Warner Brothers. Director Edward Ludwig. Screenwriters: David Duncan; Robert Blees. With: Mara Corday, Richard Denning, Carlos Rivas.

The Blob (1958). Paramount. Director: Irwin S. Yeaworth, Jr. Screenwriters: Kate Phillips, Theodore Simonson. With: Steven [Steve] McQueen, Aneta Corsaut, Olin Howlin, Earl Rowe.

The Blob (1988). Tri-Star. Director: Chuck Russell. Screenwriters: Frank Darabont, Chuck Russell. With: Kevin Dillon, Shawnee Smith, Donovan Leitch, Jeffrey DeMunn, Candy Clark.

Blue Monkey (1987). Mithras. Director: William Fruet. Screenwriters: George Goldsmith, Chris Koseluk. With: Steve Railsback, Gwyneth Walsh, Don Lake, Susan Anspach, Peter Van Wart, John Vernon.

Bug (1975). Paramount–William Castle Productions. Director: Jeannot Szwarc. Screenwriters: Thomas Page, William Castle. With: Bradford Dillman, Joanna Miles, Patty McCormack.

Caltiki, Il mostro immortale a.k.a. *Caltiki, the Immortal Monster* (1958). Allied Artists. Director: Robert Hamton (Riccardo Freda). Screenwriter: Philip Just (Filippo Sanjust). With: John Merivale, Didi Sullivan, Gerard Herter, Daniela Rocca.

The Cosmic Monsters (1958). Distributors Corporation of America. Director: Gilbert Gunn. Screenwriter: Paul Ryder. With: Forrest Tucker, Gaby Andre, Martin Benson.

The Crawling Eye (1958). Director: Quentin Lawrence. Screenwriter: Jimmy Sangster. With: Forrest Tucker, Laurence Payne, Jennifer Jayne, Janet Munro, Warren Mitchell.

Creepshow (1982). Warner Brothers. Director: George A. Romero. Screenwriter: Stephen King. With: Hal Holbrook, Fritz Weaver, E. G. Marshall, Viveca Lindfors, Ted Danson.

Cujo (1983). Taft–Sunn Classic. Director: Lewis Teague. Screenwriters: Don Carlos Dunway, Lauren Currier. With: Dee Wallace, David Hugh-Kelly, Christopher Stone, Mills Watson, Danny Pintauro.

The Cyclops (1957). Allied Artists. Director: Bert I. Gordon. Screenwriter: Bert I. Gordon. With: Gloria Talbott, Lon Chaney Jr., James Craig, Tom Drake.

Damnation Alley (1977). Twentieth Century–Fox. Director: Jack Smight. Screenwriters: Alan Sharp, Lucas Heller. With: George Peppard, Jan-Michael Vincent, Dominique Sanda, Paul Winfield, Jackie Earle Haley, Kip Niven.

Day of the Animals (1977). Film Ventures International. Director: William Girdler. Screenwriters: William and Eleanor E. Norton. With: Christopher George, Lynda Day George, Richard Jaeckel, Ruth Roman. Jon Cedar.

The Deadly Bees (1967). Paramount–Amicus. Director: Freddie Francis. Screenwriters: Robert Bloch; Anthony Marriot. With: Suzanna Leigh, Frank Finlay, Guy Doleman, Michael Ripper.

The Deadly Mantis (1957). Universal-International. Director: Nathan Juran. Screenwriter: Martin Berkeley. With: Craig Stevens, William Hopper, Alix Talton.

Deep Blue Sea (1999). Warner Brothers. Director: Renny Harlin. Screenwriters: Duncan Kennedy, Donna Powers, Wayne Powers. With: Thomas Jane, Saffron Burrows, LL Cool J, Samuel L. Jackson, Michael Rapaport.

The Devil Bat (1940). Producers Releasing Corp. Director: Jean Yarbrough. Screenwriter: John T. Neville. With: Bela Lugosi, Suzanne Kaaren, Guy Usher.

Dogs (1976). American Cinema. Director: Burt Brickerhoff. Screenwriter: O'Brian Tamalin. With: David McCallum, Linda Gray, George Wyner, Sandra McCabe.

Dragonslayer (1981). Paramount–Walt Disney. Director: Matthew Robbins. Screenwriters: Hal Barwood, Matthew Robbins. With: Peter MacNicol, Caitlin Clarke, Ralph Richardson, Sydney Bromley, John Hallam, Chloe Salamar, Albert Salmi.

Earth vs The Spider (1958). American International. Director: Bert I. Gordon. Screenwriters: Laszlo Gorog, George Worthing Yates. With: Ed Kemmer, June Kenney, Sally Fraser, Hank Patterson, Gene Roth.

Elephant Walk (1954). Paramount. Director: William Dieterle. Screenwriter: John Lee Mahin. With: Elizabeth Taylor, Peter Finch, Dana Andrews.

Empire of the Ants (1977). American International. Director: Bert I. Gordon. Screenwriter: Jack Tur-ley. With: Joan Collins, Robert Lansing, John David Carson, Albert Salmi, Jacqueline Scott.

Eye of the Cat (1969). Universal. Director: David Lowell Rich. Screenwriter: Joseph Stefano. With: Eleanor Parker, Gayle Hunnicutt, Michael Sarrazin, Tim Henry, Laurence Naismith.

Fiend Without a Face (1958). MGM–Amalgamated. Director: Arthur Crabtree. Screenwriter: Herbert J. Leder. With: Marshall Thompson, Kim Parker, Kynaston Reeves.

The Flesh Eaters (1964). Vulcan. Director: Jack Curtis. Screenwriter: Arnold Drake. With: Martin Kosleck, Byron Sanders, Rita Morley, Barbara Wilkin, Ray Tudor, Christopher Drake.

The Flying Serpent (1946). Producers Releasing Corp. Director: Sam Newfield. Screenwriter: John T. Neville. With: George Zucco, Hope Kramer, Ralph Lewis, Eddie Acuff.

The Food of the Gods (1975). American International. Director: Bert I. Gordon. Screenwriter: Bert I. Gordon. With: Marjoe Gornter, Ida Lupino, Ralph Meeker, Pamela Franklin.

The Food of the Gods II (1989). Carolco. Director: Damian Lee. Screenwriter: Richard Bennett. With: Paul Coufos, Lisa Schrage, Stuart Hughes, Jackie Burroughs.

Frogs (1972). American International. Director: George McCowan. Screenwriters: Robert Hutchison, Robert Blees. With: Ray Milland, Sam Elliott, Joan Van Ark, Judy Pace, David Gilliam.

The Giant Behemoth (1959). Allied Artists. Director: Eugene Lourie. Screenwriter: Eugene Lourie. With: Gene Evans, Andre Morell, John Turner, Jack McGowran, Leigh Madison, Henri Vidon.

The Giant Claw (1957). Columbia. Director: Fred F. Sears. Screenwriters: Samuel Newman, Paul Gangelin. With: Jeff Morrow, Mara Corday, Morris Ankurm, Edgar Barrier, Robert Shayne.

The Giant Gila Monster (1959). Hollywood Pictures Corporation. Director: Ray Kellogg. Screenwriter: Jay Simms. With: Don Sullivan, Lisa Simone, Bob Thompson, Fred Graham.

The Giant Spider Invasion (1975). Cinema Group 75. Director: Bill Rebane. Screenwriters: Robert Easton, Richard L. Huff. With: Steve Brodie, Barbara Hale, Alan Hale, Leslie Parrish, Bill Williams.

Godzilla, King of the Monsters! (1956). Toho-Embassy. Directors: Ishiro Honda, Terry Morse. Screenwriters: Takeo Murata, Inoshiro Honda. With: Raymond Burr, Takashi Shimura, Akihiko Hirata, Akira Takarada.

Goliath and the Dragon (1960). Universal. Director: Vittorio Cottafavi. Screenwriter: Marcello Baldi. With: Mark Forest, Broderick Crawford, Eleanora Ruffa, Gaby Andre.

Gorgo (1961). MGM. Director: Eugene Lourie. Screenwriters: John Lorgin, Daniel Hyatt. With: Bill Travers, William Sylvester, Martin Benson, Vincent Winter.

Grizzly (1976). Film Ventures International. Director: William Girdler. Screenwriters: Harvey Flaxman, David Sheldon. With: Christopher George, Andrew Prine, Richard Jaeckel, Joan McCall, Joe Dorsey.

The Horror of Party Beach (1964). Iselin-Tenney. Director: Del Tenney. Screenwriter: Richard Hilliard. With: John Scott, Alice Lyon, Marilyn Clarke, Allan Laurel, Eulabelle Moore.

In the Shadow of Kilimanjaro (1986). Film Corporation of Kenya. Director: Raju Patel. Screenwriters: T. Michael Harry, Jeffrey M. Sneller. With: Timothy Bottoms, John Rhys-Davies, Irene Miracle, Michele Carey, Patrick Gorman.

Island of Terror (1966). Universal-Protelco. Director: Terence Fisher. Screenwriters: Edward Andrew Mann, Allan Ramsen. With: Peter Cushing, Edward Judd, Carole Gray, Niall Magginnis.

It Came from Beneath the Sea (1955). Columbia. Director: Robert Gordon. Screenwriters: George Worthing Yates, Hal Smith. With: Kenneth Tobey, Faith Domergue, Donald Curtis.

It! The Terror from Beyond Space (1958). United Artists. Director: Edward L. Cahn. Screenwriter: Jerome Bixby. With: Marshall Thompson, Shawn Smith, Kim Spalding, Ann Doran, Ray Corrigan.

Jack the Giant Killer (1962). United Artists. Director: Nathan Juran. Screenwriters: Orville H. Hampton, Nathan Juran. With: Kerwin Mathews, Torin Thatcher, Judi Meredith, Anna Lee, Roger Mobley.

Jason and the Argonauts (1963). Columbia. Director: Don Chaffey. Screenwriters: Beverley Cross, Jan Read. With: Todd Armstrong, Nancy Kovack, Gary Raymond, Honor Blackman, Laurence Naismith.

Jaws (1975). Universal. Director: Steven Spielberg. Screenwriters: Peter Benchley, Carol Gottlieb. With: Roy Scheider, Robert Shaw, Richard Dreyfuss, Lorraine Gary, Murray Hamilton.

Jurassic Park (1993). Universal. Director: Steven Spielberg. Screenwriters: Michael Crichton, David Koepp. With: Sam Neill, Laura Dern, Jeff Goldblum, Wayne Knight, Richard Attenborough, Martin Ferrero, Ariana Richards, Joseph Mazzello.

Jurassic Park III (2001). Universal. Director: Joe Johnston. Screenwriter: Peter Buchman. With: Sam Neill, William H. Macy, Tea Leoni, Alessandro Nivola.

Killer Fish (1979). Carlo Ponti Productions. Director: Antonio Margheriti. Screenwriter: Michael

Rogers. With: Lee Majors, Margaux Hemingway, Karen Black, Marisa Berenson, James Franciscus.

The Killer Shrews (1959). Hollywood Pictures Corporation. Director: Ray Kellogg. Screenwriter: Jay Simms. With: James Best, Ingrid Goude, Baruch Lumet, Ken Curtis, Gordon McLendon.

Killers from Space (1954). RKO. Director: W. Lee Wilder. Screenwriter: Bill Raynor. With: Peter Graves, Barbara Bestar, James Seay, Steve Pendleton.

King Kong (1933). RKO. Directors: Merian C. Cooper, Ernest B. Schoedsack. Screenwriters: James Creelman, Ruth Rose. With: Fay Wray, Robert Armstrong, Bruce Cabot, Frank Reicher.

King Kong (1976). Dino De Laurentiis Productions. Director: John Guillermin. Screenwriter: Lorenzo Semple, Jr. With: Jessica Lange, Jeff Bridges, Charles Grodin, John Agar.

King Kong (2005). Universal. Director: Peter Jackson. Screenwriter: Fran Walsh. With: Naomi Watts, Jack Black, Adrien Brody.

Kingdom of the Spiders (1977). Dimension. Director: John "Bud" Carlos. Screenwriter: Alan Caillou. With: William Shatner, Tiffany Bolling, Woody Strode, Altovise Davis.

Konga (1961). American International. Director: John Lemont. Screenwriters: Aben Kandel, Herman Cohen. With: Michael Gough, Margo Johns, Claire Gordon, Jess Conrad, Austin Trevor.

The Lost Continent (1968). Hammer–Seven Arts. Screenwriter-Director: Michael Carreras. With: Eric Porter, Hildegarde Knef, Suzanna Leigh, Tony Beckley, Dana Gillespie.

The Lost World (1925). Director: Harry O. Hoyt. Screenwriter: Marion Fairfax. With: Bessie Love, Lewis Stone, Wallace Beery.

The Lost World (1960). Twentieth Century–Fox. Director: Irwin Allen. Screenwriters: Charles Bennett, Irwin Allen. With: Michael Rennie, Jill St. John, David Hedison, Claude Rains, Fernando Lamas, Richard Haydn, Jay Novello.

The Lost World: Jurassic Park (1997). Universal. Director: Steven Spielberg. Screenwriter: David Koepp. With: Jeff Goldblum, Julianna Moore, Arliss Howard, Vanesse Lee Chester, Vince Vaughn.

The Magic Sword (1962). United Artists. Director: Bert I. Gordon. Screenwriters: Bernard Schoenfeld, Bert I. Gordon. With: Basil Rathbone, Estelle Winwood, Gary Lockwood, Anne Helm, Liam Sullivan, Maila Nurmi (Vampira).

Mako: The Jaws of Death (1976). Mako Associates. Screenwriter-Director: William Grefe. With: Richard Jaeckel, Jennifer Bishop, Harold Sakata.

The Maze (1953). Allied Artists. Director: William Cameron Menzies. Screenwriter: Dan Ullman.

With: Richard Carlson, Veronica Hurst, Katherine Emery, Hillary Brooke.

Megalodon (2004). Right Coast. Director: Pat Corbett. Screenwriters: Gary J. Tunicliffe, Stanley Isaacs. With: Leighanne Littrell, Robin Sachs, Al Sapienza.

Mimic (1997). Dimension. Director: Guillermo del Toro. Screenwriters: Matthew Robbins, Guillermo del Toro. With: Mira Sorvino, Jeremy Northam, Josh Brolin, Giancarlo Giannini, Charles S. Dutton, F. Murray Abraham, Alexander Goodwin.

Monster from Green Hell (1958). DCA. Director: Kenneth G. Crane. Screenwriters: Louis Vittes, Endre Bohem. With: Jim Davis, Robert E. Griffin, Barbara Turner, Eduardo Ciannelli.

Monster from the Ocean Floor (1954). Lippert. Director: Wyott Ordung. Screenwriter: William Danch. With: Anne Kimball, Stuart Wade, Dick Pinner.

The Monster That Challenged the World (1957). United Artists. Director: Arnold Laven. Screenwriter: Pat Fielder. With: Tim Holt, Audrey Dalton, Hans Conreid.

Mosquito (1995). Acme. Director: Gary Jones. Screenwriters: Steve Hodge; Tom Chaney. With: Gunnar Hansen, Steve Dixon.

The Mysterious Island (1929). MGM. Screenwriter-Director: Lucien Hubbard. With: Lionel Barrymore, Lloyd Hughes, Jacqueline Gadsden, Montagu Love.

Mysterious Island (1961). Columbia. Director: Cy Endfield. Screenwriters: John Prebble, Daniel Ullman, Crane Wilbur. With: Michael Craig, Joan Greenwood, Michael Callan, Gary Merrill, Herbert Lom.

The Naked Jungle (1954). Paramount. Director: Byron Haskin. Screenwriter: Ranald MacDougall. With: Charlton Heston, Eleanor Parker, William Conrad.

Night of the Lepus (1972). MGM. Director: William F. Claxton. Screenwriter: Don Holliday. With: Stuart Whitman, Janet Leigh, Rory Calhoun, DeForest Kelley.

Nightwing (1979). Columbia. Director: Arthur Hiller. Screenwriter: Steven Shagan, Bud Shrake, Martin Cruz Smith. With Nick Mancuso, David Warner, Kathryn Harrold, Stephen Macht, George Clutesi.

Of Unknown Origin (1982). Warner Brothers. Director: George Cosmatos. Screenwriter: Brian Taggert. With: Peter Weller, Jennifer Dale, Lawrence Dane, Shannon Tweed.

One Million B.C. (1940). United Artists–Hal Roach Productions. Director: Hal Roach. Screenwriters: Mickell Novack, George Baker. With: Victor Mature, Carole Landis, Lon Chaney Jr.

One Million Years B.C. (1966). Twentieth Century-Fox–Hammer. Director: Don Chaffey. Screenwriter: Michael Carreras. With: Raquel Welch, John Richardson, Martine Beswick.

Orca (1977). Paramount. Director: Michael Anderson. Screenwriter: Sergio Donati. With: Richard Harris, Charlotte Rampling, Bo Derek, Keenan Wynn, Peter Hooten.

The Pack (1977). Warner Brothers. Screenwriter-Director: Robert Clouse. With: Joe Don Baker, Hope Alexander-Willis, Richard B. Shull, Bibi Besch.

Phantoms (1998). Dimension. Director: Joe Chappelle. Screenwriter: Dean Koontz. With: Peter O'Toole, Rose McGowan, Joanna Going, Ben Affleck, Liev Schreiber.

Pigs (1972). Troma. Director: Marc Lawrence. Screenwriter; F. A. Foss (Marc Lawrence). With: Marc Lawrence, Jesse Vint, Katharine Ross, Toni Lawrence, Paul Hickey.

Piranha (1978). New World. Director: Joe Dante. Screenwriter: John Sayles. With: Bradford Dillman, Heather Menzies, Dick Miller, Barbara Steele.

Piranha 2: The Spawning (1981). Carlo Ponti. Director: James Cameron. Screenwriter: H. A. Milton. With: Tricia O'Neil, Steve Marachuk, Lance Henriksen, Ricky Paul Goldin.

Port Sinister (1953). RKO. Director: Harold Daniels. Screenwriters: Jack Pollexfen, Aubrey Wisberg. With: James Warren, Lynne Roberts, Paul Cavanagh, William Schallert.

Prophecy (1979). Paramount. Director: John Frankenheimer. Screenwriter: David Seltzer. With: Talia Shire, Robert Foxworth, Armand Assante, Victoria Ramos, Richard Dysart, Kevin Peter Hall.

Q (1982). Arkoff-Larco. Screenwriter-Director: Larry Cohen. With: Michael Moriarty, Candy Clark, David Carradine, Richard Roundtree.

The Quatermass Xperiment a.k.a. *The Creeping Unknown* (1956). Hammer. Screenwriter-Director: Val Guest. With: Brian Donlevy, Jack Warner, Lionel Jeffries, Richard Wordsworth, Margia Dean.

Quatermass 2 a.k.a. *Enemy from Space* (1957). Hammer. Director: Val Guest. Screenwriters: Nigel Kneale, Val Guest. With: Brian Donlevy, John Longdon, Bryan Forbes, William Franklyn.

Reign of Fire (2002). Touchstone. Director: Rob Bowman. Screenwriters: Gregg Chabot, Kevin Peterka, Matt Greenberg. With: Christian Bale, Matthew McConaughey, Izabella Scorupco, Scott Moutter, Gerard Butler, Alice Krige.

Secret of the Loch (1934). Ray Wyndham Productions. Director: Milton Rosmer. Screenwriters: Charles Bennett, Billie Bristow. With: Seymour Hicks, Nancy O'Nell, Frederick Peisley.

The 7th Voyage of Sinbad (1958). Columbia. Director: Nathan Juran. Screenwriter: Kenneth Kolb. With: Kerwin Mathews, Kathryn Grant, Torin Thatcher, Richard Eyer.

Siegfried (1924). Decla-Bioscop. Director: Fritz Lang. Screenwriters: Fritz Lang, Thea von Harbou. With: Paul Richter, Hanna Ralph. Margarete Schon, Theodor Loos.

Squirm (1976). MGM. Screenwriter-Director: Jeff Lieberman. With: Don Scardino, Patricia Pearcy, R.A. Dow, Jean Sullivan.

Starship Troopers (1997). Tri-Star–Touchstone. Director: Paul Verhoeven. Screenwriter: Edward Neumeier. With: Casper Van Dien, Dina Meyer, Denise Richards, Patrick Muldoon, Michael Ironside, Neil Patrick Harris.

The Swarm (1978). Warner Brothers. Director: Irwin Allen. Screenwriter: Sterling Silliphant. With: Michael Caine, Katharine Ross, Richard Widmark.

Tarantula (1955). Universal-International. Director: Jack Arnold. Screenwriters: Robert M. Fresco, Martin Berkeley. With: John Agar, Mara Corday, Leo G. Carroll, Nestor Paiva.

Tentacles a.k.a. *Tentacoli* (1977). American International. Director: Ovidio Assonitis [Oliver Hellman]. Screenwriter: Tito Carpi. With: John Huston, Shelley Winters, Bo Hopkins, Henry Fonda.

Them! (1954). Warner Brothers. Director: Gordon Douglas. Screenwriter: Ted Sherdeman. With: James Whitmore, James Arness, Edmund Gwenn, Joan Weldon.

Ticks (1993). First Look International. Director: Tony Randel. Screenwriter: Brent V. Friedman. With: Peter Scolari.

Tintorera (1977). Conacite Uno. Screenwriter-Director: Rene Cardona, Jr. With: Susan George, Fiona Lewis, Andres Garcia, Priscilla Barnes.

The Unknown Terror (1957). Twentieth Century–Fox Regal. Director: Charles Marquis Warren. Screenwriter: Kenneth Higgins. With: John Howard, Mala Powers, Paul Richards, Gerald Milton, May Wynn.

The Valley of Gwangi (1969). Warner Brothers-Seven Arts. Director: James O'Connolly. Screenwriter: William E. Bast. With: James Franciscus, Gila Golan, Richard Carlson, Laurence Naismith.

Valley of the Dragons (1961). Columbia. Screenwriter-Director: Edward Bernds. With Cesare Danova, Sean McClory, Joan Staley.

Viking Women and the Sea Serpent (a.k.a. *The Saga of the Viking Women and Their Voyage to the Waters of the Great Sea Serpent* (1957). American International. Director: Roger Corman. Screenwriter: Lawrence L. Goldman. With: Susan Cabot, Abby Dalton, Brad Jackson, June Kenney, Jonathan Haze, Michael Forest.

When Dinosaurs Ruled the Earth (1970). Hammer. Director: Val Guest. Screenwriters: J. G. Ballard, Val Guest. With: Victoria Vetri, Robin Hawdon.

Willard (1971). Bing Crosby Productions. Director: Daniel Mann. Screenwriter: Gilbert Ralston. With: Bruce Davison, Elsa Lanchester, Ernest Borgnine, Sondra Locke, Michael Dante.

Willard (2003). New Line. Screenwriter-Director: Glen Morgan. With: Crispin Glover, R.L. Ermey, Laura Elena Harring, Jackie Burroughs.

Wolfen (1981). Orion. Director: Michael Wadleigh. Screenwriters: David Eyre, Michael Wadleigh. With: Albert Finney, Diane Venora, Edward James Olmos, Gregory Hines, Dick O'Neill.

X the Unknown (1956). Warner Brothers-Hammer. Director: Leslie Norman. Screenwriter: Jimmy Sangster. With: Dean Jagger, Edward Chapman, Leo McKern, William Lucas, Anthony Newley.

Bibliography

Books and Articles

Counts, Kyle B. "The Birds." *Cinefantastique*. Fall 1980.

Harryhausen, Ray. *Film Fantasy Scrapbook*. New York: A.S. Barnes, 1972.

Rovin, Jeff. *From the Land Beyond Beyond*. New York: Berkeley, 1977.

Schoell, William. *Magic Man: The Life and Films of Steven Spielberg*. Greensboro, NC: Tudor, 1998.

_____. *Stay Out of the Shower: 25 Years of Shocker Films Beginning with* Psycho. New York: Dembner, 1985.

_____. "Two Lost Worlds of Sir Arthur Conan Doyle." *Filmfax*. February-March 1999.

Warren, Bill. *Keep Watching the Skies! American Science Fiction Movies of the Fifties*. 2 vols. Jefferson, NC: McFarland, 1982; 1986 (reprint in one vol., 1997).

Weldon, Michael. *Psychotronic Encyclopedia of Film*. New York: Ballantine, 1983.

Wood, Robin. *Hitchcock's Films*. New York: A.S. Barnes, 1977.

Websites

greatoldmovies.blogspot.com.

imdb.com.

Index

Numbers in *bold italics* indicate pages with photographs.